Visions of
Human Nature

Text and Illustrations
by
Donald Palmer

Visions of
Human Nature

AN INTRODUCTION

Donald Palmer

Visiting Assistant Professor at North Carolina State University
Professor Emeritus at College of Marin

Mayfield Publishing Company

Mountain View, California

London • Toronto

Library of Congress Cataloging-in-Publication Data
Palmer, Donald.
    Visions of human nature : an introduction / Donald Palmer.
        p.   cm.
    Includes bibliographical references and index.
    ISBN 1-55934-971-9
    1. Philosophical anthropology. 2. Philosophy Introductions.
    I. Title.
    BD450.P235   1999
    128—DC21

                                                                99-31668
                                                                    CIP

Manufactured in the United States of America
10   9   8   7   6   5   4   3   2   1

Mayfield Publishing Company
1280 Villa Street
Mountain View, California 94041

Sponsoring editor, Kenneth King; production editor, Julianna Scott Fein; manuscript editor, Thomas L. Briggs; design manager, Glenda King; text designer and art editor, Robin Mouat; manufacturing manager, Randy Hurst. The text was set in 11/14 Tekton by TBH Typecast, Inc., and printed on acid-free 50# Finch Opaque by R. R. Donnelley & Sons Company.

Text Credits: pp. 104–106, excerpts from *The Age of Belief,* Anne Freemantle, ed., Ayer Company, Publishers, pp. 88–89, 153, 173. Reprinted with permission from the publisher; **pp. 128–146,** excerpts from "Meditation on the First Philosophy" by Rene Descartes, from *The Essential Descartes* by Margaret Wilson. Copyright © 1969 by Margaret Wilson. Used by permission of Dutton Signet, a division of Penguin Putnam Inc.; **pp. 219–233,** excerpts from *Marx's Concept of Man: With a Translation from Marx's Economic and Philosophical Manuscript,* by T. B. Bottomore. Copyright © 1961, 1966 by Erich Fromm. Copyright renewed 1994 by The Estate of Erich Fromm. Reprinted by permission of the Continuum Publishing Company.

Photo Credits: p. 123, Copyright © Museo del Prado, Madrid. Derechos reservados. Prohibida la reproducción total o parcial; **p. 141,** The Granger Collection, New York; **p. 225,** Mary Cassatt, American, 1844–1926, *The Child's Bath,* oil on canvas, 1893, 39½ X 26 in., The Robert A. Waller Fund, 1910.2. Detail. Photograph courtesy of The Art Institute of Chicago; **p. 253,** Signorelli, Luca (1441–1523). *Resurrection of the Flesh.* Duomo, Orvieto, Italy. Scala/Art Resource, NY.

To Natalia Nicté Brito and Daniel Tonatiuh Brito,
who, as small as they are,
already have a lot to say about human nature

Preface

This book is a somewhat unorthodox introduction to philosophy—primarily to Western philosophy, although the dramatic appearance of the Buddha in Chapter 3 broadens the horizon a bit. What is this "philosophy" to which the book plans to introduce you? I am convinced that only a loose definition is possible, so at this point I will merely say that philosophy revolves around the "Big Questions"—problems of reality, knowledge, and value—and that philosophy is an attempt to show how the components of these categories relate to one another—how all features of experience "hang together."

There are a number of ways of introducing such a baggy monster as philosophy. One typical format invites students to investigate philosophy topically: some theory of knowledge (**epistemology**[1]), some theory of reality (**metaphysics** or **ontology**), some moral philosophy (**ethics**), some philosophy of art (**aesthetics**), some philosophy of religion, and some discussion of particularly thorny philosophical problems, such as the mind–body problem or the problem of freedom and determinism. Another approach to teaching an introductory philosophy course is historical, giving a brief overview of the path along which philosophy has traveled since ancient times. Yet another entry to the domain of philosophy involves having students read three or four books by philosophers who have the rare gift (rare among philosophers, at least) of making their ideas accessible to people not already initiated into the cult (for example, Plato, Descartes, Berkeley, Russell, and Sartre). I have used this last technique in many of my classes over a period of some thirty years; in addition, I have written textbooks in each of the first two formats.[2]

Here I offer another suggestion. We will introduce ourselves to the discipline of philosophy by studying a number of philosophical theories of human nature (ten, to be exact). For better or for worse, philosophy tends to come back eventually to the human being, to the human's relation to the rest of reality, and to the "meaning" of human existence.

In the Introduction, I show how philosophy is related to the quest for a theory of human nature, and I explain why I believe that such a quest is always philosophical. I also indicate certain logical and linguistic features of such theories that students should watch out for. Then I delve into the various theories. The first two chapters of the book—on Plato and Aristotle—give us a glimpse of the notion of human nature as it emerged from the so-called Golden Age of Greece. (We will see, however, that here, too, not all that glitters is gold.) Ancient Athens is supposed to be "the cradle of Western civilization, " so we need to take a good, long look at the philosophical theories of reality, knowledge, and value that emerged from that amazingly creative and violent moment in our past and, as some claim, in our cultural birth.

Chapter 3, about the teachings of the Buddha, provides a more multi-cultural approach to our topic, as we look to ancient India for insight. And, indeed, the picture of human nature that develops there will be in many ways startling to the uninitiated Western philosophy student. At the same time, however, a number of features of Buddhism will resonate with certain Western schools as apparently disparate as Platonism, medieval-ism, Darwinism, and existentialism.

Chapter 4 on medieval Christianity, Chapter 5 on Descartes, and Chapter 6 on Kierkegaard provide three additional religious pictures of human nature that, despite their common Christian denominator, differ among themselves almost as much as do any other views in this book. It is not only the differences between the medieval world, the nineteenth-century world, and the modern world that will explain this discrepancy, nor is it the difference between Catholicism and Protestantism; rather, it is a major difference in philosophical conceptions of reality, knowledge, and value.

Chapters 7, 8, and 9—on Darwin, Marx, and Freud, respectively—each depict theories of human nature grounded not in religion but in sci-ence. Yet, despite the enthusiasm for science and its methods evinced by the three "heroes" of these chapters, and despite a number of structural agreements, these theories seem to be mutually exclusive, and even con-temptuous, of one another. Here, too, the differences are due to deep dis-agreements about the key *philosophical categories* hovering behind the sciences (biology, socioeconomics, and psychology, respectively) that these three theorists claim to exemplify.

Finally, Chapter 10, on Sartre, takes the heroic, or absurd (or both), position that there is no such thing as human nature at all. This pronouncement seems to have its roots in Sartre's strong commitment to atheism. But, in fact, it is philosophically close to the ancient Buddhist religion's claim that there is no self and to the religious claims of Søren Kierkegaard that the self must be chosen rather than simply inherited.

Often students come to college classes with a much weaker grasp of history than their professors would like. Yet, at least in my experience, students are truly fascinated by the revelation of the historical facts that determined various features of the topics they have chosen to study. Furthermore, I think it's important to demonstrate that philosophical ideas are not created in a vacuum (even though some prove to be quite vacuous). Therefore, I begin each chapter with a brief historical backdrop and a short biography of the featured philosopher.

Oh, yes, a few words about the cartoons. As a freshman in college, I declared as an art major. Then I made a horrible discovery: I didn't have any artistic talent! But as you can see, I haven't let that stop me. Sometimes, the illustrations are meant as teaching devices—either as diagrams that communicate information or as aids to help you remember the ideas of the philosophers—but mostly I hope the drawings at least add some humor to your adventure with philosophy. Studying philosophy should be fun, and I'm taking advantage of the fact that even the gravest ideas often provoke humorous images and sometimes, I hope, hilarious associations. (It is not for nothing that one of Kierkegaard's pen names is "Hilarious Bookbinder.") We are, after all, the animal that laughs. (Aristotle denied that this feature is part of the essence of human nature, but I don't see why not.)

Laughing Hyena Reads Aristotle

Acknowledgments

I want to thank a number of people who read parts or all of this manuscript while it was in its formative stage. Their queries, criticisms, and recommendations allowed me to produce a better manuscript than the one I first showed them. These contributors include Stephen Daniel, Texas A&M University at College Station; Richard M. Jaffe, North Carolina State University; Rodney G. Peffer, University of San Diego; and Robert Zeuschner, Pasadena City College. Special thanks to Thomas E. Wren at Loyola University of Chicago, whose corrections and criticisms were embarrassingly on target. His suggestions were very smart. The few that I did not take may yet come back to haunt me.

I thank my editor at Mayfield, Ken King, who was a diligent obstetrician. Also, I express my appreciation to the rest of the expert staff there in Mountain View: Robin Mouat, Glenda King, Julianna Scott Fein, and Randy Hurst. Also, Thomas Briggs' skillful copyediting has improved this book immensely. And, a nod of gratitude to Stephen Jay Gould for a short but uproarious e-mail message clarifying a point in my Darwin chapter. (The missive announced itself as Professor Gould's first e-mail message ever, even if a graduate student assistant did press the right keys to send the message on its way.)

Finally, as with all my books, my greatest debt is to my companion, friend, intellectual jouster, and wife, Leila May. She read and corrected the whole manuscript, though she did not approve of everything in it, and she certainly did not approve of the Barbie Doll™ notebook in which I wrote these words. But down here in the small jungle town of Dominical on the southwestern shore of Costa Rica, it was a choice between a Barbie™ notebook or a Tweety-Bird™ notebook, and I went for Barbie™. Kierkegaard, eat your heart out!

Tough Decisions in the Tropics

Note

1. Definitions for boldfaced terms thorughout the book can be found in the glossary.

2. Donald Palmer, *Looking at Philosophy: The Unbearable Heaviness of Philosophy Made Lighter*, 2nd ed. (Mountain View, Calif.: Mayfield, 1994), and Donald Palmer, *Does the Center Hold? An Introduction to Western Philosophy*, 2nd ed. (Mountain View, Calif.: Mayfield, 1996). The first of these is historically oriented; the second is topical.

Contents

Introduction
What Is Philosophy?

The Origins of Western Philosophy and Science

It is true that Western philosophy began with preoccupations other than those concerning human nature. Philosophy started out on the islands off the Greek peninsula in the sixth century B.C.E. (before the common era) with admirable questions posed by the so-called **pre-Socratic philosophers.** (Obviously, they did not call themselves that.) They asked questions like these:

> What is reality made of? Is it one substance or many? If one, which one? And if one, how is the appearance of many things compatible with the Oneness of everything?
> If there are ultimately many things, how could they be related in such a way as to produce one world?
> Is motion real and stability an illusion, or is it the other way around?
> What laws, if any, govern these motions or these static states?
> If there are laws, are they "creative"? Do they produce novelty? Or is there "nothing new under the sun," only infinite repetition?

So began not only philosophy but what we today call "science." However, it did not take long for the perspective to shift. Old Socrates and his opponents, known as the **Sophists,** concluded that no account of "objective reality" could be provided until philosophers were prepared to give an account of "subjective reality," defined as the human being to whom "objective reality" presents itself.

Furthermore, it soon became apparent that the two topics—objective and subjective reality—were intimately entwined. Every discourse about human nature soon stumbled back into issues of **metaphysics** and

1

epistemology. There is an apparent paradox here: It is impossible to resolve problems of objective reality until the problem of the human subject has been addressed. Yet, to address the issue of the human subject is to throw oneself again into the problem of objective reality. So in this book, too, even though our stated topic is philosophical theories of human nature, we will also encounter metaphysics, epistemology, **ethics, aesthetics,** and a full range of philosophical problems.

Philosophical Propositions and Scientific Propositions

What makes a theory or a problem *philosophical* rather than, say, scientific? Philosophical activity is often speculative and contemplative. It also typically involves conceptual analysis. I am contrasting these terms— "speculation," "contemplation," and "conceptual analysis"—with terms more closely associated with science—terms like "experimentation," "testing," and "**empirical** investigation." Philosophical questions matter to us (they make a difference in how we approach the world), but they are usually not resolved through observation, data collection, and experimentation. If they are resolved at all, it is through argumentation and **logic.** I am thinking of questions like these:

> Is there a God? Or is there no superior power that created and directs the universe?
> Are truth and knowledge possible? Or is there only opinion?
> Are there objective moral values? Or are "values" only conveniences and privileges relative to time, place, culture, group, and individual?
> Is there true human freedom? Or is there only necessity and unfreedom everywhere?

There are no observations imaginable that will answer these questions and no experiments that can confirm or refute the various hypotheses they contain. Most philosophical hypotheses are "speculative" in this sense. We can come to understand what they mean (that is, they are not just nonsense), and we can see why accepting or rejecting them might make a difference in our lives, but we can conceive of no empirical (observational, experimental) way of determining their truth, their falsity, or even their probability. So we create philosophical arguments (arguments using abstract ideas and logic) to defend or attack them. These arguments try to relate the various hypotheses to our human experience, but never in ways that can bring them any lasting resolution or scientific likelihood.

These difficulties have led some to think that engaging in philosophy is a bad idea. This was the conclusion reached by the scientifically oriented philosophers known as "logical positivists" early in the twentieth century. Their notion of doing philosophy was to show that only scientific **propositions** and **"tautologies"** (definitions and the propositions of mathematics and logic) made sense. They argued that, roughly, philosophical propositions of the type I am characterizing here were nonsense precisely because they could not be confirmed observationally and were neither definitions nor mathematical statements. The trouble with this view is that their criterion of "meaningfulness" was so strict that, according to it, much of what clearly *is* real science proved to be "nonsense." (More embarrassing for the logical positivists was the fact that their own criterion proved to be nonsense when applied to itself. The assertion "All meaningful propositions are either tautologies or empirical" is itself neither a tautology nor empirical. That is to say, it is not a mere definition of the word "meaningful," nor can observation and experimentation tend to confirm or refute it or show it to be probable. Therefore, it is nonsense according to its own standards.) Furthermore, philosophical questions seem to be intractable: Every time we lay them to rest, they come back to haunt us. Every generation, every culture, and, I suspect, every individual pose these questions anew (and I am certainly not excluding children here). On this issue, I am sympathetic with the view of the ancient Greeks. There are moments when we experience the world in wonder, and this wonder provokes us to philosophize. I also agree with the anthropologist Claude Lévi-Strauss, who, treating the "big questions" in an analogy with food, says, "These thoughts are good to think." In other words, we humans enjoy using our minds.

One more thing about the relation between science and philosophy: Sometimes ideas that start out as speculative and conceptual hypotheses eventually become scientific. That is, as information accumulates and as technological advances produce more refined instruments and tools, some philosophical ideas become amenable to experimental investigation. This is what happened with some of the speculations of the pre-Socratics. For example, by the end of the sixth century B.C.E., the philosopher Democritus had already arrived at an atomic theory of reality. But his theory was derived from speculation (analyzing all the strengths and weaknesses of the speculations of his forerunners) and from conceptual analysis (thinking out what he took to be the logical implications of the *idea* of a physical body). Such an object would have to have size, shape, and location, and be composed of something ultimately indivisible (*atomoi* in Greek). These "atoms" would be so small as to be invisible, and hence discoverable only through philosophical reasoning. (However, Isidore of Seville, recording these

Saint Isidore Studies Atoms

same ideas 1000 years later in his "encyclopedia," which summarized all knowledge available to his early medieval world, wrote that one could test the atomic hypothesis by sitting in a dark room looking at the atoms as they passed through a shaft of light entering through a small crack in the door. Today, *we* would probably call it "dust" rather than "atoms.")

At the beginning of the twenty-first century, the atomic theory is no longer part of a philosophical discipline; rather, it constitutes a large portion of the science of physics. This does not mean that scientists have figured out ways of making atoms *visible* (they haven't), but that they've figured out experimental ways of testing different hypotheses about atoms.

What I'm saying here can, unfortunately, leave the impression that philosophy is nothing but pre-science, namely, unsophisticated thinking that will be transcended as science progresses. But this generalization would be wrong. First, there are many philosophical debates even within as sophisticated a field as atomic physics (that is, problems that cannot be resolved experimentally), and it is too early to tell whether these can be remedied. In other words, a certain amount of philosophical debate may turn out to be a permanent feature of some areas of even hard-core science.

Second, often scientific theories themselves stimulate new philosophical debates about the *meaning* of those theories in other fields of human endeavor. For example, early on the question was raised whether the apparent materialism of scientific theory precluded human freedom. (If there are only atoms, and atoms necessarily behave in accordance with natural laws, how can "free will" be possible? There are no experiments that will answer this question, because human behavior as we observe it is compatible with either the theory of freedom or with the theory of **determinism.**)

Finally, I remind you about all those questions that, by their very nature, science cannot answer, such as the question of God's existence. (Again, all observable phenomena in the universe are compatible with either the hypothesis that God exists or the hypothesis that God does not exist.) Nor do moral dilemmas admit of scientific resolution. For example, we can determine scientifically whether it is possible to create atomic bombs, and perhaps "military science" and "political science" (are these sciences?) can suggest whether the use of atomic bombs is likely to contribute to efficient attainment of our military and political goals, but no science can tell us whether it is *moral* to use them.

Conceptual Analysis

Earlier I said that **conceptual analysis** is also a part of philosophy. We can (and should) analyze the key concepts that we use in daily discourse, in moral discourse, in scientific discourse, and in philosophical discourse to see what *logical* positions that use commits us to. If I call somebody my "sister," I am logically committed to recognizing that individual as *female* and as my *sibling*. (This is the case unless I am using that word in some metaphorical sense, either institutionalized—as when referring to a nun or a nurse—or personalized—as when I claim to recognize some kindred similarity between that person and myself.) To develop the point a bit more, let me say that conceptual analysis reveals that a sentence like "My sister is female" is a **necessary truth** (it can't be wrong, given the meanings and conventions of the English language), and I

Empirical Research Discovers a Trend

don't have to do any scientific experimentation to discover that truth. In fact, no empirical observation or research is even *relevant* to determining its truth.

By the way, I am not claiming to have made a profound statement or any major philosophical breakthrough when I discover the necessary truth that "sisters are female siblings." In fact, all I am giving you is the dictionary definition of "sister." Therefore, I've given you what I previously called a **tautology,** that is, a repetition of meanings, two equivalencies. The good news about tautologies is that they are necessarily true; the bad news is that they do not make any factual claims. (Compare "My sister is female" to "My sister is seven feet tall.")

So, as we study the various philosophers and their theories of human nature, keep alert to the distinctions I have drawn here between scientific, speculative, and tautological assertions. Think of them as you are trying to figure out what the philosophers mean when they make claims such as these:

1. Each individual human is an exemplification of the eternal archetype of humanity. (Plato)
2. Every living being is striving to achieve perfection. (Aristotle)
3. The acts in which we engage in this life determine what form we shall have in future lives. (the Buddha)
4. Each object in the visible world is a sign of a higher truth in the spiritual world. (medieval Christianity)
5. I think, therefore I am. (Descartes)
6. There are three forms of human existence possible: the aesthetic, the ethical, and the religious. (Kierkegaard)
7. The production of too many useless things produces too many useless people. (Marx)
8. The social propensities we have inherited from our animal ancestors are manifested in Jesus' Golden Rule. (Darwin)
9. The psyche is composed of id, ego, and superego. (Freud)
10. No action you engage in now is ever caused by any event in your past. (Sartre)

Facts and Values

OK, if philosophical theories cannot be confirmed empirically, why are we inspecting *philosophical* theories of human nature? Wouldn't it be less frustrating—and more rewarding—to study *scientific* theories of human nature? But the thing is, probably *all* theories of human nature are "philo-sophical" in the sense I've been outlining here, even those that purport to be scientific, such as those of Freud, Marx, and, perhaps, Darwin. And there is a rather striking reason this is so—namely, that the answer to the question "What is a human?" is itself a construction rather than a discovery. We are in the process of creating the concept of human nature, of negotiating it. To consider the ten traditions represented in this book is to enter into the great social, philosophical, and legal debate—sometimes a very contentious one—that is now taking place in courtrooms, classrooms, and living rooms, in churches and temples, and in bars, art studios, and street demonstrations around the world.

Let me put the same point differently. The quest for a theory of human nature *appears* to be a factual investigation. The question seems to be, "What are the facts about human nature?" But it soon becomes obvious that the quest is **"normative"**—that is, it is a moral investigation. Theories of human nature do not simply describe what humans are; they also advocate, recommend, and even cajole. Each theory we study here will have moral and behavioral implications for how we *ought* to behave.

Ever since the problem was first identified in the eighteenth century by the Scottish philosopher David Hume, moral philosophers have puzzled over the vexed relationship between facts and values. Hume's revelation of the problem is usually worded like this: "No IS implies an OUGHT." That is to say, one cannot logically deduce any value statements from mere state-ments of fact. This is a difficult point, but an important one. Consider this logical argument:

(A) All mammals are warm-blooded.
(B) Dogs are mammals.
(C) Dogs are warm-blooded.

Proposition (C) follows necessarily from (A) and (B). That is, (A) and (B) imply or entail (C). Furthermore, if (A) and (B) are true, then (C) is true.

Now compare the following argument:

(D) Vivisection of unanesthetized mammals causes pain.
(E) Dogs are mammals.
(F) Vivisection of unanesthetized dogs is morally wrong.

Do (D) and (E) entail (F)? If (D) and (E) are true, is (F) necessarily true? No. Not unless we sneak in another premise, such as (X) "Causing pain to animals is morally wrong." Then (X), together with (D) and (E), does entail (F). But where would we get (X)? In fact, people who agree that propositions

(D) and (E) are true often disagree about whether (X) is true. But the issue here is not merely that people often disagree about moral sentiments, because we can't resolve this logical problem simply by assigning a moral value that everyone shares. For example, does proposition (I) logically follow from (G) and (H)?

    (G) Every animal with a sensitive nervous system suffers pain if its limbs are forcefully twisted.

    (H) Human babies are animals with sensitive nervous systems.

    (I) Forcefully twisting the arms of unanesthetized human babies for the fun of it is morally wrong.

Most philosophers answer in the negative—not because they disagree with (I) but because they do not believe it follows logically from (G) and (H). You might be considered a monster if you denied (I), but you would not be logically contradicting yourself if you denied that (I) follows from (G) and (H). So, again, on what grounds can we base a moral judgment like (I)? If Hume is right—

PHILOS. 208: ETHICS

NOW, STUDENTS, WE'RE GOING TO HAVE SOME FUN!

and most philosophers seem to agree with him on this—we can't base it on the observation or description of mere facts without committing what has come to be known as the **naturalistic fallacy,** that is, the fallacy of thinking that premises containing no statements about values can entail conclusions containing moral judgments. (By the way, according to this line of reasoning, even the fact that most people are outraged by the idea of sadistic baby-torturing does not entail the judgment that baby-torturing is *morally* wrong—unless, of course, we smuggle in premise, [Z], "Whatever causes outrage in most people is morally wrong." But, as I hope you see by now, there are no facts from which we can derive a premise like [Z].)

This dilemma has forced some philosophers to the radical extreme of saying that all statements of value (other than merely instrumental ones, such as "This pen is no good") are virtual nonsense. This is the conclusion reached by the aforementioned logical positivists in the first half of the twentieth century. And the dilemma has driven others to the radical extreme of claiming that there are no value-free descriptions whatsoever, that *all* language is "value-laden." This is what some "postmodern" philosophers seem to have asserted in the second half of the twentieth century.

We will not be able to resolve this problem here. I remind you that it *is* a problem for us because most theories of human nature make both moral and factual claims. Therefore, we must acknowledge the "is/ought" problem as one of the barriers to any exclusively scientific resolution of the question of human nature. To the extent that the quest for a theory of human nature is a normative quest, it cannot become scientific without committing the naturalistic fallacy.

But this does not mean that there is *no* connection between observable facts and values. Even if it is true that "No IS implies an OUGHT," it does not follow that "No OUGHT implies an IS." For example, our judgment (F) about the morality of vivisecting dogs *does* entail propositions (D) and (E). That is, if animals cannot experience pain—and whether they do is a factual issue—then it is nonsensical to assert that it is immoral to cause them pain. Take another example suggested by the philosopher Arthur Danto.[1] Think about the Ten Commandments issued to Moses by God in the Bible.[2] If there were no gods, if the institution of marriage did not exist, if humans were immortal and could not die, if people were not born of parents, if there were no such thing as property—then the Ten Commandments would be meaningless because they *presuppose* all those conditions to be factual. So, even though you will not be able to confirm or refute the various theories of human nature you are about to study by trying to deduce them from scientific evidence, you can bring scientific and other observational facts to bear on the question of the conditions presupposed by each of these theories. Unfortunately, of course, not all of the conditions that are presupposed by these theories to be factual can be established observationally. For example, some of these theories presuppose **theism** (that is, the existence of God); others, **atheism** (that is, denial of the existence of God). Some presuppose human freedom; others, determinism. Some presuppose that human beings are essentially social; others, antisocial. None of these assumptions is easily confirmed or refuted by scientific evidence, and some of them totally escape the bounds of science. So, on these issues, as well as on the moral issues we've been discussing, philosophical reasoning rather than scientific theories will have to predominate.

Ducks and Rabbits

Sometimes theories of human nature do not seek to promote values (that is, they are not intentionally normative), nor do they claim to have discovered new scientific facts about human existence. Rather, they urge us to look at old facts in new ways. Consider the now-famous figure usually called "Wittgenstein's duck/rabbit." (A certain Dr. Jastrow, a psychologist, first published it, but the philosopher Ludwig Wittgenstein made it famous.)

The facts are all before you, and there is no more information to be had. So, does the figure represent a duck or a rabbit? Clearly, no scientific analysis can resolve the issue, nor will anything else. In this case, it's completely up to you. Now, look at the little indentation on the right-hand side of the head of the duck/rabbit. If this is a duck, what is that indentation? A place where a few feathers were lost? A cowlick? (The duck had a "bad hair day"?) It's nothing very significant, in any case. But what if this figure is a rabbit? Then this indentation is a *mouth*. Very important! A rabbit without a mouth will not last long.

In a similar fashion, many of the theories of human nature will ask you to reread old ciphers. Furthermore, they will claim that features of human experience that previously seemed important in fact have only minimal significance, while features that previously were marginalized will prove

**Wittgenstein's Duck Having
a Bad Hair Day**

central. What was a duck becomes a rabbit. (Plato: What seemed to be original is only a copy; what seemed to be a fleeting image is the permanent original. The Buddha: What seemed to be pleasure is pain; what seemed to be deprivation is salvation. Medieval Christianity: What seemed to be Other is the Same; what seemed to be the Same is temptation. Descartes: What seemed to be certain is uncertain; what seemed to be fleeting is permanent. Freud: What seemed to be accidental is intentional; what seemed to be "me" is "it." Darwin: What seemed to be different is the same; what seemed to be intentional is accidental. Sartre and Kierkegaard: What seemed to be smugness and complacency is terror; what seemed to be desired is feared, and what seemed to be feared is desired.) These issues are not resolved scientifically, if ever. Yet they can be ignored only at risk. They are philosophy.

Summary

This book is a presentation of ten influential theories of human nature. It is at the same time an introduction to philosophy because the various theories of human nature presented here turn out to be more philosophical than scientific in nature. That is, they have more the features of a philosophy than of a science, even when their authors claim to be scientists. These theories do not provoke us to formulate scientific experiments or to seek natural laws so much as they invite us to meditate on general philosophical ideas—concepts of reality, knowledge, and value—as they apply to our own case as humans. In the final analysis, these theories cannot be formulated in ways that could be confirmed or refuted empirically or experimentally. Rather, they tend to be speculative, contemplative, and normative. We understand their meanings and can meditate upon them, but we cannot determine what observations would show them to be true or false. Under logical scrutiny (conceptual analysis), they reveal themselves as normative rather than descriptive, and therefore as being unlike theories in the natural sciences. This means that their main categories prove to be value-laden, bristling with value judgments that are in some cases blatant and in other cases hidden. But even when these moral judgments that support the various theories prove to be compelling, they cannot be shown by scientific methods to be true or false—as, indeed, no moral theory can be. The gap between "facts" and "values," while not necessarily absolute, is still wide enough to be a barrier to scientific demonstration. Furthermore, many theories of human nature do not have the effect of revealing new realities, but they reorient our way of looking at old realities (the duck becomes a rabbit). The cases we will inspect here try to change our way of perceiving ourselves and our fellow humans.

Yet, despite their inability to achieve certainty or even consensus, these attempts at gaining knowledge of human nature are important. The ancient Greeks were right—we humans are the philosophical animal. It is good to think, and it is necessary to try to figure out who we are, even if our tentative answers are challenged on all sides.

Notes

1. Arthur C. Danto, *Mysticism and Morality: Oriental Thought and Moral Philosophy* (New York: Harper & Row, 1973). See especially pp. 10–11.
2. The Ten Commandments, found in Exodus 20, are roughly these: (1) Place no other gods before God himself. (2) Worship no idols. (3) Do not take the name of God in vain. (4) Observe the seventh day of the week as a holy day. (5) Honor your father and mother. (6) Do not kill. (7) Do not commit adultery. (8) Do not steal. (9) Do not bear false witness against your neighbor. (10) Do not jealously desire your neighbor's possessions, including his wife.

1

The Platonic Conception
of Human Nature

Historical Backdrop

The Athens of the fourth and fifth centuries B.C.E. found itself at the end of the epoch that some now call "the Golden Age of Greece." Three hundred years earlier, the Greek peninsula had been submerged in chaos and barbarism, during what the nineteenth-century philosopher and classicist

Chronus Eating His Children
(After Francisco Goya)

Friedrich Nietzsche called "the Age of Titanism." (Nietzsche associated this period with the generation of the Titans, dread gods who predated the Olympian gods in ancient Greek mythology. This period was dominated by gods like Chronos, who ate his own children to prevent them from usurping his power, and vicious monsters like the one-eyed, man-eating Cyclops Polyphemus, who was finally blinded by Odysseus, hero of the Trojan War. What the Greeks were doing in these tales, according to Nietzsche, was mythically narrating their own brutal history.) By the fourth century B.C.E., however, Greece had emerged from its Dark Age and, as Nietzsche put it, was basking in the brilliant clarity of Apollo—the god of light. By then, the Greeks had organized themselves into

13

a number of prosperous city-states that formed political and economic networks. Of these city-states, Athens was the crown jewel. Two hundred years earlier, the great political reformer and leader Solon (640–558 B.C.E.) had created a democratic system that allowed all male citizens the vote in the assembly and obligated them to sit as jurors. This political equality marked a victory of the newly emerging middle classes over the old aristocracy. Versions of this system and its new name—*demokratia*—spread throughout the city-states, with a few notable exceptions, especially Sparta, whose cowed peasants were ruled by an oligarchy of aristocratic warlords. Twice in the previous century, the Athenian democracy had repelled invasions by the powerful Persians. The Greeks defeated the numerically superior army of King Darius at Marathon in 490 B.C.E. and, ten years later, destroyed the fleet of Darius's son, Xerxes, in the battle of Salamis, after the Persians had already caused the abandonment of Athens by occupying the Acropolis, the hill rising above the city.

The Acropolis itself was a crowning achievement of Athenian art and culture. Its marvelous temple, the Parthenon, dedicated to Athena, the patron goddess of Athens, had been built between 447 and 438 B.C.E., and it still triumphantly gazes down upon Athens, perched there, as Nietzsche says, as "a permanent citadel of the Apollonian,"[1] a force of clarity and cool aloofness. The Parthenon contained a gigantic gold and ivory statue of Athena fashioned by the great sculptor Phidias (500–c. 431 B.C.E.), who, along with Praxiteles (born c. 390 B.C.E.) and an army of talented sculptors, left some of the most impressive works of art. Athens during the fifth

century was also blessed by some of the greatest dramatists of all time. Writers like Sophocles (c. 496–405 B.C.E.), Aeschylus (525–456 B.C.E.), and Euripides (480–406 B.C.E.) synthesized their creative genius with the Greek religious tradition, dramatizing the great events in which gods and humans interacted heroically to create the foundational moments of the history of the human race. (We now call it "myth," and our study of it, "mythology.")

**Oedipus Answers the Riddle of the Sphinx
(After Jean-Auguste Ingres)**

Yet, despite all this, despite "the glory that was Greece," as some enthusiasts have called it, the gold of the Golden Age was tainted with base metals that compromised the happiness of its leaseholders and foretold its eventual demise. Not only did the democracy of the city-states disenfranchise women (who were mere property of their fathers or husbands), but much of the "wealth of the nation" originated and was perpetuated in the institution of slavery and the policy of imperialism. The two programs were related, because slaves were considered to be the rightful spoils of war. And the colonialism of Athens was no light yoke to bear. The most notorious example of Athenian imperialistic zeal was the assault on the island of Melos. When Melos declared neutrality in the "cold war" between Athens and Sparta, it was put to siege by Athens, which, after accepting the surrender of

All men are free

. . .and I do mean men.

(Ahem.) Actually I mean landlords.

the island, betrayed the conditions of capitulation and massacred the male inhabitants and sold the women and children into slavery. This sordid affair was a prelude to the disastrous Peloponnesian War (431–404 B.C.E.), a prolonged internecine military clash that eventually favored the Spartans but that decimated both sides. During the the war, Spartans pillaged the countryside around Athens. The decomposition of corpses from the slaughter and the overcrowding of Athens by fleeing refugees produced a plague that killed a quarter of the population of the city, including its most illustrious politician-general, Pericles (c. 490–429 B.C.E.).

Furthermore, and related to the turmoil of the war, the Athenian democracy was overthrown twice. In 411 B.C.E., the "Dictatorship of the 400" was established, and in 404 B.C.E., after the dissolution of the first dictatorship, the rule of the "Thirty Tyrants" brutally suppressed the hard-won Athenian liberties before being finally overturned. However, even after the restoration of democracy, political troubles of the type that provoked the war with Sparta and the tyrannies of the dictatorships continued, foreshadowing the eventual demise of Athens and the Greek city-states. The Greeks' inability to maintain political unity and stability provoked their powerful northern neighbor, Macedonia, to force a peace upon the city-states. That artificial peace collapsed with the death of Macedonia's young leader, Alexander the Great. In the ensuing political chaos, Greece's greatest admirer and imitator, Rome, invaded the peninsula and imposed the notorious *pax romana* of the second century B.C.E.

Biography

Surprisingly little is known about Plato's life—partly due to controversy concerning the authenticity of certain letters purportedly written by him and partly because of a strange Athenian reluctance to write publicly about living or recently deceased persons. (Aristotle, Plato's student, rarely mentions him by name, referring to him with phrases like "friends of our own.") Plato was born in Athens, probably in 428 B.C.E., into a wealthy, aristocratic, antidemocratic family. Evidence suggests that he had political ambitions as a young man, but any such aspirations were forestalled by the success of the democratic parties in Athens and the taint of his family connections. His uncle, Critias, reputedly was the cruelest of the Thirty Tyrants, who temporarily overturned the democracy in 404 B.C.E. Critias was killed while fighting against the resistance forces the following year. Plato almost certainly fought in the Peloponnesian War, even though he is sometimes accused of having sympathies for the Spartan cause.

There is also evidence that, in his youth, Plato aspired to be a dramatist and even wrote several plays but that, when he fell under the influence of the old philosopher Socrates, he destroyed them. Plato was thirty-one years old when, in 399 B.C.E., Socrates was tried and executed, obstensibly for teaching doctines deemed atheistic, libelous, and untrue. Immediately after Socrates' death, a number of his followers, including Plato, found it wise to leave Athens. Plato may have journeyed to Egypt a few years later, and in 382 B.C.E. he made the first of three lengthy visits to Sicily, where he was handsomely paid to tutor the son of Dionysos the Elder, the king of Syracuse. Once back in Athens, Plato founded a small school called "the Academy," which is in some ways the ancestor of the modern university. He returned

Plato (c. 428–347 B.C.E.)

twice to Sicily, where he apparently hoped to influence politics along the lines of his philosophical theories. And he may well have intended that his most famous book, *The Republic,* be first presented there. (In Plato's day, books were not so much read as *presented*—that is, read out loud to an audience. This fact partially explains the dramatic

**The Death of Socrates
(After Jacques-Louis David, 1787)**

form that most of Plato's twenty-four books take.) But Plato became entangled in a dangerous political battle between his old student, Dionysos the Younger, and Dionysos's rival, Dion. One tradition has Plato's Athenian friends paying ransom to release Plato from prison or, some say, from slavery. At any rate, Plato's writings on politics became more somber after his final visit to Sicily. He died in Athens in 347 B.C.E. at the age of eighty-one.

Plato's Theory
The Social Conception of the Self

To appreciate Plato's theory of the self, let us contrast it with a very different conception of the self taken from our own era. Perhaps we could call it a peculiarly American conception (though not *the* American conception, since there are many of those), which goes something like this: The self is the individual. All people who are born psychically and emotionally whole are, or eventually become, individuals unless they somehow fail to do so out of cowardice or some other moral weakness. A true individual stands alone—perhaps against the crowd. He (typically "he," a masculine self) looks into his own heart to discover what is right. As John Wayne says (in how many movies?): "A man ought

The Individuality of George Custer

to do what he thinks is right." (When Wayne says this, typically a number of Native Americans are about to be slain.) Often, or maybe always, the individual is at odds with the state, for according to the belief system of exaggerated versions of this conception of the self, the state (government) has been taken over by forces allied against individualism: aliens, communists, minority lovers, subversives, perverts. Yet this same conception sees individuals as automatically having certain natural rights simply by virtue of their having been born of human parents—rights that, ironically in the case of those who see the individual as pitted against the state, are more or less those embodied in the Declaration of Independence, Constitution, and Bill of Rights. In this American conception, "society" is nothing more than the totality of individuals. Society thus has no life of its own—or, if it *does* take on a life of its own, that life should be resisted, for it may tend to drain the rights of individuals in terms of taxes and laws imposed upon them and governing their behavior (hence the suspicion of the state).

Yet, despite its claim to be "natural," this conception of the self is a historical product. It represents hard-fought victory—but a victory over what? Perhaps over

This country ain't big enough for both of us!!

the frontier. It is a conception that is partially the cause and partially the effect of the collective experience of a group of mostly European immigrants in a new and hostile land. Perhaps this is why this conception of the self is bound up with the idea of violence and even with the idea of guns, for it emerges from a history necessarily filled with violence.

Yet it was not always so. In ancient Greece, there predominated, among both the common people and the philosophers, a more social conception of the self in particular and of human nature in general, one in which the idea of the individual in opposition to the social body would be incomprehensible. We will begin our survey of various philosophical theories of human nature with what may be the most famous of such social conceptions, that of Plato, who claimed that the social body, the *polis* (from which we get our word "politics"), is the individual writ large. Conversely, the individual is a small political unit, a microcosmic reflection of the social macrocosm. (Needless to say, the macrocosm that Plato had in mind was a relatively small one—the size of the typical Greek city-state. Athens had a population of about 100,000 at the time that Plato wrote.) Even though the Greek city-state roughly fitted Plato's idea of the exemplary political body, Plato was not in love with the Athens of his day. As we saw, it had endured many political upheavals and had suffered from war and plague. Power was now in the hands of a new class of landholders and merchants who in the previous century had managed to wrest control from the old aristocratic class and had established the first political democracy. As we also saw, Plato was no friend of the democrats. He preferred the old aristocratic oligarchy, and what he took to be its respect for tradition and honor, over the new and unstable democracy, in which (as he saw it) private interest and political chicanery held sway. Yet, in his own depiction of the ideal state (and hence the ideal individual), he looked neither to the past nor to the present as his guide; rather, he imagined an ideal city governed by certain rational ideas that he believed the philosophical mind could discover, much as it could discover the secrets of nature.

Before describing Plato's philosophical theory of the polis, we must take two short side trips, one to inspect Plato's general metaphysical view of reality (this will illuminate why Plato could "look into the sky" for the guidelines of his ideal city), and one to discern his method of communicating his ideas.

The Doctrine of the "Forms"

Plato's most complete statement of his overall metaphysical view appears in Book VI of *The Republic*, where he has his spokesman, Socrates (more about him in a moment), draw with a stick in the sand a line around which he traces a design that looks like this:[2]

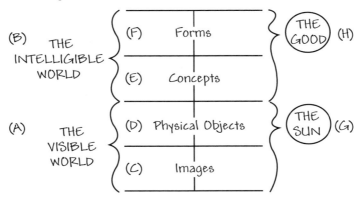

The Simile of the Line

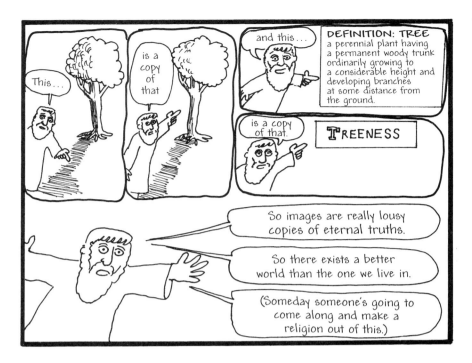

Luckily, for our purposes, we need only the barest outline of this complicated vision, now usually called "the simile of the line," though it has exercised such an influence over Western thinking that we allude to it constantly in subsequent chapters.

Plato's main division is between (A) the visible world and (B) the intelligible world. (A) is a copy or imitation of (B), so the implication is that the visible world (that is, the physical world we inhabit) is somehow less real than the intelligible world it imitates. As you can see, each main division, (A) and (B), is further broken down into two subdivisions that reflect the structure of the main divisions. That is, (C) images (such as reflections, shadows, and paintings) are copies of (D) physical objects.

FORM	$f = ma$
CONCEPT	"Force equals mass times acceleration"
PHYSICAL ACT	
IMAGE	

Mathematical Version of "the Line"

Hence, images are less real than physical objects. Similarly, (B) is broken down into (E) concepts (basically theories and definitions) and (F) Forms; here, the former are imitations of the latter. Plato's key notion, Forms, is also his most puzzling one, and scholars have struggled with its meaning for 2000 years. The **Forms** are often understood to be kinds of mathematical truths, and therefore mathematics is what imposes order on the flux of the physical world. (Note that there is a kind of mathematical formula governing the whole of Plato's system here: [A] is to [B] as [C] is to [D], as [E] is to [F], as [G] is to [H].) Whatever else they may be, the Forms are eternal, unchanging archetypes of everything that exists in the worlds below them. They can be grasped not by the eye but by the mind, the intellect—though they are grasped intellectually analogously with the way the eye "grasps" the visible world.

Thus, we have the further analogy of (G), the Sun, which rules over the physical world and whose light allows us to grasp via the senses the physical world, and (H), the Good, which rules over the intelligible world and whose "light" allows us to grasp the Forms intellectually. The acquisition of knowledge, then, is the movement from what most translators call *opinion* (basically, the nonconceptual grasping of the images and objects of the physical world) to *knowledge* (basically, the grasping of reality through concepts and, ultimately, through the Forms.) The pursuit of knowledge in itself is finally a *moral* pursuit, as the goal is the grasping of the Good, the source of all reality and knowledge. It is the light of the Good shining on the Forms, Plato believed, that allows one to "see" the ideal city, and hence the ideal human being.

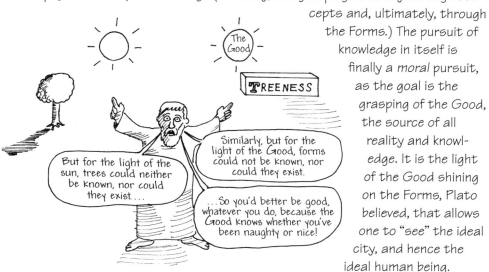

But for the light of the sun, trees could neither be known, nor could they exist....

Similarly, but for the light of the Good, forms could not be known, nor could they exist.

...So you'd better be good, whatever you do, because the Good knows whether you've been naughty or nice!

Socrates (c. 470–399 B.C.E.)

And now, a few words about Plato's method of philosophizing: Plato wrote most of his philosophy in the form of dramatic dialogues, which were to be presented to the students of his Academy and were meant to provoke philosophical discussions among the students. The characters in these dialogues were usually real people whom Plato had known in his youth, when he was a disciple of the eminent Athenian philosopher, Socrates (470–399 B.C.E.). Socrates had been condemned to death by a jury of his peers for impiety, for teaching false doctrines, for slander, and for corrupting the youth of Athens. Part of Plato's antipathy for democracy stems from this unjust sentence passed on his martyred teacher, and Plato honored Socrates by making him the main spokesman for the key philosophical ideas in Plato's dialogues. The problem for both ancient and modern readers of these dialogues is determining how many of those ideas were really Socrates' and how many were put in his mouth by Plato. Unfortunately, Socrates wrote nothing because he was suspicious of the written word, a sentiment clearly not shared by Plato. Luckily, there is much overlap between the ideas of these two men, because Plato agreed with most of what Socrates taught—at least, as he understood it. But as the years passed and memory faded, Plato's own ideas no doubt displaced those of his teacher. Much scholarly work and much debate have been dedicated to sorting out all

Never trust a book . . . except this one, of course.

this. A commonsense assumption is that the earlier dialogues report more accurately the actual ideas and discourse of Socrates than do the later dialogues. For our purposes, we will treat the words put into Socrates' mouth by Plato as *Plato's* words, and not try to determine how well they reflect the views of his teacher.

The Origin of Society

Having said that, let us now return to Plato's understanding of the relation between the individual and the *polis* as it is explained in his most famous work, *The Republic*, in order to determine Plato's specific vision of human nature. There, Plato has Socrates imagine the origins of the social unit. He says, "A city, I take it, comes into being because each of us is not self-sufficient. Can you think any other beginning could found a city?" he asks his young friend, Adeimantos. Plato assumed that individual humans have needs but are unable to supply those needs by themselves. Therefore, they enter voluntarily but naturally (we are naturally social beings) into mutually

advantageous relations with other human beings. "Then one man gives a share of something to another or takes a share . . . because he thinks he will be better for it?" Socrates asks.[3] He then describes a society based on a simple division of labor, whereby each individual contributes his or her skills and reaps the benefits of the skills of others. The result is an uncomplicated, almost "spartan" social unit. (Remember, some critics believe that Plato secretly sympathized with the Spartan cause in the Peloponnesian War.) They will produce "food and wine" and, for winter, "clothes and shoes," for in summer they will work "stripped and barefoot" (p. 168). They will grow barley and wheat for bread and cakes, which they will consume with small amounts of wine. At this point, Socrates' friend Glaucon interrupts, complaining that the city described is *too austere*. Socrates agrees to add salt, olives, cheese,

onions, and greens, and perhaps figs for dessert, "So they will spend their days in health and peace, living to old age" (p. 169). This simple social unit is what Socrates calls a "healthy city." But now Glaucon complains that, even with these additions, the city is still too simple. He objects that the people will not be comfortable because they do not have couches upon which to recline (a very Greek thought!).

Socrates says that he sees that the question has now been changed from "How does the city come into being?" to "How does a luxurious city come into being?"—a city that no longer contains only the bare necessities, but one that requires "fine foods . . . ointments . . . incense . . . pretty girls and cakes . . . gold and ivory" (p. 169). Such a "swollen city" by implication produces swollen individuals, and it requires more land, which must be taken from its neighbors. There is a reciprocity

between greed in the individual and greed in the city—and greed is the origin of war (and hence the source as well of a certain kind of violence within the individual psyche).

The Social Divisions of the Ideal City

At this point, Plato moves from a discussion of greed to a discussion of war and the class of warriors that must be generated to wage war, whether just (presumably in the defense of a "healthy city" against a greedy, "feverish city") or unjust (in the case of feverish aggression). This discussion initiates Plato's analysis of the Ideal City—certainly not the same as the "feverish city," but apparently not identical to the "healthy city" either. Rather, this city imitates a plan that exists in the heaven of Forms. By extension, his analysis is also one of the ideal human individual. This ideal city thas three castes: a working and artisan class, making up the majority of the population; a military and police class, which protects

The Three Castes

the city from its enemies, external and internal; and a ruling class of "guardians," philosophers who will guide the city according to rational principles. Despite the worrisome nature of this caste system, it is to Plato's credit that, unlike the Athenian democracy into which he was born, he respected the intellect and capacity of women enough to place no barriers between them and leadership positions. The best of them (but only the best, as his republic was an elitist philosophical oligarchy) could become members of the ruling class. Plato devotes several chapters of *The Republic* to explaining the complicated relations among these three classes and the education of the members of the two upper classes (involving so much regimentation and censorship that it seems obnoxious to the modern reader, and surely to many of Plato's contemporaries as well).

For our purposes, we need only concentrate on the fact that Plato claims that each class has its own virtue—its own kind of "excellence" (*aretê* in Greek)—and that the truly *good* city (that is, the just city) results from each class dedicating itself to its specific *aretê* and submitting to the rule of Reason and Law. The prime virtue of the working class is that of *moderation* or *temperance*, of the military class is *courage* or *spirit*, and of the ruling class is *wisdom* or *intelligence*. In a curious, almost mathematical way, the

Reading the News in Plato's Republic

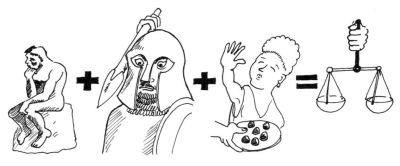

Wisdom *plus* Courage *plus* Moderation *equals* Justice

sum total of these three virtues is a kind of harmony that is somehow equal to *justice*. Having established this argument to his own satisfaction, Plato now has Socrates return to the topic that was the original source of the discussion: the individual.

The Psychological Divisions of the Soul

Just as the city is composed of three hierarchically structured social classes, so is the human soul composed of three hierarchically structured psychical elements. Plato calls these, in the order of their priority, the rational soul, the spirited soul, and the appetitive soul. Reason, which Plato associates metaphorically with the head, is that faculty capable of seeing beyond the flux and illusions of appearance and of grasping that which is eternally true, of grasping the structure of Being itself. However, despite its intellectual power, Reason by itself is impotent. It can provide justifications for actions, but no real *motives*—that is, it can't move us to action. By contrast, Spirit (which is vaguely associated with the heart) is the seat of action— it transforms reasons for actions into causes for actions. Spirit is capable of embodying the reasons of Reason and acting upon them, but unfortunately, it is also capable of embodying the reasons (or the unreason) of Appetite. Appetite, which can be associated vaguely with a region of the body somewhere below the midriff, is the animal self.

DOWN BOY!

Its "reasons" are derived from desire—sexual, nutritive, or aggressive—and so it connects us more immediately with the animal world than with the divine. Left to its own devices, Appetite would produce chaos in the individual. A passage in Book IX of *The Republic* reveals both this possibility and the extent to which Sigmund Freud's conception of the id (to be discussed in Chapter Nine) was influenced by Plato. Speaking of the "lawlessness" of certain "unnecessary desires and pleasures," Socrates says:

> . . . they are born in everyone, it is true, but when they are chastened by the laws and the better desires with reason's help, some people can get rid of them wholly, or only a few remain. . . .
> [These desires] are those that are aroused in sleep . . . whenever the rest of the soul, all the reasonable, gentle and ruling part, is asleep, but the bestial and savage, replete with food and wine, skips about and, throwing off sleep, tries to go and fulfill its own instincts. You know there is nothing it will not dare to do, thus freed and rid of all shame and reason; it shrinks not from attempting in fancy to lie with a mother or with any other man or beast, shrinks from no bloodshed, refrains from no food—in a word, leaves no folly or shamelessness untried. (pp. 369–370)

Glaucon's response to this amazing description of dream life, involving incestuous and homosexual rape, bestiality, impiety, murder, and gluttony, is simply to say, "Only too true" (p. 370). No wonder Plato believes that the animal side of human nature must not be given free rein. Unfortunately, Plato finds that art relates to Appetite roughly as philosophy relates to Reason. Art is a dream for those who are awake. Therefore, in the name of Reason's rule over the entire soul, the arts must be suppressed—or at least highly censored—lest they motivate the passions to rebellion.

The three partitions of the soul stand in the same relation to one another and to the psychic whole as the three social classes stand to one another and to the social body. Just as the class of philosophers must guide the soldiers and the workers, so must Reason guide both Spirit and

Appetite. Spirit must implement the rules revealed by Reason, and Appetite must submit to the rational controls imposed upon it even though these rules go against Appetite's natural inclinations.

Here is where political science returns to psychology. The three social classes have the same virtues as do the three aspects of the soul.

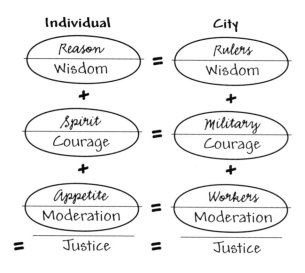

The excellence of Reason is wisdom; the excellence of Spirit is courage; the excellence of Appetite is temperance. The correct balance of these three virtues produces a kind of exceptional goodness, called *dikaiosyne* in Greek and awkwardly translated as "justice." (Perhaps a term such as "morality" or even "moral ecology" communicates the idea better.) The truly good human self for Plato is the self that allows itself to be dominated by Reason; it is the self of the passionate person who has rational mastery over his or her passions. But in a certain sense, this rational mastery comes from outside. That is, a plan exists eternally in the heaven of Forms that Reason must grasp, and once grasped, the plan must be imposed upon the soul. This plan involves a kind of

The Dictatorship of Reason

dictatorship of Reason, which may be less offensive in Plato's psychological model than in his political model, in which the ideal society is literally a dictatorship.

Yet Plato, and Socrates before him, did not live in such an "ideal" society. They lived in a flawed society—very flawed from Plato's point of view, for it was a democracy, and hence a society dedicated to individual self-interest and to short-range goals. And according to his theory, such a society must produce individuals with the same "virtues," or lack of them. Now, here is a paradox for Plato. On the one hand, his psychological/political model entails the view that there is a reciprocal relation between the individual and the city—they create each other in their own image. (If the city is the individual writ large, then the individual is the city writ small.) On the other hand, the actual individuals of his day inhabited a city that he believed was incapable of creating the social conditions that would enhance the moral qualities of the individual. So what was Plato's attitude toward the individual Athenian citizen—a man or woman who does not inhabit Plato's ideal republic? Should such persons oppose the authority of the state that has created them? In fact, how would such an antagonistic relationship be possible if the individual was both the creation and the reflection of the social body?

The Individual Is the City Writ Small

The Relation between the Individual and the Law

Perhaps the answer to this question is best developed through an inspection of some of the ideas that Plato puts in the mouth of Socrates in the much-read dialogues called *The Apology* and *Crito*. *The Apology* is the dialogue dramatizing the trial of Socrates and his response to his accusers.[4] (The English word "apology" is a very misleading translation of Plato's *apologia*, which means "defense"; Socrates is not even slightly disposed to apologize for his behavior.) He has been charged by his enemies with corrupting the young and with impiety (that is, disbelief in "the gods whom the state believes in" [p. 430]). Socrates denies the charge—denies that he is a criminal. He admits that his views have been provocative and have annoyed "the state," but he claims that he has merely been a "gadfly" whose bite wakens the noble steed that is the state, so that in fact his philosophical critique has been of service to the state. For Plato's Socrates, the *idea* of the state is higher than any of its manifestations. Socrates is loyal to the idea of the state even when he is in disagreement with its contemporary embodiment. The idea of the state incorporates a higher law, namely,

Socrates as Gadfly

that law embodied in the *Form of the State* that exists in the top segment of the divided line. Every state—even those that reflect that idea poorly—imitates that higher law. To that law, Socrates is faithful. And for the same reason that Socrates is loyal to the state, he is loyal to himself; he believes that he has wronged no man by his actions, and he certainly will

not wrong himself by groveling before the jury to save his life. In precisely this way, he refutes the charges that he does not believe in "divine and spiritual things" (p. 434).

But if Socrates thinks that the charge brought against him by the state is unjust, as is the state's punishment of him, why does he not escape from jail when his friend Crito bribes the guard? If there really is a "higher law," does it not command him to disobey temporal laws that are unjust? Certainly, we, who have been brought up with an awareness of the tradition of the doctrine of civil disobedience set forth by Thoreau, Gandhi, and Martin Luther King, Jr., may well ask this question. But Socrates' views on this topic lead him to a different conclusion. He believes that what dis-

tinguishes humans from the rest of the animals is that we create communities governed by law rather than by instinct. Even though each community is an imperfect embodiment of the Law, it is the Law that makes us what we are. Socrates will prove the injustice of the temporal law's punishment by accepting that punishment. He believes that, in escaping, he would be breaking the law and would thereby set himself in opposition to the Law—and hence in opposition to humanity itself (because humanity is what it is by virtue of its acceptance of Law). Socrates presents Crito with two arguments to prove that he must submit to the unjust death sentence. First, because he has accepted the benefits offered to him by the laws of his state, he has entered into an implied contract with the state. Therefore, he is obligated to obey even the law that condemns him to death. Second, if an individual has the right to break any law that he sees as inconvenient to him (and "inconvenient" here includes the belief that the law is unjust), then he is attacking the concept of Law itself. (He has declared war against the Law and is therefore an outlaw.) Law cannot exist if any individual has the privilege of ignoring it.

To understand Socrates' argument, think of the analogy between the laws of a state and the rules of a game. What if we were playing chess and either of us could ignore any rule that we found "unjust"? For instance, you move your queen two spaces from my king and say, "Check!" I reach down, pick up your queen, and swallow her. You reach over, grab my king, and throw him through the window. Whatever is going on in this mad episode, it is *not* chess. It is like a scene out of *Alice Through the Looking-Glass*. Such a world, in fact, cannot exist. And an individual, even a "gadfly to noble

Chess, Anyone?

steeds," cannot exist as a member of the human community if he arrogates to himself the right to be an outlaw. The individual is the Republic writ small. So believed Plato.

Summary

In Plato's theory of human nature, the human being, like everything else in the universe, is the manifestation of a sublimely real **essence.** The double key to the essence of humanity is its rationality and its sociability. The human being is—or ought to be—governed by Reason, which is the ability to search for, grasp, and act on eternal truths. That is, Reason is the human capacity for wisdom. Or, to put it yet another way, Reason is the capacity to grasp the Good—and hence to become identified with the Good—that makes one human. Success in this endeavor requires that Reason, the rational aspect of the tripartite human soul, dominate the other two parts, Spirit and Appetite, creating a harmonious whole in which each part fulfills its function. Reason provides wisdom, Spirit generates courage, and Appetite (needed for physical sustenance, procreation, and sensual pleasure) exhibits moderation. A function of such a harmony is *justice*.

But justice, wisdom, courage, and moderation are not merely individual virtues; they are also social virtues. Because humans are by nature social, there must exist an eternal Form for the virtue of social justice, just as there is a Form for the other virtues. A major part of the philosopher's desire to seek wisdom is a need—indeed, a duty—to discover the proper manner in which sociality ought to be organized. That is, the philosopher must discover the nature of the *polis*—the republic. Based on what has been said so far, we might expect such a society to be a republic of arts and letters, in which all individuals are encouraged to pursue to the fullest their natural

What about this bust of you, Plato? Shall we destroy it too?

Well, no.... Let's keep that.

Art Whose Function Is More Noble

capacity for philosophy and the arts. But it turns out that this is not so. The arts are not greatly cherished in Plato's ideal world; in fact, they are highly censored, being, as Plato believes, aligned not with Reason or Spirit, but with Appetite—with the dangerous passions that encourage humans to revolt against their natural ruler, Reason. Nor is philosophy pursued on a universal scale in *The Republic*, because it turns out, surprisingly—indeed, contradictorily—that most people are incapable of philosophizing. It is this contradiction in Plato's theory of human nature (namely, that it is part of human nature that the soul should be guided by Reason, yet most humans do not have enough Reason to be so guided; therefore, they must be guided by someone else's Reason) that results in Plato's ideal republic being a rigid dictatorship that holds a strict caste system in place by force of arms. What Plato's philosophers discover when they look to the heavens in pursuit of the Good is that, in the good society, most people are not good.

Topics for Consideration

1. How does Plato's political philosophy in general relate to the political conditions of fourth-century B.C.E. Athens?

2. What features of fourth-century B.C.E. Athens provoke various enthusiasts to refer to the period as "the Golden Age of Greece"? What features undermine that attribution?

3. In what ways does so-called American individualism contrast with the ancient Greek conception of selfhood and citizenship?

4. What does Plato mean when he says that the city is the individual writ large?

5. Select a concept such as "beauty" and analyze it from the perspective of Plato's metaphysics as exhibited in "the simile of the line."

6. What is the status of "the Good" in Plato's system? How does it relate to the various components of "the simile of the line"?

7. Trace the development of the city from its origin in its simplest form to Plato's ideal republic.

8. What are the four main virtues in Plato's moral theory? Show the parallelism between these virtues as personal moral qualities and as public, social qualities.

9. Write a paragraph in which you attack art from Plato's point of view; then write another in which you defend art from Plato's attack.

10. Take sides in the debate over whether Socrates' refusal to escape from jail is consistent with the Socratic/Platonic philosophy set forth in this chapter.

11. If Plato could be made to agree that *all* people are capable of philosophy *and* that art is in the service of truth, how different would his ideal republic be from the dictatorship he imagines?

Suggestions for Further Reading

I. Plato's Main Works

Great Dialogues of Plato. Trans. W. H. D. Rouse. New York: Mentor, 1984. (Includes *The Republic, Apology, Crito, Phaedo, Ion, Meno,* and *Symposium.*)

II. Secondary Sources on Plato

Cavalier, Robert. *Plato for Beginners.* London and New York: Writers & Readers, 1996.

Grube, G. M. A. *Plato's Thought.* Indianapolis, Ind.: Hackett, 1980.

Stone, I. F. *The Trial of Socrates.* Boston and Toronto: Little, Brown, 1988.

Vlastos, Gregory. *Studies in Greek Philosophy,* Vol. II, *Socrates, Plato and Their Tradition.* Princeton, N.J.: Princeton University Press, 1995.

Notes

1. Friedrich Nietzsche, *The Birth of Tragedy,* trans. Clifton F. Fadiman (New York: Dover, 1995), p. 12.

2. There is some disagreement concerning the mathematical proportions in this diagram. We will ignore that debate and make the divisions equal in size. Also, there has been much controversy over the translation of Plato's key terms. Obviously, I have selected the ones that I find truest to the spirit of his philosophy.

3. Plato, *The Republic,* in *Great Dialogues of Plato,* trans. W. H. D. Rouse (New York: Mentor, 1984), pp. 165–166. Page numbers of future references to *The Republic* will be included in the main body of the text in parentheses.

4. Plato, *Apology,* in *Great Dialogues of Plato,* p. 430. Page numbers of future references to *Apology* will be included in the body of the text within parentheses.

2

The Aristotelian Conception of Human Nature

Historical Backdrop

The main historical development between the overlapping generations of Plato (c. 428–347 B.C.E.) and Aristotle (384–322 B.C.E.) is, on the one hand, the failure of the Greek city-states to terminate the kind of internecine conflict that had decimated Athens and Sparta in the Peloponnesian

Ancient Greece

War, and, on the other hand, the parallel expansion of the political and military might of Macedonia. Macedonia was a landmass to the north of the Greek peninsula between the classical city-states and the "barbarian"

Philip of Macedonia (382–336 B.C.E.)

tribes of the Balkans. The Macedonians were a people on the fringe of the Greek-speaking world. The city-states treated Macedonia as either barbarian or as part of the Greek world, depending on their purpose of the moment. Politically, Macedonia did not fit in. The city-states were, as we have seen, small democracies or oligarchies; by contrast, Macedonia was an unwieldy political giant (about twice the size of the state of Massachusetts) governed by a line of hereditary kings that had not changed in hundreds of years. Also, unlike the city-states, it did not organize its substructure of labor

around slaves or serfs—most Macedonians were free farmers tilling their own soil. These "primitive features" of the Macedonian social world provoked their southern neighbors to mock the Macedonians as barbarians. However, what the Macedonians *did* have was an ambitious, politically astute, and militarily brilliant leader, King Philip II. Philip could boast of excellent Greek aristocratic credentials, tracing his lineage to Heracles, son of the god Zeus. A contemporary historian, Theopompus, has summarized the way Philip was able to exploit the various factions in the politics of the city-states and take advantage of the power shifts in the wars among those republics between 358 and 354 B.C.E.:

> While the city-states of Greece longed individually to exercise power over others, they ruined their own power one and all. Rushing headlong into mutual annihilation, they realized only when they were subjugated that the very thing individual states were losing was being lost by them all; for Philip indeed, king of Macedonia, perched as it were on a watch-tower, having laid his ambushes against the liberties of them all, while he fed the flames of inter-state rivalries by affording help to the weaker party, compelled conquerors and conquered alike to accept enslavement to a king.[1]

In 362, the city-states, exhausted by the turmoil they had unleashed upon themselves, had tried to form a pan-Hellenic unity pact, the Common Peace, but within a year it had collapsed. In 357, Athens and some allies declared

The Macedonian Phalanx

war on Macedonia, but Philip proved to be a formidable opponent. He had invented the Macedonian phalanx, which was a formation of 16,000 soldiers, 1,000 across and 16 deep, each carrying a heavy, fifteen-feet-long pike. The pike had a steel spearhead at the point and was counterweighted at the butt so that it could be held with both hands near the butt. The soldiers each carried a shield only two feet in diameter, so they could stand closely together and create a shell above them to defend against barrages of arrows. The phalanx advanced slowly but relentlessly, like some kind of bristling mechanical monster. Nothing could stand in its way—not infantry or cavalry or even elephants. The phalanx secured the defeat of the anti-Macedonian alliance of city-states, and it would shortly permit Philip's son, Alexander (Alexander "the Great," if you admire slaughter and pillage in the name of conquest and glory), to defeat Persian armies vastly superior in number. Philip was assassinated in 336 by one of his officers at the celebration of his polygamous marriage to a beautiful young bride. There has been suspicion that the assassin, Pausanias, was in league with the Athenians, or

Alexander in Battle

with the Persians, or with Philip's first wife, mother of Alexander, or even with Alexander himself. But Pausanius apparently was a jealous and vengeful officer in Philip's army who as a young man had been Philip's lover and who more recently had not received justice from Philip after he reported being raped by some officers who were members of the king's inner circle.[2]

Alexander, only nineteen years old, inherited his father's throne, but the city-states took advantage of Philip's death to try to free themselves from Macedonian rule. Alexander marched to southern Greece to put down a rebellion in Thebes, one of the city-states. He utterly destroyed Thebes to set an example to the other contentious republics. Having thus resecured Macedonia's grip on the Greek peninsula, Alexander invaded Asia Minor, conquering all of the Middle East as far as India and having himself declared a god by priests in Egypt, where he set up his only truly lasting monument, the city of Alexandria. In one battle alone, he left the corpses of 300,000 men, in addition to those of horses and elephants. Because there were too many corpses to allow for burial or cremation, the rotting remains created a pestilence that killed many thousands more. A nineteenth-century biographer of Alexander, writing prior to the horrors of the American Civil War and World War I and the Holocaust of World War II, could say:

> In fact, it is probable that Alexander's slaughter of the Persian army at Arbela, and the subsequent spoliation of Susa, constitute, taken together, the most gigantic case of murder and robbery which was ever committed by man. . . . That these deeds were really crimes there can be no doubt, when we consider that Alexander did not pretend to have any other motive in this invasion than love of conquest, which is, in other words, love of violence and plunder.[3]

In 321, at the age of thirty-two, Alexander died in Babylon of general dissolution and debauchery (shortly before falling mortally ill, he had twice drained the gigantic, wine-filled Bowl of Hercules to the enthusiastic applause of his guests). At the news of his death, there was great mourning in Babylon and Macedonia, but in the streets of Athens, a wild celebration broke out. Yet neither on the Greek mainland nor in Alexander's Persian Empire was there to be peace, for he had done nothing to ensure political continuity upon his death. Thus, upon his burial in Alexandria, the various nations in the region fell into bloody civil strife. Alexander's sudden fall from power left all Macedonians living in Greece in mortal danger, vulnerable to reprisal from vengeful Greeks who had suffered under the Macedonian yoke. Included in this group of frightened individuals was Alexander's former tutor, the philosopher Aristotle.

Biography

Aristotle was born in Stagira, Macedonia, in 384 B.C.E. His father and his grandfather had been personal physicians to the kings of Macedonia. Both

Aristotle (384–322 B.C.E.)

of Aristotle's parents died young, and at the age of seventeen, Aristotle went to Athens to study at Plato's Academy, where he remained for almost twenty years. After Plato's death in 347, he left the Academy, complaining that Plato's successor had tried to "turn philosophy into mathematics." How much *direct* influence Plato had on Aristotle is still debated (Plato flitted about quite a bit during those years). But it is fairly clear that, in his earliest writings, Aristotle followed Plato almost completely, only later becoming critical of many of his mentor's main ideas.

In 343, King Philip invited Aristotle to return to Macedonia to tutor his son, Alexander. This tutelage ended in 335 when, upon his father's death, Alexander became king. As a gift for the new king, Aristotle had an elegant copy of Homer's poems made. The young ruler took it with him on all his campaigns and tried to style himself after the Homeric heroes. For example, in his invasion of Asia Minor, Alexander insisted on making his first landing at what he took to be the site of the ruins of Troy, scene of the Trojan War described by Homer. Despite stories that have Alexander sending Aristotle meteorological and astronomical data, as well as scientific specimens from the lands he conquered, there is little evidence of Aristotelian influence on Alexander's thinking. For instance, Aristotle's political thought was confined to the idea of the city-state, but Alexander thought BIG (as we saw, perhaps a little too big).

Aristotle returned to Athens in 335 and opened his own school, the Lyceum, successfully competing with the Academy. Because he would lecture while walking along the *peripatos* (covered pathway) of his garden, he became known as "the Peripatetic." He taught there until the news of Alexander's death reached Athens, at which point strong anti-Macedonian sentiment was unleashed and cries for a declaration of war against Macedonia were heard. Fearing for his life, Aristotle fled Athens, "lest the Athenians sin twice against philosophy." He was

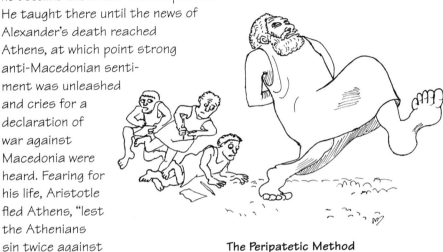

The Peripatetic Method

indeed charged with the capital crime of "impiety" (the same vague charge leveled against Socrates), tried *in absentia,* and sentenced to death—probably because of his ties to Philip and Alexander—but by then he was safe on the island of Eubia, which had granted him refuge. Twice married, Aristotle had a daughter with his first wife, Pythias, niece of the king of Assos, a colony on the coast of Asia Minor (today's Turkey); after her death, he had a son, Nicomachus, by his second wife, Herpyllis of Stagira. He dedicated to his son *The Nicomachean Ethics,* the book we will reference in our review of Aristotle's theory of human nature. Aristotle apparently suffered from delicate health throughout his life. He died in 322 B.C.E. in exile at Eubia. His will shows that, at the time of his death, he was moderately wealthy. He owned several slaves, some of whom he freed in his will.

Unfortunately for readers of Aristotle, he was a poor stylist, writing in a repetitive and clunky manner. Most of his works were not intended for publication and were probably his lecture notes. Nevertheless, they cover a remarkable range of topics—including logic (a science he almost single-handedly established), drama, rhetoric, biology, psychology, ethics, physics, and metaphysics. (The word "metaphysics" was coined by Aristotle's editor, who, after Aristotle's death, bound together a collection of his essays containing general speculations on reality at large, placed the collected essays after the book on physics, and called it simply *Metaphysics*. The Greek word *meta* means "after.")

Aristotle's Theory

Aristotle shared with his teacher, Plato, the general Greek assumption about the social nature of humans. His main objection to his mentor's philosophy concerned its abstract and otherworldly nature. He tried to bring Plato's philosophy down to earth. For Aristotle, there was no need to imagine an ideal republic-in-the-sky in order to understand human nature. It could be studied by meditating on empirical observations of human beings both in everyday situations and in extreme conditions.

Teleology

Notwithstanding Aristotle's anti-Platonic concern for concrete facts, his philosophy is dominated by a guiding abstract concept—that of **teleology,** the study of goal-oriented behavior. For Aristotle, all events, natural or human, must be understood as purposeful. Thus, the rain falls *in order to* water the grasses, and the grasses grow *in order to* feed animals. These goals do not exist external to the world in some realm of eternal Forms (as in Plato's view), nor in the mind of some transcendent God who has created the natural world to fulfill His wishes (as in Judaism, Christianity, or Islam). Rather, these goals are implicit in nature itself. There is a god in Aristotle's system— a "prime mover"—but this deity does not exist as a creator (what Aristotle would call an "efficient cause"). The prime mover's only activity is pure thought. It thinks only about those things that are unchanging; that is, it thinks only about itself. It is, in fact, the perfection toward

Aristotle Bringing Plato's Philosophy Down to Earth

which all reality strives as its objective. It is what Aristotle calls a "final cause"—"final" in the sense that it is reality's goal, the *telos* of the universe. Every object in nature is unconsciously striving for perfection, striving to be godlike insofar as that is possible within the constraints of its essential makeup. In fact, every object in the universe is defined in terms of the *purpose* it is trying to fulfill, which is to say, in terms of its maximum excellence (once again, as with Plato, we have the Greek word *aretê*).

Teleology: Actions Are like Arrows— They Are Aimed at Some Target.

This, of course, is exactly the kind of view of nature that Charles Darwin's theory of evolution is thought to refute. As we will see in Chapter 7, Darwin believed he could show that what we take to be purpose in nature is, in fact, merely the fallout from random statistical probability (as we would say today) coincidentally resulting in living organisms that survive because they have features that respond well to the envi-

ronmental conditions in which they find themselves. Darwin called this arbitrary process "natural selection." Darwin did not deny that teleological concepts are the correct ones for understanding individual human actions. People (but not carrots) do things because they have purposes and goals. But Aristotle went much further: Not only do humans have purposes, they have a purpose. In the same way that rain and crops can become self-actualized by fulfilling their purposes, so can humans become self-actualized by fulfilling theirs.

Later in the book, we will see arguments that constitute a radical critique of Aristotle's views (especially by Darwin in Chapter 7 and by Jean-Paul Sartre in Chapter 10). Despite those arguments, Aristotle's teleological conception of human nature has a power of its own. Let us now develop his conception by looking at some of the key ideas in his *Nicomachean Ethics*.[4]

Carrot Teleology

Every action and choice seem to aim at some good. [p. 1]

The Meaning of Life

Actions are instruments for achieving goals. I get up in the morning in order to shower, dress, and eat. I shower, dress, and eat so I can go to work. I go to work so I can earn money. I earn money so I can pay my utilities and buy food and clothes and a bed. BUT WAIT A MINUTE!

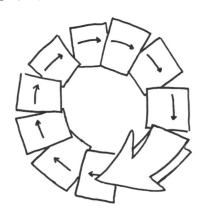

Circular System

A Tale Told by an Idiot

Is this all there is to life—this circular system of goals forever feeding one into the other? If so, says Aristotle, "then our desire would be futile and pointless" (p. 15), and life would be, as Shakespeare's Macbeth says two thousand years later, "a tale told by an idiot, full of sound and fury, signifying nothing." If, on the other hand, there is some supreme good that is desirable for its own sake—a goal under which we can subsume all other

Oh goody! I've fallen from the tree. Now I can become a butterfly!

Acorn Unclear on the Concept

goals, goals that would prove to be only means to this supreme end—then we have an obligation to ourselves to discover what that supreme goal is. That is, we have an obligation to philosophize, for only through philosophy can we identify that supreme goal.

According to Aristotle, all beings and all systems have built into them an **entelechy,** namely, a goal-oriented mechanism of self-actualization. Acorns, for example, strive to fulfill themselves as oak trees, while caterpillars direct themselves toward becoming butterflies. Of course, this is not conscious motivation on their parts; it is an unconscious organic process. In fact, in one sense, acorns and caterpillars have an advantage over humans precisely because their goal-seeking is unconscious. They may have bad luck (an acorn may fall on the pavement, or a caterpillar may be crushed by a chariot), but they can't err. Because consciousness is part of the human essence, humans must *choose* goals to

PARKING

BY THE MILLENNIUM
$50 PER HOUR

Oh Oh!

pursue, and humans can make mistakes—
sometimes *big* mistakes. A person could
spend his or her whole life pursuing
false goals, and, for Aristotle, this
would be the greatest tragedy
imaginable. Death is sad, but it
is not tragic. However, if a man
on his deathbed looks back
over his time on earth and
says, "I have wasted my life," no
greater misfortune can be imagined. So, again, we *must* philosophize to avert this tragedy. We
must find out if there is such a
supreme goal, and if so, what it is.

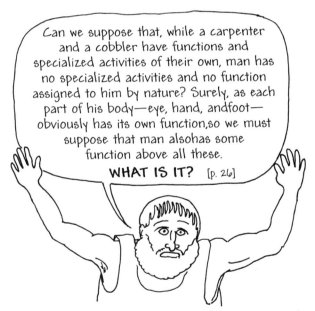

I cudda been
somebuddy.
I cudda been
a contenda.

Aristotle asks:

Can we suppose that, while a carpenter
and a cobbler have functions and
specialized activities of their own, man has
no specialized activities and no function
assigned to him by nature? Surely, as each
part of his body—eye, hand, andfoot—
obviously has its own function,so we must
suppose that man alsohas some
function above all these.
WHAT IS IT? [p. 26]

Now, in one sense, we already know the answer, according to Aristotle. Each
of us already knows what we want out of life: happiness. (Note that the
Greek word for "happiness," *eudaimonie*—roughly, "good genius"—does not
seem to have an exact English counterpart. Translating it as "well-being" or
as "human flourishing" might better express Aristotle's idea.) But this
really gets us nowhere; we still don't know exactly what happiness is and
how it can be achieved. Therefore, asserts Aristotle, saying that the goal of
human life is happiness is the beginning of the investigation, not its end.

Before stating his own view, Aristotle cannot resist taking a swipe at his old master, Plato, saying:

I wonder how the weaver would be aided in his craft by a knowledge of the form of the good, or how a man would be more able to heal the sick or command an army by contemplation of the pure form or idea. It seems to me that the physician does not seek for health in this abstract way but for the health of man—or rather of some particular man, for it is individuals that he has to heal. [p. 22]

If we are to determine what "the function of man" is, we will have to know what a human being is. What if we said that the human being is the animal capable of blushing or the animal capable of getting corns on its feet? Would we be able to deduce the human function from these definitions? No, because despite being exclusive (no other animal blushes or gets corns), these characteristics do not name the human essence. But Aristotle is able to deduce our function from the following definition—"man is the rational animal"—which does name our essence. "The function of man is an activity of soul in conformity with reason," and "the good of man is an

Oooh, how embarrassing.

activity of his soul in accordance with virtue, or, if there be more than one, in accordance with the best and most complete virtue" (p. 26). What, then, is this *rational activity of the soul in accordance with virtue* whose realization constitutes hap-

piness? Well, first some qualifications. One must live a relatively long life to achieve happiness. It cannot be like a momentary pleasure or joy, for, as Aristotle says, "one swallow does not make a spring" (p. 26). Furthermore, luck matters, just as it did in the case of the acorn or the caterpillar. And certain "external goods" are needed, for "it is impossible, or at least not easy, to act nobly without some material goods" (p. 30). What "material goods" are these? Aristotle's list may annoy you.

> There are some things whose absence takes the bloom from our happiness, as good birth, the blessing of children, personal beauty. A man is not likely to be happy if he is very ugly, or of low birth, or alone in the world, or childless, and perhaps still less if he has worthless children or friends or has lost some good ones that he had.   [p. 30]

It gets worse! Not only must you have noble birth and personal beauty to be happy, you also must be *tall*. Aristotle says, "Small men may have appeal and be well proportioned but cannot be called beautiful" (p. 97). Furthermore, apparently one must be independently wealthy to achieve happiness. Aristotle writes, "No man can practice virtue who is living the life of a mechanic or labourer."[5]

And when Aristotle says "man," he means MAN. His prejudices—in sharp contrast here with those of Plato, who believed that women in principle were no different from men in their capacity to become philosophers and rulers—lead him to suspect that women cannot fully pursue the required "activity of soul" because they do not have complete souls. They are not fully human! Like undeveloped children, they can have pleasures and joys, but they can never achieve human happiness.

Do all these obnoxious qualifications that Aristotle attaches to the idea of happiness mean that we must part company with him and can derive no benefit from reading his theory of human nature? Fortunately, this is not the case. We can register strong objections to his sexism or his classism and then move beyond them. Nothing

else in his theory commits a contemporary "Aristotelian" to his narrow-mindedness on these topics. However, the issue of his list of "material needs" is a bit more complicated. We can write off his *specific* list (noble birth, wealth, physical beauty, tallness, good children), attributing it to his personal elitism and snobbery. But the question remains as to whether happiness is in some ways dependent on such material conditions and whether access to these material conditions depends partially on "luck." We can contrast Aristotle's "material goods" argument with the views of more **ascetic** thinkers, the most radical of whom believe that any material possessions stand in the way of true blessedness. For my own part, I think that Aristotle's notion of "moral luck" should be taken seriously.

Saint Jerome in the Desert

Let us return now to Aristotle's definition of happiness. Remember, he told us that happiness is what is produced by a rational activity of the soul in accordance with virtue. There are three concepts we need to look into in this definition: *soul, rationality,* and *virtue*. We'll start with the last.

Virtue: Moral and Intellectual

There are two kinds of virtue according to Aristotle: moral and intellectual. Moral virtue (*ethike*) derives from habit (*ethos*). Intellectual virtue derives from a combination of education and biological inheritance.

MORAL VIRTUE This kind of virtue "is involved with passions and with actions," and its key notion is that of *moderation*. Concerning action and passion, "Excess and deficiency are wrong but the intermediate amount is praised and right. . . . Virtue, then, is a kind of mean" (p. 46). This is the famous "golden mean" that Aristotle recommends. For every category

Doesn't do a thing for me...

The Temptations of Saint Anthony

of action or emotional expression, there is some behavior that would constitute excess, another that would constitute *deficiency*, and another that would prove to be the correct act in the circumstance, *the mean.* For example, in the case of facing danger, "cowardliness" would be deficient, "foolhardiness" excessive, and "courage" the golden mean. In the case of the pursuit of pleasure, "self-indulgence" would be excessive, "emptiness of feeling" deficient, and "self-control" virtuous. Let's chart out other examples given by Aristotle:

ACTION	VICE		VIRTUE
	EXCESS	DEFICIT	MEDIUM
expenditure of money	extravagance	stinginess	generosity
large-scale donation	bad taste, vulgarity	miserliness	magnificence
expression of emotions	wrathful	apathetic	amiability
stating facts about oneself	boasting	self-deprecating	truthfulness
expressing humor	buffoonery	humorlessness	wittiness
emotional relations to others	obsequiousness	grouchiness	friendliness
expressions of feelings about undeserved prosperity of others	envy	spite	righteous indignation
pursuing aspirations	overambition	unambition	no proper name for this

In some ways, this chart may appear to be trivial; that is, Aristotle's solutions may seem merely verbal or facile. Everybody already knows, for example, that courage is morally superior to cowardliness and that friendliness is better than grouchiness. We didn't need to read Aristotle to figure that out. The question is, What exactly is a courageous act, and what is a cowardly or foolhardy one? And it may even seem that Aristotle provides an empty, mathematical answer to this question. (A virtuous act is halfway between two vicious acts. Draw an arc of ninety degrees, and divide it into two; that's virtue!) But such interpretations miss a number of Aristotle's important points. First, moral philosophy cannot be "scientifically exact" (p. 39)—it cannot be mathematical. Second, practical morality is *situational*. The same act that is courageous in one case (stepping between your family and a roaring lion) is in another case foolhardy (stepping into a lion cage at the zoo to confront a lion that has

just roared at your family). Therefore, practical morality is experimental. It is neither inherited nor learned from books. One must *engage in life*; one must make a few mistakes before one learns what success entails. The person who, after much practice in life, develops habits of courage, who develops a disposition to act courageously, creates for himself (or herself, as *we* should add) *moral character* if similar dispositions have been developed in the other categories of behavior. But Aristotle is not arguing that this should become rote or unconscious habit; rather, it should become voluntary habit, willed habit. The person we are speaking of acts for *reasons*. This person is, in fact, the man (or woman) of "practical wisdom."

Virtue, then, is a disposition involving choice, the characteristic of which lies in moderation or observance of the mean relatively to the persons concerned, as determined by reason, that is, as the man of practical reason would determine it. [p. 46]

In one way, there is circular reasoning here:

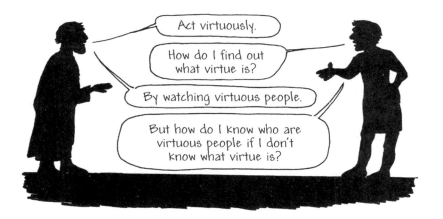

Act virtuously.

How do I find out what virtue is?

By watching virtuous people.

But how do I know who are virtuous people if I don't know what virtue is?

But it's not a *vicious* circle. There *are* people who do have "practical wisdom," people who have developed skills to make the right decision at the right moment and to act efficiently on those decisions. We can usually recognize these people because they succeed in both the moral and the practical sphere. The issue is a practical one, after all.

There is an important example that Aristotle gives in the context of his discussion of "the golden mean" and of moral virtues that tells us something interesting about the difference between his world and ours. In speaking of actions performed in the pursuit of honors or avoidance of disgrace, Aristotle says that the excess is "vanity," the deficiency is being "small-souled" (in Greek, *mikropsychia*), and the mean is being "great-souled" (in Greek, *megalopsychia*). The Greek words have no exact English equivalents, but let's look at some of Aristotle's examples of *megalopsychia*.

> The great-souled man, then, exhibits his character especially in the matter of honors and dishonors. When he receives great honors from good men he will be moderately pleased as he will be getting nothing more than what he deserves, or even less, because no honor can be adequate to complete virtue. But honor from ordinary men on trivial grounds he will utterly despise. . . . Thus, great-souled men seem to look down upon everything. . . . A haughty demeanor in dealing with the great is quite consistent with good breeding, but in dealing with those of low estate it is crude, like showing off one's strength on a cripple. . . . [The great-souled man] does not do many things but only great and notable things. . . . He will not hesitate saying all that he thinks, since he looks down on mankind. . . . Nor is he easily moved to admiration because nothing appears great to him. . . . Further, the character of the great-souled man seems to require that his gait should be slow, his voice deep, his speech deliberate. A man is not likely to be in a hurry when there are few things in which he is deeply

interested, or excited when he holds nothing to be of very great importance. These are the causes of a high voice and rapid movements. (pp. 98–99)

Aristotle's "small-souledness" now looks very much like our idea of *humility*, and his "great-souledness" seems very much like *pride*. Perhaps because of two thousand years of Jewish and Christian moral traditions in the West, Aristotle's "great-souled" man will seem to many of us today as quite obnoxious—the kind of person we might name not by calling him "great-souled," but by calling him a "jerk."

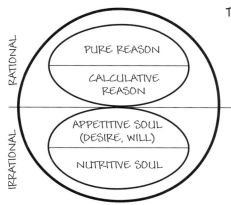

The Faculties of the Soul

THE SOUL We have now had a look at moral virtues. Recall that there were also "intellectual virtues" to be dealt with. But before we can discuss them, we should say something about Aristotle's conception of the soul. Remember that Aristotle's teacher, Plato, had divided the soul into three aspects: reason, spirit, and appetite. Aristotle, too, divides the soul, though his partition is more complicated than Plato's. Luckily, we don't have to follow all of Aristotle's details in order to arrive at the basic point. The simplified version is this: The soul is divided into two main parts, the *rational* and the *irrational*. The irrational is further divided into *appetite* (desire and will) and *nutritive* (nourishment). These are irrational in that their governing principles are not those of reason, but those of pleasure and satiety. The rational soul is also subdivided into *pure reason* and *calculative reason*. Aristotle says: "There are two rational faculties: (1) that by which we know those things that cannot be other than what they are, (2) that by which we know

Deliberation

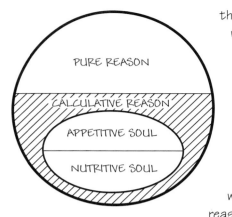

those things that can be other than what they are" (p. 105). Calculative reason (which Aristotle also calls "deliberative reason") is that form of reason that deliberates over which actions are to be performed in specific circumstances. As we have just seen, it is this form of deliberation that must become habitual in the person of practical wisdom. In other words, if calculative reason can impose its rule over appetite and nutrition, then the irrational soul will become rationalized. (This is not so different from Plato's view, after all. It is merely more "down to earth.")

Think about Aristotle's original definitions. Happiness is the supreme good for humans, and that state of blessedness is the result of achieving one's function as a human. And the function of the human "is an activity of soul in conformity with reason" or "an activity of . . . soul in accordance with virtue, or if there is more than one, in accordance with the best and most complete virtue" (p. 26). So we have now covered most of the features of these definitions. Aristotle asserts:

It is evident, then, from what has been said that it is impossible to be good in the full sense without practical wisdom or to have practical wisdom without moral virtue.   [p. 108]

INTELLECTUAL VIRTUE But there is still one more item to deal with—that "best and most complete virtue." This has to do with the aspect of the soul we have not yet reviewed—pure reason. If the virtue of calculative reason is practical wisdom, then the virtue of pure reason is philosophical wisdom. Pure reason contemplates those features of reality about which we can do nothing, as we have seen. It produces "theoretical knowledge or philosophical contemplation" (p. 138).

Contemplating That about Which We Can Do Nothing

Aristotle says:

> Only the life of contemplation is desired solely for its own sake; it yields no result beyond the contemplation itself, while from all other actions we get something more or less besides the action itself. [p. 139]

. . . and

> Since, then, it is reason that in the truest sense is the man, the life that consists in the exercise of reason in pursuit of theoretical wisdom is the best and pleasantest for man, and therefore the happiest. [p. 140]

If the human being is "the rational animal"—if reason is the human essence—then philosophical contemplation proves to be the highest goal of human life, the "function" of human existence, and the happiest human being is THE PHILOSOPHER (the philosopher, it is important to note, who does not simply sit around thinking, but who engages actively in everyday life with "practical wisdom").

Of course, we may be a little suspicious to find a philosopher writing a book in which he tries to figure out what the best form of life is and discovering it to be . . . his own! (Would someone from a different profession have arrived at a different conclusion?) But it is comforting, at least to me, to learn that the human being is *Homo philosophicus*.

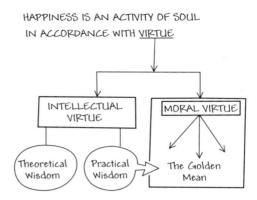

HAPPINESS IS AN ACTIVITY OF SOUL
IN ACCORDANCE WITH VIRTUE

INTELLECTUAL VIRTUE

MORAL VIRTUE

Theoretical Wisdom

Practical Wisdom

The Golden Mean

Summary

Aristotle's philosophy is guided by a central idea—that of *teleology*. Only by determining the *function* of any object can we evaluate its success, so the "function of man" must be established if we are to know "the good life" for human beings. For Aristotle, this function, this goal, turns out to be happiness, but happiness is itself a complicated concept. As in the theories of Aristotle's teacher, Plato, and as for most ancient Greek thinkers, the idea of happiness involves both rationality and sociability. But Aristotle's investigation of these notions is much less abstract and otherworldly than Plato's, and much more empirical—that is, based on careful observation of actual human behavior.

Because human beings are unique in having choices—in other words, because they are free—it is easy for them to choose false goals or to misconstrue happiness. Therefore, in order to avoid the greatest of all tragedies, the wasted life, it is important to *philosophize*. Philosophy leads Aristotle to the conclusion that the "function of man" is "an activity of soul in accordance with virtue." The activity of soul that Aristotle has in mind turns out to be philosophical contemplation, an activity that for Aristotle is godlike, because the activity of god—Aristotle's "prime mover"—is the contemplation of things that do not change. (Shades of Plato!) But humans are not endowed only with godlike reason. Unlike the prime mover, but like the gods of Mount Olympus, they also are social and active. A philosopher's work takes place not in hermitlike isolation, but in midstream of the flow of life in the republic. There, too, happiness requires the pursuit of excellence.

This excellence (practical wisdom) can only be achieved experimentally. It is situational and contextual. It involves striving for a certain equilibrium, a middle ground between excess and deficiency, a perfect balance between what Friedrich Nietzsche—also looking back to the Greek gods of Olympus—calls "the Dionysian" (frenzy and ecstasy) and "the Apollonian" (cool intellectual aloofness). The moral life, for Aristotle, is composed not of dedication to certain absolutist moral demands but of a seamless series of actions, each type of which is exemplified in a parallel series of virtues, connecting individuals with their fellow humans and always placed in the context of the philosophically contemplative stance toward the universe. The person who has both the intellectual and the physical skills (and the *luck*) to achieve such a balance procures happiness, and thereby, complete self-realization as a human being.

Topics for Consideration

1. Explain Aristotle's conception of "teleology" as you understand it from reading this chapter. Show how it links all objects—birds, rain, plants, and humans, for example—in a general pursuit of excellence.

2. Select some process in nature (such as the evolution of the eyeball over many generations or the sunflower's turning toward the sun), and characterize it first from an Aristotelian perspective and then from what you take to be a Darwinian perspective.

3. What is "the wasted life," according to Aristotle, and how can it be avoided?

4. Discuss the idea of "luck" in Aristotle, and especially the idea of "moral luck."

5. What would you say is Aristotle's objection to Plato's metaphysics and, by extension, to Plato's views on "the good life"?

6. Write a paragraph explaining the two kinds of wisdom: practical and speculative.

7. Explain Aristotle's view of the "golden mean," and employ some examples from your own life to clarify it.

8. What is your opinion of Aristotle's "great-souled man"?

9. What features of Aristotle's philosophy do you find to be Platonic?

Suggestions for Further Reading

I. Aristotle's Main Works

Introduction to Aristotle. Ed. Richard McKeon, trans. W. D. Ross. New York: Modern Library/Random House, 1992. Contains *Posterior Analytics* (complete), *Physics* (Book II of eight books), *On the Soul* (complete), *Metaphysics* (Books I and XII of fourteen books), *Nicomachean Ethics* (complete), *Politics* (Books I and III of eight books), *Poetics* (complete).

A Guided Tour of Selections from Aristotle's Nicomachean Ethics. Ed. Christopher Biffle, trans. F. H. Peter. Mountain View, Calif.: Mayfield, 1991.

II. Secondary Sources on Aristotle

Adler, Mortimer J. *Aristotle for Everybody.* New York: Simon & Schuster, 1997.

Barnes, Jonathan. *Aristotle.* Past Masters Series. Oxford and New York: Oxford University Press, 1991.

Kenny, Anthony. *Aristotle on the Perfect Life.* Oxford and New York: Oxford University Press, 1995.

Rorty, Amélie Oksenberg, ed. *Essays on Aristotle's Ethics.* Berkeley and Los Angeles: University of California Press, 1984.

Notes

1. Theopompus, "Justin 8," trans. by and quoted in N. G. L. Hammond, *Philip of Macedon* (Baltimore: The Johns Hopkins University Press, 1994), p. 29.
2. Hammond, *Philip of Macedon,* p. 176.
3. Jacob Abbott, *The History of Alexander the Great* (New York: Harper and Brothers, 1857), 208–209.
4. Aristotle, *Nicomachean Ethics,* in Christopher Biffle, ed., *A Guided Tour of Selections from Aristotle's Nicomachean Ethics,* trans. F. H. Peter (Mountain View, Calif.: Mayfield, 1991), p. 14. Page numbers of future references to this work will be included in the body of the text.
5. Aristotle, *Politics,* 1278, a 20, in Richard McKeon, ed., *The Basic Works of Aristotle,* trans. Benjamin Jowett (New York: Random House, 1968), p. 1183.

3

The Buddhist Conception of Human Nature

Historical Backdrop

At about the same time that Greece emerged as the main conduit of knowledge and culture in the Mediterranean basin, India was playing that role in Asia. Greek philosophy culminated in the figures of Socrates, Plato, and Aristotle, while India's dominant philosophical personage was a man who would come to be called "the Buddha"—literally, "the Enlightened One." In fact, in terms of sheer numbers of people influenced by him, the Buddha may have been the most persuasive thinker in human history. His ideas flourished for 1500 years in their Indian birthplace before receding. By then, however, they had become a prominent guide to behavior in China, Tibet, Sri Lanka, Korea, and Japan, where today they still hold sway over many. Indeed, a community of Buddhists has existed for 2500 years, making Buddhism one of the oldest continuously existing religious or philosophical traditions in the world.

The India into which the Buddha was born sometime in the sixth or fifth century B.C.E. already housed a very old culture; unfortunately, rela-

Ancient India, Including Today's Nepal,
Bangladesh, Pakistan, and Sri Lanka
(Modern Cities in Parentheses)

tively little is known about it. In ancient times, a dark-skinned people known as the Dravidians occupied much of India. They spoke a language completely separate from the roots of today's European, Slavic, Chinese, and Japanese tongues. These Indians may have been related to the present-day aborigines of Australia. In about 1500 B.C.E., they were invaded by the lighter-skinned Indo-Europeans, speakers of the precursors of the present-day European and Slavic languages.

These Indo-Europeans, or Aryans, probably arrived in India through the mountain passes of today's Iran and Afghanistan. Though they left little by way of material culture to be investigated by archaeologists, they did bring religious traditions and writings that still survive in the form of the *Vedic hymns*. These holy words were supposedly exhaled by *Brahman*, a creator god. They became the founding literary documents of **Hinduism,** a religion that was adopted by the newly merged Indo-European and Dravidian peoples. But except for the erstwhile Hindu common denominator and the uneasy political union forged (and ruptured) in the twentieth century, the Indian amalgamation of peoples, cultures, and languages has always been difficult. As late as 1911, the official *Census Report* of India listed 220 languages.

One attempt to resolve the contradictions of such conflicting values involved the development of a system of social classes, or "estates," once there were kings in place. Four large groupings were installed below the kings: (1) the priests and pastors charged with religious matters (*brahmans*), (2) the aristocratic warrior class (*kshatriyas*), (3) the merchant class (*vaishyas*), and (4) those who tilled the land or were slaves (*shudras*). This system was the precursor of the much more complicated caste system still in place in India today. This

India as the Tower of Babel

rigidly defined class system had to exclude certain newcomers and members of slippery categories. By 500 B.C.E., a class of hunters and gatherers emerged (perhaps from a hitherto unidentified more "primitive" tribe) that did not fit into the preexisting niches. Therefore, they were identified as "out-caste" and as "untouchables" by those on the inner rungs of the caste structure.

The Buddha arrived on the Indian scene at a time of social upheaval. The old estate system was groaning and straining to contain all its disparate components. The feudal and agrarian economy was giving way to a new system, involving for the first time real cities, with all their advantages and disadvantages (very much in the way that

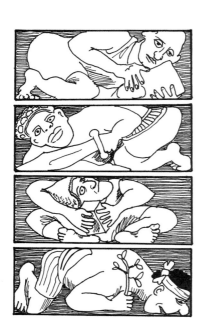

The Caste System

Socrates found himself born into a new "citified" culture in the West). These cities produced more complex human relations and institutions than could have been imagined in the estate system. Urban economies required the institution of coinage (money) and all the attendant complications—debt, credit, capital, investment, profit, loss, bankruptcy. The caste system produced different responses to these

Socrates and the Buddha Observe Urban Chaos

new factors, trying to find adjunct categories (identities), as well as formulas of transition from the old to the new. (How else could it explain the dramatic, sometimes overnight, acquisition or loss of power by a member of a "static" class?)

The philosophical import of this social structure was effectively the denial of anything we could call "human nature." There was only "caste-nature" and total exclusion. One could define the essence of a warrior or of a slave, but not of a "human being." There were, in fact, no "human beings," only members of specific classes.

Besides the groups in the estate system and the untouchables, another group emerged—homeless religious beggars. These "ascetics," who had renounced

society and the world, wandered the periphery of civilization denouncing the world in the name of a higher good. By the time of the Buddha's birth, these ascetics had already established a "fifth estate" and, ironically, were the only ones in a position to discourse about "human nature" in general. Such a discourse, examples of which we find in the dialogues attributed to the Buddha, constitute a revolutionary step because, as one scholar of Buddhism puts it, prior to the philosophizing of the ascetics, "the Indians had no way of speaking of human life beyond the narrow local conception of estates, bound to the older order of Indian society."[1] The Buddha took advantage of this breakthrough and elevated the level of discussion to new heights. He set forth a conception of human nature that turned into a major worldview.

Biography

In the religious tradition that he established, the Buddha can be thought of from three perspectives: (1) as a historical person (in which case one can speak of his birth, life, and death), (2) as a spiritual principle (in which case the Buddha-nature predates and postdates his physical body, which is

merely a manifestation of that principle), or (3) as an entity known as the "glorified body" (which is a combination of the first two, a kind of **mystical** yet physical Buddha that is twenty-seven feet high and does not experience the physical limitations of normal bodies). In this section, we are concerned with the first of these possibilities, the physical Buddha.

The information about the life of the Buddha is very meager, and what little is available is uncertain and often contested. For instance, there is much controversy over the dates of his birth and death. Buddhist literature most typically puts his birth at 563 B.C.E., though some documents move this back 350 years and others move it up 250 years. All versions of the tradition claim he lived for eighty years, so most sources make his dates 563 to 483 B.C.E. But recent scholarship has placed his birth closer to 450 B.C.E. (Remember that Socrates was born about 469 B.C.E., so this date would make the Buddha almost an exact contemporary of the Greek philosopher.)

The Buddha was born in the town of Lumbini outside the city of Kapilavastu, in northeastern India, on the lowlands below today's Nepal. He was born into the elite warrior class (the *kshatriyas*) and no doubt had all the advantages of wealth and status. His family name was Gautama, and his first name may have been Siddhartha. He was not called "Buddha" until after his "awakening," any more than as a child Jesus was called "Christ" (a Greek word standing for the Hebrew term for "the anointed one").

The Buddha Statue, Yün Kang, China (c. 500 C.E.)

What did the Buddha look like? We really have no good idea because images were not made of him until about 300 or 400 years after his death. Tradition has it that he was very handsome, but certain iconographic conventions, such as closed eyes, a bun, and extraordinarily large ears, have come between us and a realistic portrait. Also, Buddhist art has allowed rather comical caricatures of the Buddha to exist alongside more solemn representations.

When the Buddha was about thirty years old, he began to feel a deep disquietude about his life. He renounced his wealth and family (including his wife and son, according to some traditions) and adopted the life of a wandering beggar. Traveling freely through forests and towns, he was able to view all levels of society. He studied meditation with two masters and then practiced asceticism for a number of years. Then, when he was about thirty-five years old, something important happened to him. As he sat under a great Bodhi tree on a spring night lighted by a full moon, he suddenly experienced a moment of profound illumination, an "awakening," that provided him with an insight into the human condition. He was shown the nature of salvation and, at the same time, was guaranteed that he himself had achieved release from suffering.

For the next forty-five years, the Buddha wandered the region of the Ganges River basin teaching the path to enlightenment that he had discovered. By the time of his death, he had established a saffron-robed order of monks and another of nuns whose mission it was to pass on their master's teachings. This they did with extraordinary success.

The Awakening

The Buddha's "Theory"

There already existed among the community of religious ascetics a body of philosophy of which the Buddha availed himself, clarified, amended, and then preached in a new form. Included in this philosophy developed by the Buddha were the beliefs that (1) existence always involves suffering; (2) **reincarnation** is everywhere in effect, such that current living beings have lived previous lives and, after physical death, will be born again into new bodies; (3) the kind of future life one will have is determined by how one lives one's current life; and (4) salvation from misery in this life and in future lives is best achieved through a combination of meditative practices and asceticism (the choice of poverty and the flight from worldly pleasures).

Suffering

Let us look first at the doctrine of necessary suffering as the Buddha developed it. According to this view, all the goals we pursue as committed members of the worldly community—namely, seeking fulfillment of our personal desires, sexual and gastronomic gratification, wealth and material objects, popularity and prestige, and power over others—are **"karmic"** acts. That is, they have unseen consequences; they have the power to generate a future life for us, causing us to be reborn to yet another life of striving.

By renouncing all these pursuits, by living a solitary life of medita-tive inaction, one not only escapes the "rat race" of

Each Act Produces Worlds of Repetition of the Same

this life but may place oneself in a position to avoid prolonging that "race" into an interminable series of failed lives. By pursuing a life of meditative asceticism, one does not build up a bank account of "bad" karma. This, along with certain acts producing "good" karma, results in eventual libera-tion from suffering and from continual rebecoming.

Now, this platform presumes that its audience will agree that life is experienced as suffering. And surely in the Buddha's time, as in our own, many did experience life as a fundamentally unhappy experience. But there is another level of analysis in Buddhism that addresses those who either do not see life in such purely negative terms or think that the solution to unhappiness is the pursuit of pleasure and worldly goods. This is a philo-sophical exposé of the notion of desire showing that, by its very nature, it is insatiable and frustrating; therefore, its pursuit can only lead to un-happiness. Discontent will necessarily be our lot if the fulfillment of desire is our goal. In fact, rather ironically, this part of the Buddhist doctrine sounds very much like that of the Western Existentialists we will read about later in this book—Kierkegaard and Sartre—who argue that "anxi-ety" is, in fact, the foundation of consciousness. And just as Existential-ists assert that those who reject this insight are in a state of "bad faith," denying in fear what they are in fact aware of (a denial that is itself in fact a form of anxiety), so does the Buddha hold that sometimes the recogni-tion that everything is suffering is one that can only be made by the wise. In short, ignorance is the cause of denial.

Still, as if fearing that Buddhist monks would fail to grasp this mes-sage, the teaching called for them to remind themselves constantly of the

Caption: Kierkegaard, the Buddha, and Sartre

misery caused by their encasement within a physical body. The monk is urged to consider just how repulsive the body is by thinking about "stomach, excrement, brain, bile, digestive juices, pus, blood, grease, fat, tears, sweat, spittle, snot, fluid of the joints, urine."[2] The monk is aided in feeling disgust at and shame for his body by being exhorted to meditate on "the Nine Apertures," which produce filthy substances: the two ears, nostrils, and eyes, and the mouth, anus, and urethra. As one Buddhist scholar summarizes it, "It is a fundamental thesis of Buddhism that there is nothing which is not either directly experienced as ill, or in some way bound up with ill—past or future, one's own or another's."[3]

Caption: The Human Body

Meditation

The release from suffering is attained through **meditation.** After rejecting the meditative solution offered by his two teachers as too superficial, narrow, and temporal, the Buddha developed a form of meditation whose practice can lead to **Nirvana,** the state of release achieved by the Buddha in his "awakening."

But even meditation requires preparatory training, as explained in the "Great Discourse on the Foundations of Mindfulness," one of the most important Buddhist texts. One must practice a form of introspection in which one is attentive in a dispassionate mode to one's every thought and sensation, clearly aware of the smallest perception or feeling. One learns to be acutely conscious of them without responding automatically to them. If

one is aware of a hunger pang, for example, one does not necessarily search for food. If one perceives a fly alighting on one's nose, one does not swat it or even necessarily brush it aside.

After a thorough training in this technique of detached introspection, one is ready to meditate. The meditator finds a place of silence. He or she sits cross-legged with a straight back—that is, in a position not necessarily completely comfortable. In the primary form of meditation, sometimes called "calm meditation,"[4] the meditator concentrates attention on some object placed in the field of vision—a bowl of water, a circle formed out of flower petals, or the image of the Buddha. The same procedure can be applied to a repeated sound instead of a visible object. In either case, concentration eventually reduces the object of awareness to its mere image. The training in introspection allows the meditator to view in a detached way the annoyances, irritations, and distractions attached to this physical state (the desire to scratch one's nose, the stiffness of one's leg, the buzzing mosquito, and so on). One becomes absorbed in the object of awareness; all other sensations are suppressed. This concentration produces a mild state of well-being, a slight "high." This is, in fact, the first in a hierarchy of five kinds of joy that can be achieved in this state:

. . . the initial stage of "slight joy" simply raises the hairs of the body; "momentary joy" comes like repeated flashes of lightning, while "descending joy" is stronger and washes over the body again and again and then subsides; "transporting joy" has the power to lift the body into the air. . . . Eventually, the mind settles in "suffusing joy"; this kind of joy pervades the whole body touching every part and is likened to water flooding into a rock cave.[5]

But even this pleasure must not be allowed to distract one from the next meditative plateau, sometimes called "insight meditation."[6] The mind of the meditator achieves a condition of pure consciousness, a limpid and translucent receptivity in which the distinction between subject and object is dissolved. Eventually, there occurs a consciousness of emptiness, or an emptiness of consciousness, as one approaches the Buddhist goal of Nirvana—a release from a repetitive existence of suffering created by our cravings, our greed, our desires, into an emptiness of nonbirth and nondeath.

Selflessness

However, one of the Buddha's insights at his "awakening" was that these ecstatic, exalted **mystical** states are not the ultimate goal. True salvation comes solely with the discovery of the "not-self." This is sometimes described as the need to obliterate the self, but this formulation is misleading, because the Buddha's discovery was that there is no self to obliterate. The doctrine in question is a departure from the Hindu tradition of India, which, like Western religions, sought an immortal, eternal, unchanging Self (âtman in Sanskrit) liberated from suffering. But the Buddha's insight was that the very notion of striving for such a self as an escape from suffering is itself a major source of suffering.

In denying that there is a Self (with a capital S), the Buddha did not deny that we have an experience of "ourselves" (with a small s). But a correct analysis of this "self" shows it to be a criss-crossing, overlapping artifice of what the Scottish philosopher David Hume (1711–1776) would later call "bundles of perceptions." The Buddha called them "heaps" or "aggregates," and he listed five of them: (1) matter (our body, our possessions), (2) feelings, (3) perceptions, (4) impulses and emotions, and (5) acts of consciousness. But, as in Hume, there is no underlying unity; rather, there are only converging streams of histories, and this convergence is unified by

The Self as "Heaps"

the combination of *craving* and *suffering*. As one of the early Buddhist scriptures says, describing the First Noble Truth:

> This is the noble truth of suffering: birth is suffering, ageing is suffering, sickness is suffering, dying is suffering, sorrow, grief, pain, unhappiness, and unease are suffering; being united with what is not liked is suffering, separation from what is liked is suffering; not to get what one wants is suffering; in short, the five aggregates of grasping are suffering.[7]

The idea of "individuality" is a product of desire ("*I* want this; *I* need that; *I* must have those"). The subject ("I") of these cravings is a grammatical fiction. Similarly, the notion of belongingness ("*my* car, *my* house") is also an imaginary construct. Nothing *belongs* to anybody or anything. Hence, both the positive and negative possessives (mine/not-mine) are illusions, forms of ignorance, but ignorance that can be dispelled by (Buddhist) wisdom. That is, it is possible to *see* how the artifice that is the self comes about and to see that this artificial construct is the cause of suffering. And, through discipline and meditative practices, it is possible to overcome that artificial self, to unravel it. It is possible to arrive at a state of not-self (*an-âtman* in Sanskrit, or *an-attâ* in the Pali of the early Buddhist manuscripts).

This idea of an *an-âtman* is, perhaps, the main contribution to religious thought by Buddhism. It places consciousness in an "emptiness" that is inhabited by Truth (Dharma). This emptiness is a mystical space "between affirmation and negation, existence and nonexistence, eternity and annihilation."[8] It is as if this "space," this "Dharma," this "Nirvana," is the ultimate reality for the Buddhist.

Comparison is sometimes made between this mystical space and the idea of the "Absolute" in the writings of Western mystics such as Saint Teresa of Avila—which is roughly their term for God. Indeed, in some strains of later Buddhism, the Buddha is

**Saint Teresa in Ecstasy
(After Gianlorenzo Bernini, 1652)**

seen as the personal embodiment of this Nirvana, and as such is the object of worship. Certainly, the historical Buddha left no evidence of a desire to be worshiped. Even where the term *worship* is appropriate in Buddhism, it cannot be in the ancient Greek sense of demanding gifts and sacrifices, nor in the Judeo-Christian sense of eliciting love or fear or of issuing commands to be obeyed. Some have gone so far as to argue that Buddhism is literally an atheistic religion. Others have declared that it is not a religion at all.

Buddhist Ethics

All this raises the question of whether there can be a "Buddhist ethics," where **ethics** is understood as a system of rules governing human relations. Certainly, some features of Buddhist doctrine appear to undermine such a possibility. For example, the centrality of meditative practices seems to place the emphasis in Buddhism on a solitary state of inaction rather than on the kind of behavior that Western ethics addresses, namely, praiseworthy and blameworthy actions. Furthermore, its "egoistic" concerns (salvation for the meditating monk) seem to ignore the plight of others, as does the embracing of a state of selflessness. Indeed, the goal of Buddhism—the achievement of a state of Nirvana—seems to annul the very entities to which ethics directs itself (namely, persons).

Moral Tranquility

Yet, there is indeed a Buddhist ethics. It is based on the karmic doctrine that the universe really demonstrates a fundamental moral order. According to Buddhist morality, one cannot simply "go along the banks of the Ganges striking, slaying, mutilating and commanding others to mutilate, oppressing and commanding others to oppress."[9] Or, at least, one cannot do so without paying the price of creating for him- or herself a future life on an even lower rung of the wheel of suffering, where one will be engulfed ever deeper in misery.

Although a great part of Buddhist thought could be described in morally neutral terms, much of the actual language of Buddhism is distinctly moral in nature. For instance, the explanation of suffering is some-

The Great Wheel of Suffering

times rendered like this: ". . . in-flamed by greed, incensed by hate, confused by delusion, overcome by them, obsessed in mind, a man chooses for his own affliction, for the affliction of both, and experiences pain and grief."[10] To counter this, Buddhism teaches strategies for moderating the emotions. They are composed of lessons in friendliness, compassion, sympathetic joy, and even-temperedness. The goal of these exercises is to dissolve the boundaries between oneself and others, regardless of whether those others abide by the same rules. In this respect, the Buddhist strategy is like Jesus' "Love thy neighbor" and "Love thine enemy." It is also consistent with the goal of dissolving the self because a false sense of "self-interest" is what engenders vices.

Buddhism is often summarized in terms of its **Four Noble Truths:** (1) Everything involves suffering; (2) the cause of suffering is craving or desire; (3) craving must be overcome; and (4) craving can be transcended by following the **Noble Eightfold Path.** This path is clearly a moral trajectory:

Right outlook: understanding the Four Noble Truths
Right purpose: to reach liberation
Right speech: not to lie, not to slander
Right behavior: not to kill, not to steal, not to drink intoxicants, not
    to be unchaste (or, for laypersons, not to be promiscuous)
Right self-discipline: to practice the monastic life (or, for laypersons,
    to practice a moral life)
Right effort: to exercise willpower
Right self-knowledge: to examine constantly one's behavior
Right self-transcendence: to meditate on the ultimate truth

As in Socratic and Platonic thought, the highest moral virtue in Buddhism is Wisdom. Wisdom is understood as the systematic contemplation of the Dharmas, or truths. But it also filters down to everyday actions,

whereby a certain kind of practical knowledge guides all actions, bringing them to a level of perfection. The Greek word for this perfection, or excellence, is *aretê;* the Pali word is *kusala.* According to this concept, every act worth undertaking can be done with absolute grace and competence. In Buddhist thought, the act is somehow detached from the agent. (This idea traces back to the notion of the unraveling of the self.) The graceful yet powerful exercises of tai-chi and other Asian "military arts" might provide examples of this idea. Each act—whether greeting a friend, pouring a glass of water, or begging food—can be done with perfection. Note, however, that the Buddhist who spends long periods in meditation probably engages in many fewer acts than does the Western agent.

**Exhibiting Excellence (Kusala)
While Flossing**

Ultimately, then, the Buddha's ethics, like Plato's, strives to synthesize **egoism** and **altruism.** Every action (or nonaction) should be for the benefit of the agent *and* for the benefit of others. There may be, however, an unresolvable core of self-contradiction in Buddhist ethics because Buddhism insists both that barriers between persons should be broken down and that there are no persons as such. But at the least, the Buddha cannot justifiably be charged, as he sometimes is, with being concerned only with the individual's salvation.

Monks and Laity

The monks are the true Buddhists in the strict sense of that term. The life they are expected to lead is in many ways incompatible with the everyday demands placed on those who own houses, who marry and have children, who go off to work or till the fields. The Buddha's primary message thus is directed to the monks—an elite that steps back from society and whose universalization would make society impossible.

What life were the monks originally supposed to lead? Most obviously, one of poverty. A monk could not even touch gold or silver. He was to own no private property, with some minimal exceptions. A monk could wear a robe—originally rags from junk heaps stitched together and dyed saffron,

and later a garment do-
nated by laypersons. A
monk carried a bowl for
begging and from which
to eat and drink. He was
allowed to have a filter to
remove insects and float-
ing matter from his drinking water. He could carry
a needle and thread and
prayer beads. He had to
be homeless, and his food
had to come from begging.
(Note that begging in Asian
countries traditionally has been
accepted as a way of life, and

nomadic monks actually bestowed a kind of nobility upon it. Begging was
not viewed as a result of laziness or idleness, because everyone knew that
the beggar led a hard life. In fact, it was a form of virtuous activity, in that
the beggar used it to control his desires.) The monk had to accept whatever was offered to him and consume it without making a judgment about
its quality. He could not feel either joy or disappointment over what he was
given. Nor could he seek out wealthy donors
over the poor in his
quest for aid. And
if a woman provided
food, he had to
accept it without
looking at her, and
certainly without
judging her beauty or
ugliness. By begging,
the monk also
allowed others
to practice virtue
through the exercise
of generosity.

The monk also
had to be celibate. If he
succumbed to temptation
and became unchaste, he was

immediately expelled from the order; he was allowed to think about the sexual act only in terms of how beastly and disgusting it was. This attitude reflected a certain contempt for women. The monks had to remain especially vigilant and distant in their relations with the nuns whom they instructed—as one commentator has put it, "especially in hot climate."[11]

As Buddhism spread from India to the rest of Asia, these strict requirements about monkish poverty and celibacy eventually were loosened and, in places, abandoned. But even in the thousand years before that happened, there grew up around the monastic community of propertyless, celibate monks a large community of Buddhist householders. How is that possible? What could Buddhism offer those who did not spend their lives seeking Nirvana in chaste poverty? And what could the laity offer to Buddhism? Of course, from the perspective of Buddhist theory itself, only the community of meditative philosophers seeking salvation could justify the existence of society at large. But how could such a view come to be accepted by that society, which was expected to provide the material support for that elite community?

The community of monks and nuns offered the **laity,** or lay community, a kind of spiritual wealth. The householders achieved a spiritual reward for feeding the monks and for hearing their sermons, which contained wisdom that could guide the life of the householders, explaining how their future good fortune depended on the actions in which they engaged in daily life. Thereby, the laity came to understand why they should not kill, lie, steal, or drink intoxicants; why they should not eat after midday and should sleep on a mat on the ground; and why they should be considerate, temperate, and prudent in all their worldly engagements. Even though liberation could be achieved only by the monk, laypersons could acquire "merit" and hope to earn a better rebirth in a future life—including the hope that they would finally be reborn in the conditions that would lead them to monkhood and, ultimately, liberation. In fact, in later Buddhism, the Mahayana sect, which became the dominant one, allowed that laypersons could become **Bodhisattvas.** Bodhisattvas have vowed to achieve Buddhahood. They strive for and eventually achieve a nonpermanent Nirvana, a state into which they continue to be reborn in order to help others. Even though they could pass over permanently into Nirvana, they have chosen to delay that transition in order to help others do it, too. Bodhisattvas thus are somewhat akin to saints in the Christian tradition.

Moreover, the monks could provide a compelling account of suffering and human destiny and—that big philosophical conundrum—of the meaning of life. Also, as Buddhism developed, moving from country to country over the centuries, its peculiarly otherworldly nature allowed it to accommodate myth, magic, and ritual from the host communities that for generations had depended upon these factors for stability and understanding.

Laypersons could—and still can—call themselves disciples of the Buddha if they were willing to make this declaration:

I go to the Buddha for refuge.
I go to the Dharma for refuge.
I go to the Sangha [monastic community of monks or nuns] for refuge.[12]

Developments after the Death of the Historical Buddha

Hinayana and Mahayana Buddhism

It would be foolish to assume that any system as old as Buddhism would remain unchanged through time. Indeed, more than eighteen different schools have achieved prominence, each claiming to be true Buddhism, but the two main early branches are the "Hinayana" and the "Mahayana." According to tradition, this division was formally recognized early in the second century C.E at the Fourth Buddhist Council, which took place in Kashmir, India.

Hinayana Buddhism is more closely related to the original, at least in terms of historical proximity. It recognizes only certain early scriptures as authentic. However, to assert that the Hinayana are doctrinally closer to the Buddha's original intentions would be problematic, for, as in Judaism, Christianity, and Islam, the "original" documents are subject to interpretation. If you believe that those documents must be accepted literally and revered as absolute authority (as fundamentalist Christians believe about the Bible), then you will be siding with the Hinayana. But if you think that the scriptures require interpretation and adaptation to changing times, you will be closer to the **Mahayana.** Hinayana, which translates literally as "small vehicle," was a somewhat derogatory name bestowed by their opponents, the Mahayana, which means "large vehicle." According to the

The Small Vehicle and the Large Vehicle

Mahayana, the fundamentalists saw Buddhism as carrying only one individual at a time across the duplicitous sea of existence, whereas the Mahayana themselves professed to transport whole groups. Because of the negative connotations originally intended by those who coined the term *Hinayana*, modern scholarship often replaces it with the term *Theravada*, which designates the Buddhism of Southeast Asia, where the Hinayana school dominates today.

(A word of caution: When speaking of various "schools" of Buddhism, be aware that, unlike some competing "schools" in Western religion, we are not talking of "sects" or "denominations," with adherents each declaring the others to be heretical and attempting to "excommunicate" them. Thus, a monk who advocates Mahayana ideas may inhabit the same monastery as a monk who disagrees with him. In fact, even today, monks or nuns cannot be expelled from the Buddhist community based on their religious opinions. The only grounds for expulsion are *moral errors*—for example, murder, theft, or sexual intercourse.)

The holy texts of the Hinayana are restricted to early manuscripts in the Pali language, an artificial canonical language based on the dialects spoken by the historical Buddha and the early Buddhists. By contrast, the Mahayana scriptures comprise a massive and amorphous group of writings, most of which are in Sanskrit, or in Chinese or Tibetan translations from Sanskrit. They are the largest collection of holy scriptures in history but are so undefined that no one can say with certainty what is included within them and what is excluded.

One reason for this mass of material is the absorption of earlier sources into Mahayana Buddhism—hence the admission of some works that are of Hindu origin. Not only was the scriptural body more open than that of the Hinayana, but in every way Mahayana was more comprehensive and elastic. The Mahayana reconceptualized the idea of the Buddha and Nirvana in such a way as to universalize the goal of Buddhahood to encompass all sentient beings. Disciplinary rules were interpreted less strictly, so Buddhism became more compatible with the life of the average layman, who did not have to restrict his activities as much nor part with as many of his possessions. Women were viewed with less suspicion, and their spirituality was valued. Place was made for less talented candidates for monkhood.

The absorption of earlier Indian traditions also resulted in the subtle introduction of Hindu polytheism into Buddhism, though the names of the many gods were changed as these divine entities became "buddhas" or "bodhisattvas" who were manifestations of Buddhahood. As a result, the idea of "worship" was also introduced into Buddhism in a serious way—an idea that had little significance to the Hinayana sect. Nevertheless, even among the Hinayana, there had always been great respect for certain holy sites, such as the Bodhi tree under which the Buddha had been "awakened," or certain relics, such as prayer bowls, robes, bones, or teeth believed to have been the Buddha's. (The most notorious case was a tooth several inches long—apparently much more animal-like than human—which was taken to be a tooth of the Buddha. The tooth traveled the Buddhist world, appearing in Ceylon, then in Persia in 405 C.E., and even later in Portuguese Goa, where a Catholic archbishop had it pounded into dust, which was then burned, and the ashes scattered over the sea. Soon after its destruction, Buddhist monks declared the tooth to have been inauthentic, and two "legitimate" ones appeared in its place.)

The very elasticity of Mahayana Buddhism was seen by its Hinayana opponents as a form of degeneration and decadence, but it is also this feature that accounts for Mahayana's eventual dominance. By 800 C.E., the Mahayanists considerably outnumbered the Hinayanists. Yet by this time, Buddhism was already in decline in India due to purges, invasions, and, some say, degeneration. By the time of the Muslim invasions into India from Persia in 1000 C.E., there was little left of Buddhism in India to be oppressed. Islam and a revival of Hinduism filled the gap. Nevertheless, it was the Mahayana doctrine that traveled well, reaching to China and beyond, and most contemporary versions of Buddhism are descendants of the Mahayana philosophy. Even so, the more austere Hinayana is still practiced today in Sri Lanka, Burma, Cambodia, Thailand, and Laos.

Tantric Buddhism

One of the most extreme versions of Buddhism outside India proper took hold in Tibet, where by about 500 C.E., it began to develop out of the Mahayana doctrine. Because of the elasticity of that doctrine, in Tibet Buddhism was able to incorporate magical beliefs and practices that probably went back to pre-Hindu Dravidian times. Magical forces, demons, and deities were a large part of this tradition, and they became part of Tantric Buddhism.

There is much secrecy in **Tantra,** and, unlike earlier Buddhism, it relies on esoteric knowledge—that is, on what purports to be mystical knowledge transmitted between master and student in secret rituals and symbols. Little attention is paid to holy manuscripts, even though there is a massive Tantric literature, originating in India and then emerging from Tibet. According to this tradition, books cannot teach us salvation; rather, we must each attach ourselves to a "guru," a religious master, to whom we turn over our will in absolute obedience. Only the guru can transmit the secrets that can lead to our salvation. We are taught certain spells to recite, called **mantras,** and their repetition gives us power over the malevolent forces that threaten our well-being. The repetition of this mantra also becomes a meditative tool to lead us to the vast emptiness that has always been at the center of the Buddhist vision; in that emptiness, all opposition between malevolence and benevolence disappears.

Another aid in this quest is the drawing of magic circles, or **mandalas,** which are symbols of the spiritual system of reality. In effect, by using certain hand gestures (body), mantras (speech), and mandalas (mind), the practitioner is creating the body, speech, and mind of a Buddha, thereby achieving awakening in one lifetime. If we avail ourselves of these tools, and apply them under the direction of our guru, we will learn that:

The world is nothing but a reflection of the Buddha's light, more concentrated in one place, and more diffused in another, as the case may be. The Buddha is the secret reality in all things, their heart, the living and central truth in them. We ourselves are not strange elements external to it, and all we have to do is to realise that we ourselves are the Buddha and the cosmos.[13]

An Eighteenth-Century Mandala from Rajasthan

Tantra is divided into two groupings, called "Left-Handed Tantra" and "Right-Handed Tantra." This distinction derives from an earlier division in Hinduism, in which a feminine principle was associated with the goddess Shakti (this is the left hand) and a masculine principle with Shakti's consort, the divine Shiva (the right hand). The emphasis on female spirituality in Left-Handed Tantra may well date back to Dravidian times.

Sculpture, Devī Jagadambū Temple, Khajurāho, India (c. 1000 C.E.)

Left-Handed Tantra continues this ancient tradition, worshiping "Shaktis" (female deities), representing them in amorous union with male deities, and consequently incorporating elaborate rituals of sexual intercourse into the quest for salvation.

This idea is obviously in direct and shocking contrast with the strategies of salvation addressed to the Buddha's original disciples, according to which sensual pleasure in general, and sexual pleasure in particular, were seen as temptations away from salvation. But Tantra recognized that the state of sexual bliss was similar to the ecstatic moment of deliverance promised by the meditative trance and so incorporated sexual intercourse into its discipline. In fact, Left-Handed Tantra has identified liberation with the passions. Thus, the readers of the *Guhyasamaja-tantra*

Developments after the Death of the Historical Buddha ◆ 87

are told "the passions are the same as Nirvana."[14] Not surprisingly, Buddhist opponents of Tantra strongly disapprove of these developments, seeing them as a perversion of the doctrine of the Buddha. The vegetarian propensity in traditional Buddhism leaves some adherents outraged at the Tantric instruction to eat horse, elephant, and dog meat, and they are shocked at the

Here, have a little something to eat.

suggestion that all food be mixed with meat, urine, and dung. Those impressed by Buddhist asceticism will not be pleased to be counseled to engage in "daily intercourse in out of the way places with twelve-year-old girls" of a caste other than one's own.[15] The purpose of these recommendations, however, was to overcome all divisions and oppositions in an experience of unity.

Buddhism in China and Japan

By 1200 C.E., Buddhism had disappeared from India but had become strong in China, where it had been patronized for several hundred years by Chinese emperors. One of the main developments there grew out of the Mahayana tradition and became known as Ch'an, a Chinese word meaning "meditation." By 900 C.E., it had already achieved dominance over the other forms of Chinese Buddhism. Four centuries later, it had taken root in Japan under the Japanese name of **Zen,** where it left an even greater imprint than it had in China. It influenced not only religious practice but art, poetry, calligraphy, dancing, social ceremony, gardening, flower arrangement, archery, and the art of war.

Ch'an or Zen is antirationalistic (that is, it refuses to follow a model of logically structured rationality), occasionally choosing a path of paradox and self-contradiction to achieve a direct understanding of the Buddha's teachings. It seeks immediate awakening and disdains time-consuming methods for achieving it, including the scholarly study of ancient texts. It stresses, then, the sudden enlightenment of the Buddha. Such an awakening, even if maintained for only a second, reveals that all living existence is identical with the Buddha. This perfect wisdom transforms the meditator into Buddha himself.

To arrive at the emptiness that constitutes this insight, one must transcend not only desire but reason itself. In Zen training, the student is aided in this endeavor by submitting to the master's use of koan, a series of paradoxical questions, or to blows to the body, or combinations of both. "What is the sound of one hand clapping?" is the most well known koan. Sometimes, pulling on the student's nose or hitting the student with a stick achieves the same effect. The awakening produces Satori, roughly equivalent to the Nirvana of the Indian Buddhists. The nothingness and emptiness experienced there also teach lessons for the guidance of

everyday life. Actions undertaken, whether arranging flowers, painting a landscape, or slaying an enemy warrior, become in a certain sense "agent-less" actions, as the self disappears. Therefore, the opposition between actor and act dissolves, and the act becomes an expression of a total nothingness that is purity.

Summary

What kind of picture of human nature and of selfhood does Buddhism leave us with? It leaves a picture that must be startling to the uninitiated Western mind. According to Buddhism, there is indeed a universal human nature, but one whose correct articulation leaves us with no substantial self. Human nature turns out to have something in common with all forms of life—an idea we will see again in Chapter 7, "The Darwinian Conception of Human Nature." But here, what human nature shares with the rest of life is not some common ancestors or a common genetic endowment, but the fact that all life is suffering and all life is connected in a karmic system of reincarnation. These two common denominators—suffering and karma—are, in fact, directly related, because the greatest suffering is the knowledge of the infinite tedium of rebirth, life, and death. Furthermore, human life is a kind of inexorable grasping, craving, and desiring that always is insatiable, and the so-called self that is "ours" is nothing but bundles of such cravings.

Buddhism offers an escape from this terrible karmic wheel of suffering. A certain kind of meditative stance, carried out in conjunction with a set of moral rules, offers the followers of Buddhism a dissolution of the self that is part of the suffering, and it offers a transcendence over karmic rebirth. It transports its adherents into a state of Nirvana, a vast emptiness of mystical peace and release. This doctrine is truly universal, and the silent ecstasy and tranquility it promises must seem as attractive to many people in today's hectic world as it did in the Buddha's time 2500 years ago. One might agree with Edward Conze's judgment that

The Unraveling of the Self

"[i]n Buddhism there is nothing that cannot easily be transported from one part of the world to another." And, indeed, as Conze reminds us, Buddhism did adapt itself as easily "to the snowy heights of the Himalayas as to the parched plains of India, to the tropical climate of Java, to the moderate warmth of Japan and the bleak cold of outer Mongolia."[16]

Yet there seems to be a strange paradox in the story of Buddhism's attraction and historical success, for the path to the release, tranquility, and peace along which the doctrine leads us wanders through a metaphysical landscape that few people outside the Indian religious tradition would likely find enticing. The central doctrine of infinite suffering and cosmic rebirth must seem to many outsiders extremely and unwarrantedly pessimistic, despite disclaimers from Buddhists themselves. Furthermore, the key assumption of eternal rebirth must strain the credibility of most people who were not raised in the metaphysical tradition of ancient India. (One must recognize, of course, that many of the metaphysical assumptions behind Western religions would seem equally puzzling and unattractive to non-Westerners.) Though it is certainly possible today to experience some of the "world-weariness" suffered by the Buddha, it is likely that Western admirers of Buddhism are taken not so much by these dark metaphysical doctrines as by the joyfulness often found in Buddhist communities and by the offer of a path out of the postindustrial chaos of modern life and toward peace, calm, and tranquility.

No doubt this path can be approached pragmatically. It can be traversed experimentally without committing oneself to the complicated cosmic doctrine from which it sprang 2500 years ago. Much of what is attractive in Buddhism is most obvious in the way it is actually lived, rather than in the way it is spelled out in its texts. In Buddhist communities, we find that the sense of the importance of the individual diminishes, and there is more emphasis on transindividual realities, such as friendship groups, family, and society. As a result, there is much less of the grandstanding, rudeness, and road rage that seem to be endemic to Western societies, as well as less emphasis on trying to "be all that you can be" (as the Army ad enjoins). Buddhist communities also make a great deal of the rituals of politeness, so that the social fabric is not shredded by impoliteness. Furthermore, Buddhists generally accept what life has to offer and maintain a light-hearted atti-

Buddhist Road Rage?

tude toward difficulties. At the bottom of this is the sense that problems are an inevitable part of life but that humans can ride out the storms. Some of the Buddhist texts may seem gloomy to outsiders, but skeptical visitors to actual Buddhist communities are often forced to admit that the people they meet there are among the most cheerful in the world.

Of course, it would be simplistic to assume that Buddhism's historical success can be accounted for purely in terms of the content of its ideas or customs, any more than we could say that about other religions such as Christianity or Islam or about partially successful nonreligious doctrines like Marxism or capitalism. Unlike certain periods of historical Christianity, Buddhism was neither inquisitional, nor imperialistic and militaristic, nor did it often seem motivated by missionary zeal.

Nevertheless, patronage by royal power, which was itself zealous, militaristic, and imperialistic, has played a large role in Buddhism's spread. And in medieval Japan, Buddhism's natural nonaggressiveness did not prevent hordes of Buddhist monks from descending from their mountain retreats to attack their enemies. Also, where Buddhism did succeed in promoting a kind of passivity and pessimism about the physical world, it has sometimes played into the hands of tyrants. Furthermore, some have claimed that certain features of Zen Buddhist philosophy were incorporated into very nonBuddhist practices, such as the ceremonial execution of captured enemy aviators in Japan during World War II.[17] But then, there is probably a version of this story applicable to each of the great "isms" in world history. Perhaps the only thing that prevented abuses in the names of Plato, Aristotle, Sartre, and others discussed in this book is that their thoughts did not become the basis of major world socio-politico-religious systems.

Topics for Consideration

1. Why, according to the material introduced early in this chapter, were the ascetic religious beggars of ancient India in a better position than most to philosophize about human nature?

2. According to the Buddhist tradition, how is it possible that a man named Siddhartha Gautama became the Buddha while sitting under a Bodhi tree?

3. What response might a Buddhist have to a Western critic who says that her experiences in life make her skeptical of the Buddhist doctrine that life is always a form of suffering?

4. What is the connection between the Buddhist doctrine of suffering and its doctrine of karma, as best you understand it?

5. Defend one (or, if possible, both) of these theses:

   a. Buddhism is a philosophy of pessimism.

   b. Buddhism is a philosophy of optimism.

6. Set aside some time to experiment with the process of meditation as presented in this chapter. Then write a "phenomenological" account of your experiment; that is, write a descriptive memoir of the kinds of unusual experiences of consciousness that you encountered.

7. What does it mean to say, with the Buddhists, that there are selves but no true selfhood?

8. Lay out your own ideas about the meaning of the terms *god*, and *religion*. Then decide whether one can accurately attribute either term to the Buddhist system of belief and behavior.

9. Show how the moral recommendations associated with Buddhist ethics are related to the doctrine of karma.

10. The American philosopher Arthur Danto argues that Buddhist ethics make sense only if one accepts the metaphysical presuppositions on which they are based (the doctrines of karma and reincarnation). He believes that, for most educated Westerners, these doctrines cannot be seriously entertained, and that, therefore, the Buddhist way of life cannot be a genuine option here in the West. Respond to Danto's assertion by agreeing or disagreeing with it or by finding some middle ground.

Suggestions for Further Reading

I. Main Buddhist Works

Beyer, Stephen. *Buddhist Experience: Sources and Interpretations*. Encino, Calif.: Dickenson, 1974.

Burtt, E. A. *The Teachings of the Compassionate Buddha*. New York: New American Library, 1955.

Warren, Henry C. *Buddhism in Translations*. New York: Atheneum, 1963.

II. Secondary Sources on Buddhism

Carrithers, Michael. *The Buddha*. Oxford and New York: Oxford University Press, 1988.

Conze, Edward. *Buddhism: Its Essence and Development*. New York: Harper & Row, 1959.

Danto, Arthur C. *Mysticism and Morality: Oriental Thought and Moral Philosophy*. New York: Harper & Row, 1973.

Feibleman, James K. *Understanding Oriental Philosophy*. New York: New American Library, 1977.

Gethin, Rupert. *The Foundations of Buddhism*. Oxford and New York: Oxford University Press, 1998.

Rawson, Philip. *The Art of Tantra*. New York and Toronto: Oxford University Press, 1978.

Notes

1. Michael Carrithers, *The Buddha* (Oxford and New York: Oxford University Press, 1988), p. 20.
2. Quoted in Edward Conze, *Buddhism: Its Essence and Development* (New York: Harper & Row, 1959), p. 97.
3. Conze, *Buddhism*, p. 113.
4. Rupert Gethin, *The Foundations of Buddhism* (Oxford and New York: Oxford University Press, 1998), p. 174.
5. Gethin, *Foundations of Buddhism*, p. 183.
6. Gethin, *Foundations of Buddhism*, p. 187.
7. Quoted from the *Samyutta Nikaya*, in Gethin, *Foundations of Buddhism*, p. 59.
8. Conze, *Buddhism*, p. 132.
9. Quoted from the *Dîgha Nikâya*, Vol. I, in Carrithers, *The Buddha*, p. 54.
10. Quoted from the *Anguttara Nikâya*, Vol. III., in Carrithers, *The Buddha*, p. 68.
11. Conze, *Buddhism*, p. 58.
12. Gethin, *Foundations of Buddhism*, pp. 107–108.
13. Conze, *Buddhism*, p. 188.
14. Quoted in Conze, *Buddhism*, p. 195.
15. Quoted from the *Guhyasamaja-tantra*, in Conze, *Buddhism*, p. 195.
16. Conze, *Buddhism*, p. 77.
17. James K. Feibleman, *Understanding Oriental Philosophy* (New York: New American Library, 1977), p. 202.

4

The Medieval Christian Conception of Human Nature

Historical Backdrop

The city of Rome was founded in the year 753 B.C.E., and therewith were laid the foundations of an empire that eventually would achieve the unity and power that the Greek city-states were never able to accomplish, and that Alexander achieved only in an artificial and temporary manner. Always admiring Athens, Rome borrowed its religion, copied its art and architecture, and, by 510 B.C.E., emulated its political structure, declaring itself a republic with democratic institutions. Despite these institutions, Rome derived much of its wealth from slavery and imperialism, as had Athens before it. But it wisely created a system of provinces into which conquered peoples could be absorbed and easily granted Roman citizenship. As in Athens and Macedonia, there were in Rome political intrigues aplenty. One

Caligula (12–41 C.E.)

of these eventually propelled the popular consul and general Julius Caesar into an absolute dictatorship, which soon evolved into a hereditary emperorship that would last for five centuries, producing at least one great philosophical mind (Marcus Aurelius, 121–180 C.E.) and at least two deranged monsters (Caligula, 12–41 C.E., and Nero, 37–65 C.E.). Like Athens, Rome had a "Golden Age" (70 B.C.E.–14 C.E.), one as fraught with deceit and cynicism as the Golden Age of Athens. At its height, the Roman Empire extended from Gibraltar in the west to Armenia in the east and from Scotland in the north to North Africa in the south.

An imperial edict in 313 C.E. guaranteed freedom of religion throughout the empire and legitimized the Christian faith, which had been suppressed for hundreds of years. Furthermore, the emperor Constantine's conversion in 323 guaranteed Christianity's dominance in the empire. But soon after, Constantine transferred the seat of the empire to Byzantium—thereafter called Constantinople (until 1930, when it became Istanbul)—and split the empire into two parts, with each having its own emperor. This schism also signaled the beginning of the end of the Roman world. The Eastern empire distanced itself from the West, becoming increasingly Greek in culture and language and eventually producing the Eastern Orthodox churches (Greek, Ukrainian, and Russian), while the Western empire began to totter.

The Fall of Rome in the fifth century resulted from numerous factors in addition to the great schism—factors both internal and external. Internal problems that have been cited by various historians include (1) Christianity's otherworldliness, (2) paganism's penchant for vice, (3) geographic overextension, producing a cumbersome and ever more inefficient bureaucracy, (4) an increasingly irrational and corrupt tax system, and (5) the restlessness of retired soldiers flocking back to Rome. The external factor was the push into the empire by the "barbarian" Teutonic tribes that inhabited the forestlands of present-day Germany and Hungary. Sometimes these pushes were simply massive immigrations of pagan tribes desiring the advantages of Roman citizenship—as in December of 406 when the Rhine River froze over and the soldiers of the Roman Legion's border guard could not prevent the influx of thousands of Germanic peoples. Other times the pushes were literally invasions of marauding tribes, as in the sack of

Germans Crossing the Rhine

Rome by the Visigoths in 410 and again by the Vandals a few years later. Some of these tribes had themselves been displaced by the even more barbaric Huns from Asia who were swarming over the ancient homelands of the Teutons.

In most cases, the new arrivals had been converted to one form or another of Christianity, believing that to become Christian was to become Roman. However, in the eyes of the Romans, most of these new converts were not only barbarians but heretics, having been won over to a version of Christianity known as **Arianism,** which denied the **doctrine of the Trinity** (Father, Son, and Holy Ghost) and thereby the divinity of Jesus. The missionaries of the founder, Arius, would stand on the banks of the rivers being crossed by the invaders and declare them baptized as they emerged from the water.

At any rate, hordes of new arrivals took over the

How the Germans Became Christians

old empire: The Franks and Burgundians occupied today's France; the Jutes, Angles, and Saxons, England; the Ostrogoths, Italy; the Vandals, North Africa; and the Visigoths, Spain. The Roman legions abandoned England in 409. Meanwhile, at the other end of the empire, as the great philosopher and bishop Augustine (later, Saint Augustine) lay dying in his cathedral in the North African city of Hippo, the Vandals were burning the city all around him, preserving only the cathedral out of respect for him. By 476, the Roman emperor himself was an Ostrogoth. For all practical purposes, Rome had fallen, and the Dark Ages had commenced. The countryside became dangerous, as roving bands of marauders terrorized the population. All libraries disappeared, and learning was scorned. And the old Roman provinces broke up into feudal principalities where illiterate Gothic warlords ruled over illiterate peasants.

**The Invasion of the Germanic Tribes
in the Fifth Century C.E.**

The "darkness" of the Dark Ages was to last some three hundred years, relieved by only a few pockets of illumination, usually in remote monasteries on craggy mountaintops or on rocky promontories in the Atlantic Ocean or the Irish Sea. Eventually, a brief rebirth of learning took place in the court of the king of the Franks, Charlemagne, whom the pope had named Holy Roman emperor on Christmas Day of the year 800. (Do not be deceived by the title; the eighteenth-century French writer Voltaire described the Holy Roman Empire, late-blooming successor to the original Roman Empire, as "Not holy, not Roman, and not an Empire.") Charlemagne, who could write his own name but nothing more, called scholars from the Irish monasteries to his court in Aachen. Here, Greek texts were translated into Latin, and for the first time since the execution of the philosopher Boethius by the Ostrogothic emperor Odovicar in 525, real philosophical innovation took place—particularly in the work of John Scotus Eriugena (c. 810–877), "Sean the Irishman from Ireland" (the Irish were referred to as the Scoti), who worked at the court of Charlemagne's son, Charles the Bald.

During this era, Christianity was on the rise partly because the Irish monks, in whose hands the remnants of classical knowledge rested during the Dark Ages, returned to the Continent to set up a chain of abbeys and monasteries that became cultural and even political centers. The office of bishop was one of the few institutions that had survived the transition from the Roman to the medieval world, and in the fifth century, the bishop of Rome had managed to become designated the leader of (Western) Christendom as "pope" (father). Over the years, the power of the popes increased, as they called together councils that determined the content of the Holy Scriptures, declaring some to be apocryphal (that is, falsifications) and others authentic, and solidifying Christian

The Romanesque Saint-Just de Valcabrère (Haute Garonne, France)

dogma. A major event had been the conversion of the Frankish king, Clovis, from paganism to Catholicism in 496. The conversion of the Irish Celts by Saint Patrick in 461 brought Ireland into the Catholic fold, and Isidore of Seville's conversion, in about 600, of the king of the Visigoths from Arianism designated Spain as a Catholic stronghold. This meant that the bulk of the old Roman Empire had been re-Christianized by the seventh century and brought under the spiritual rule of the new Rome.

At the seat of each bishopric, a cathedral was built, first in the powerful style of Roman architecture (hence, "Romanesque"), and, after 1200, in the new, lighter, soaring Gothic style. Towns grew up around these cathedrals and became commercial, political, and academic centers, several of which had produced universities by the twelfth century. The bloodthirsty Vikings of Scandinavia, who, from the end of the eighth century on, had plagued the European countryside with their murderous raids, were finally defeated and even Christianized in the eleventh century. Also, the

The Gothic Style

wars with the Muslims in Spain (who had invaded and conquered the Iberian Peninsula in 711) had dwindled and become localized. Scholarly exchanges between Christian academics—including future popes—and the Muslim and Jewish philosophers of the great libraries of Seville, Toledo, and Cordoba had reintroduced documents believed long lost and augmented the few works of antiquity—Greek and Roman philosophy, medicine, science, and art—that had been hidden in the monasteries and abbeys during the Dark Ages. The Muslims were finally expelled from Spain only after the Catholic army of Queen Isabel won its last battle against the caliph of Granada in 1492, a year of many thought-provoking events.

Because of the religious obsession of the medieval era—that thousand-year period after the Fall of Rome—and the domination in Europe of Christian ideas, all of the recovered books from antiquity, particularly the works of Plato and Aristotle and the brilliant commentaries on them by the Arab and Jewish philosophers of Spain, such as Averroës (1126–1198) and Maimonides (1135–1204), had to be "sanitized," shown not only to be compatible with Christianity but to be versions of the Christian message. Part of the problem stemmed from the fact that people in the book-depleted Middle Ages—at least after its chaotic beginning—worshiped books. The words *auctor* (author) and *auctoritates* (authority) had the same connotation for medieval readers. As one scholar put it, "They find it very hard to believe that anything an old auctor has said is simply untrue."[1] Nor could they believe that two books could ultimately contradict each other. Therefore, the work of reconciliation governed scholarly activity. In fact, this bookish idea of reconciliation guided Western thinking, and, as we shall see, the world itself

Moses Maimonides (1135–1204 c.e.)

was seen as God's "Book of Nature," with each aspect of the world a sign to be read in deciphering the divine message that was hidden therein. This literary metaphor inspired not only the monkish scholars who copied actual manuscripts, illuminated them, and commented upon them but also the great mass of illiterate peasants who looked to the priestly class for guidance. Therefore, the artworks of the Middle Ages—the churches, murals, statues, and stained glass—had to be rendered in terms of visible images that were signs transmitting instructions on how to read the Book of Nature that was the world.

Out of all of this arose new ideas about human nature. Because the medieval period lasted a thousand years, and because it featured so many different phases and dramatic upheavals, there really isn't any single "medieval conception of human nature," nor any one philosopher who could claim to be a complete representative of the period. (That is why in this chapter we will skip our usual biographical section.) Nevertheless, there are prominent common denominators that allow for the possibility of a composite picture of human nature that accurately reflects some of the medieval world's most cherished and most interesting ideas.

Medieval Christian Theory

The Biblical Story of the Creation and Creation's Aftermath

According to the medieval Christian tradition, human beings are the intentional creation of a supernatural, all-powerful, all-knowing, benevolent, but

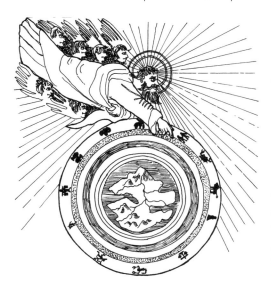

wrathful God. God also created the universe, and, as the medieval mind understood it, placed humans smack dab in the middle of it and gave humans custodianship over large segments of it. (In the biblical Book of Genesis, sacred to both Jews and Christians, humans are given dominion over the fowl of the air, the fish of the seas, and the beasts of the earth. They are also allowed to name all of the animals.)

The Creation of the World
(After an Anonymous Medieval Painting)

God gave human beings free will and the ability to choose between good and evil, which, in the case of the first humans, Adam and Eve, meant the choice of obeying or disobeying God's commandments. Unfortunately, humans might be tempted into disobedience by Satan, a dissident angel whom God had banished from Heaven. Because the first humans did indeed disobey God, he punished them and all their descendants. First, he expelled them from Eden—the paradise in which he created them (present-day Iraq)— and then he condemned them (and us) to "work by the sweat of the brow" and eventually to die.

However, God also had created humans with immortal souls. To give them a second chance, he sent his son, Jesus, who would assume the burden of human guilt and make possible salvation and eternal life in God's very home, referred to as a "New

Jerusalem." (Old Jerusalem was the capital city in ancient Palestine during biblical times and has been a destination for Jewish, Christian, and Muslim pilgrims ever since.) Those who repented by begging for God's mercy, acknowledging Jesus as God's son and as their savior, submitting themselves to God's will, and living the kind of life entailed by such a submission could hope to be judged favorably by God on a Day of Judgment. The specific date was known only by God himself, but the prophecies of Saint John the Divine in the New Testament Book of Revelation placed it after a period in which Satan would have strong influence, a period of great social turmoil and violence. (The medieval world mistakenly

The Final Judgment
(Tympanum, Saint Foy, Conques, France)

believed Saint John the Divine to be identical with the author of the Gospel of John, who was assumed to be one of the twelve disciples of Jesus, so the prophecies of Revelation were accorded a tremendous degree of respect.) Those who were so judged—both "the quick and the dead"—would receive their eternal recompense. Those who were judged positively would be elevated to the New Jerusalem, where they would enjoy eternal blessedness. Those who were judged negatively would be consigned to eternal punishment in hell, where they would be "burned by the eternal flame and gnawed by the eternal worm." (The bliss of the blessed would be increased by the enjoyment they would derive from watching the torment of the damned, in the opinion of Saint Thomas Aquinas, one of the greatest spokesmen of the Middle Ages.[2])

According to medieval Christianity, after his crucifixion and resurrection, Jesus

The Damned Dragged Down
to Hell by Demons
(After Luca Signorelli)

returned to his heavenly father, but before doing so he appointed his disciple Peter as custodian of his divine work. A hierarchy of authority grew up around this work. After much theological struggle over the course

of several centuries, as we have seen, the bishop of Rome convinced the Christian world that his office had inherited the mantle of Saint Peter, and he became the pope, spiritual leader of Christendom.

Medieval Proofs of God's Existence

The central idea in the medieval discourse, then, is the idea of God—an idea that goes virtually unchallenged. In the Middle Ages, there are many "heretical" views concerning God's nature, but there is no atheism. Once it is determined that the world is God's Book of Nature, then every feature of the world becomes incontrovertible evidence of God's existence—as when Saint Patrick, examining the flowers in his garden, exclaims: "I see his blood upon the rose."[3] Yet medieval philosophy is full of rational *proofs* of the existence of God. That is because for the philosophers of the Middle Ages, human reason, too, is a *sign* of God's existence.

One of the most famous of the attempts to prove God's existence is that of Anselm (1033–1109), an Italian priest who later become archbishop of Canterbury and was eventually sanctified as Saint Anselm. His proof of God is now called the **ontological argument.** This curious, but in some ways powerful, argument is addressed not to atheists (as I said, there weren't any) but to God himself! It's hard to believe that God needed proof of his own existence, but Anselm was probably offering his meditation as a form of worship or gift that could not possibly add anything to God's store (nothing could) but that nevertheless would be pleasing in God's sight. This is Anselm's introduction: "I do not seek to understand that I may believe, but I believe in order to understand. For this also I believe, that unless I believed, I should not understand." Anselm goes on to refer to the "fool" mentioned in Psalm 53:1, who "says in his heart, 'There is no God.'" Even this fool is convinced that something exists in the understanding, at least, than which nothing greater can be conceived. For when he hears of this he understands it. And whatever is understood exists in the understanding. And assuredly that than which nothing greater can be conceived, cannot exist in the understanding alone. For suppose it exists in the understanding alone: then it can be conceived to exist in reality, which is greater.

Therefore, if that than which nothing greater can be conceived exists in the understanding alone, the very being than which nothing greater can be conceived, is one than which a greater can be conceived. But obviously this is impossible. Hence, there is no doubt that there exists a being than which nothing greater can be conceived, and it exists both in the understanding and in reality.

And it assuredly exists so truly that it cannot be conceived not to exist. For it is possible to conceive of a being which cannot be conceived not to exist. Hence, if that than which nothing greater can be conceived, can be conceived not to exist, it is not that than which nothing greater can be conceived. But this is an irreconcilable contradiction. There is, then, so truly a being than which nothing greater can be conceived to exist, that it cannot even be conceived not to exist; and this being thou art, O Lord our God.[4]

Let's try to simplify this argument a bit, even though in so doing, we will lose the effect of the marvelous Latinate poetic style.

(A)   It is possible to think of an absolutely perfect being.
(B)   If that absolutely perfect being exists only in the mind of the thinker, then it is *not* the most absolutely perfect being that can possibly be thought of (because a being that existed both in the mind and outside of it would be superior to one that existed only in the mind).
(C)   Therefore, the possibility of conceiving of an absolutely perfect being entails its necessary existence.
(D)   This absolutely perfect being that must necessarily exist is the being we call God.

This argument looks suspicious. It appears as though it should be pretty easy to knock it over, but it is a slippery argument and more resistant to criticism than you might think. Its main weakness from *our* point of view— namely, its presupposition of a neo-Platonic metaphysical scheme—would not have been considered a liability in Anselm's time. It assumes the validity of Plato's "hierarchy of being," in which that which is "most real" is equivalent to that which is "most perfect." It is a purely **a priori** argument— that is, its appeal is exclusively to logic and never to empirical evidence. Seemingly, if Platonic ontology is correct, then Anselm's argument is valid; if that ontology is incorrect, then the argument is dubious. But in the year

1100, very few doubted the neo-Platonic picture of reality as a "great chain of being."

Yet, only 150 years later, after contact with the philosophers and libraries of Muslim Spain, scholars brought Aristotle's critique of Plato rather suddenly into the mainstream of medieval Christian thought. Consequently, some of that thought became more Aristotelian, and hence more empirical. Contrast, for instance, the **cosmological argument** for God's existence written by Thomas Aquinas (1225–1274) with Anselm's Platonic ontological argument. Aquinas writes in his *Summa theologica*:

> In the world of sense we find there is an order of efficient causes. There is no case known (neither is it, indeed, possible) in which a thing is found to be the efficient cause of itself; for so it would be prior to itself, which is impossible. Now in efficient causes it is not possible to go on to infinity, because in all efficient causes following in order, the first is the cause of the intermediate cause, and the intermediate cause is the cause of the ultimate cause, whether the intermediate cause be several or one only. Now, to take away the cause is to take away the effect. Therefore, if there be no first cause among efficient causes, there will be no ultimate, nor any intermediate cause. But if in efficient causes it is possible to go to infinity, there will be no first efficient cause, neither will there be an ultimate effect, nor any intermediate efficient causes; all of which is plainly false. Therefore it is necessary to admit a first efficient cause to which everyone gives the name of God.[5]

The term *efficient cause* is one Aquinas borrowed from Aristotle, and it is roughly equivalent to what we mean today by the word *cause*. Therefore, Aquinas's argument seems to boil down to this:

(A) Every event in the observable world is caused by some event prior to it.

(B) Either (1) the series of causes is infinite, or (2) the series of causes goes back to a first cause, which is itself uncaused.

(C) But an infinite series of causes is impossible.

THE BUCK STOPS HERE

(D) Therefore, a first cause, which is God, exists.

Perhaps the modern mentality would challenge each step in this argument, as did the eighteenth-century Scottish philosopher David Hume, but to the medieval mind of the mid-thirteenth century, such a critique would probably be unintelligible. Despite the differences between the arguments of Anselm and Thomas (roughly the differences between the twelfth and the thirteenth centuries), both philosophers agree that human reason itself is a sign of a higher order, and that therefore its study must lead to God.

Collective Memory and Salvation History

The medieval Christian idea of human nature did not dwell exclusively on the faculty of reason, however; it also involved the faculty of memory—particularly the idea of collective memory. Human beings find out who they are by remembering their past, by placing themselves in history. In the Middle Ages, the job of priests, scholars, philosophers, historians, theologians, poets, dramatists, sculptors, architects, and glasspainters was to show that present events are made meaningful by relating them to the complete picture of the cosmos, and especially that the history of individuals and societies belongs to **salvation history,** with Christ's passion (the story of his trial, torment, and crucifixion) at its center. The scholars could communicate this idea to other scholars, but in a world of widespread illiteracy, it fell to the artists to communicate

Luxury, Pride, and Cowardice (Nôtre Dame, Paris)

to laypersons that their world mirrored God's presence in history and that they therefore needed to subordinate the worldly to the heavenly. The work of art, then, not only had to be a symbol of something divine, but it had to communicate the idea that human actions and nature itself were symbols of higher things. The medieval individual was taught to read nature as a book written by the Creator in such a way that its correct reading would reveal its hidden meaning. Part of what would be revealed is

God Writing in the Book of Nature

that each life is a microcosm reflecting the whole. As the historian Rodolphus Glaber of Cluny (c. 1030) said:[6]

Pilgrimages and Holy Relics

If the life of each individual repeats the whole of salvation history, then history is circular. However, this does not mean there is no progress. Jerusalem may be the "umbilicus of the world," but Rome, the home of the pope, becomes a New Jerusalem (thereby alluding to the past and foreshadowing the future). And so, for the French, the city of Orleans—the early medieval seat of the kings of France—would also take on universal historical dimensions. When, in the year 999, Orleans was destroyed by fire, it was rebuilt even more gloriously as an ever-finer New Jerusalem.

Orleans also had the advantage of being closer to home for the Christians of northern Europe than Jerusalem

The Umbilicus of the World

and Rome. It was necessary to bring the divine story home because travel was so difficult during much of the early Middle Ages (though Jerusalem still had its appeal, as evidenced by the Crusades of the twelfth and thirteenth centuries). This explains the importance of certain tombs, such as Santiago de Compostela in northern Spain, believed to house the body of Saint James. It explains the importance of certain historical sites, such as Roncesvalles in the Pyrenees, where the mighty Count Roland had been killed, and where, it was believed, Emperor Charlemagne had avenged Roland's death against Muslim infidels. It explains the importance of certain holy relics— for example, clothing, parts of the body, or bones of men and women who had led exemplary, saintly lives, such as the girdle of Saint Foy at Conques in southern France, or even garments of Christ himself, such as the holy shroud at Turin, a visit to which would somehow verify

ACTUALLY, THEY WEREN'T MUSLIMS AT ALL. THEY WERE BASQUE BANDITS.

The Mighty Roland Fights Off Hordes of Muslim Warriors

the truth of the divine story and allow pilgrims to experience that truth in their own lives. Sites in Spain (for example, Santiago and Roncesvalles) and in France (for example, Blaye, Le Puy, Conques, Rocamadour and Mont Saint Michel) became part of a system of signs that might be read in terms of the Book of Revelation, thereby linking the reader of these signs to salvation history.

Divine Signs and Terror

The medieval human being, then, was a creature who existed on two different planes at the same time, a natural and a supernatural one. Because humans were essentially symbolizing beings—makers and readers of signs—they could bridge the apparent gap between these two planes.

**A Bridge of Signs between
the Natural and the Supernatural**

Medieval philosophers were able to use what little they knew of Plato and Aristotle to develop this divine **semiology,** or theory of signs. Plato, you will recall, divided reality into an eternally unchanging spiritual or intellectual sphere and an ever-changing physical sphere, with the latter a poor copy of the former. The **neo-Platonic** medievals emphasized the fact that the sensual world was a cryptic version of the spiritual world. Therefore, far from despising physical nature, they tried to read it as a symbol of the spiritual. Philosophers like Pseudo-Dionysius ("pseudo" because he was incorrectly believed to be the Dionysius converted in Athens by Saint Paul, mentioned in Acts 17:34, and also to be Saint Denis, Christianity's first martyr and patron saint of France during the early Middle Ages) and John Scotus Eriugena developed this idea into a complete coherent system of sign reading, such that it was almost impossible for medieval humans to view history and nature without seeing them as signs of higher things. Consider, for example, the soliloquy of Adam of Saint Victor, a twelfth-century poet, as he discourses about a walnut he holds in his hand in the monastery refectory:[7]

What is a nut if not the image of Jesus Christ? The green and fleshy sheath is His flesh, His humanity. The wood of the shell is the wood of the cross on which that flesh suffered. But the kernel of the nut from which men gain nourishment is His hidden divinity.

This picture of human nature must seem in many ways alien to us at the turn of the century (even to those of us who have deep religious sentiments). But it has numerous positive features, not the least of which is the *meaning* that it bestowed on everybody's life, down to that of the simplest **villein.** Even if one's life was sheer misery, it was *meaningful* misery, played out as it was on the center stage of the universe and associated symbolically with Christ's passion and the salvation story. (No wonder the Church panicked when Galileo threatened this view by providing strong evidence that the earth revolved around the sun!) Another advantage was the weakening of the distinctions between self and world and between self and other. Even in a world of rigid social class divisions, a world in which nature must often have seemed hostile, it was understood through symbolic reading that, after all, reality was a seamless whole.

There were, of course, some extreme disadvantages as well. The same symbolic system that created meaning and offered promise also generated terror. It was not without excited passions that men and women of the Middle Ages on their way to morning services passed under tympana carved with the demons, monsters, and other horrible beasts. Both the Book of Revelation and the Gospel of Matthew on which the carvings were based promised horrible

punishments for the wayward. The proliferation of mysterious signs in the form of strange fauna from the Bestiaries (books explaining the symbolic meaning of animals—familiar ones, exotic ones, mythical ones) caused much confusion. Perhaps the contemporary philosopher and fiction writer Umberto Eco best captured the potential for that panic in his best-selling novel, *The Name of the Rose*. The book's narrator, the fourteenth-century monk Adso of Melk, catalogues the beasts depicted in the tympanum of his monastery. Let me quote Adso (and urge you to read the novel, which will not only teach you something about the medieval world but offer you a good detective story as well):[8]

> ...sirens, hippocentaurs, gorgons, harpies, incubi, dragopods, minotaurs, lynxes, pards, chimeras, cynophales who darted fire from their nostrils, crocodiles, polycaudate, hairy serpents, salamanders, horned vipers, tortoises, snakes, two-headed creatures whose backs were armed with teeth, hyenas, otters, crows, hydrophora with saw-tooth horns, frogs, gryphons, monkeys, dog-heads, leucrota, manticores, vultures, paranders, weasels, dragons, hoopoes, owls, basilisks, hypnales, presters, spectafici, scorpions, saurians, scitales...and sea turtles.

Another disadvantage of this system of signs was that it needed to be grounded in the certainty of a powerful authority. Of course, the original authority was supposed to be the voice of the Creator himself ("In the beginning was the Word"). But because the original language of Adam had been lost at the **Tower of Babel,** and because the divine word was ambiguous, an authoritative interpretation was needed. (For example, it was decided that every passage in the Old Testament could be interpreted in four ways: (1) *historically* [having a literal meaning], (2) *allegorically* [showing the Old Testament as prefiguring the New], (3) *tropologically* [unveiling a hidden moral truth], and (4) *anagogically* [foreshadowing the mystery of a future life and eternal bliss].) In the search for an authoritative interpretation, certain early texts had been declared canonical, but often they themselves required interpretation.

The hierarchy of the Church, culminating in the proclamations of the pope, was authoritative. But the Middle Ages were full of dissension, sometimes producing bloody inquisitional trials and even pogroms (such as the crusade against the Knights Templar in the twelfth century and against the Albigensians in the thirteenth) as the fear of heresy contaminated the world. Especially in the fourteenth century, authority began to crumble as several popes clashed with large constituencies within

the Church, including numerous monastic orders, and the legitimacy of various popes was questioned. A power struggle in the early fifteenth century resulted in three papal claimants, with each excommunicating the other two and all of their followers.

This collapse of authority paralleled the collapse of the medieval period itself. The anxiety concerning interpretation in the last century of the Middle Ages is captured splendidly in Eco's aforementioned novel. The nar-

FIRST MEANING [HISTORICAL]: ADAM, the first man (this really happened!).

SECOND MEANING [ALLEGORICAL]: ADAM as a sign of Christ (Adam, the first man, Christ, the second man).

THIRD MEANING [TROPOLOGICAL]: ADAM, as disobedient (the wages of sin is death).

FOURTH MEANING [ANAGOGICAL]: ADAM, lost, recovered (cast from Paradise at the beginning of time, re-enters at the end of time).

"...And God said unto Adam..."

rator, Adso, having witnessed one inquisitional burning, is terrified by the possibility of misinterpreting the signs he finds around him in nature, art, and society. He slips into a hallucinatory trance filled with images of hell after staring at the tympanum in the monastery where he is residing. (The tympanum Eco describes is the actual one at the Church of Saint Pierre in Moissac.) He has just been gazing at the figure of Christ sitting in judgment surrounded by four beasts, one with the head of a man (symbolizing Saint Matthew), one a bull (symbolizing Saint Luke), one an eagle (symbolizing Saint John), and one a lion (symbolizing Saint Mark). The lion symbolizes Mark because, in the beginning of his Gospel, he speaks of "a voice crying in the wilderness," which in medieval times was associated with a lion. But it turns out that the lion also stands for Christ's resurrection (both because the Bestiaries asserted that lions sleep with their eyes open and because the lion cubs are born dead and brought to life on the third day by the breath of their father). Also, the lion stands for courage and for strength, and sometimes for temperance. Furthermore, the lion is associated with the sainthood of Gerasimus and Jerome (two saints whom the Middle Ages constantly confused) and with Pepin the Short, father of Charlemagne, as well as with the biblical tribe of Judah. However, the lion is

The Lion, Symbol of Saint Mark, as Depicted in the Tympanum, Saint Pierre's, Moissac, France

Daniel in the Lions' Den
(Capital—La Magdeleine de Vezelay)

burdened with less positive meanings as well. It is the zodiacal figure standing for the heat of August that ravages the fields. It is also associated with the attempted execution of Daniel in the lions' den in the Old Testament and with Saint Denis's martyrdom. Even in the Book of Revelation, there are contradictory signals. There, though the lion symbolizes Saint Mark, its head is also found on the pestilent beasts issuing fire, smoke, and sulfur out of their mouths at the end of the world, and the beast with seven heads referred to there has a lion's mouth. And in some medieval statues, Christ is shown treading a lion underfoot; the lion thus was also understood as symbolizing the **Antichrist.** Small wonder that poor Adso is confused. How's a (medieval) guy to know? He stares at the lion carved in the columns supporting the tympanum and says, "Its figure suggested to me both the image of the Enemy and that of Christ our Lord, nor did I know by what symbolic code I was to read it, and I was trembling all over."[9]

It is curious that, in so many ways, the Greek pictures of human nature (Plato's and Aristotle's, for example) seem easier for us to identify with today than does the medieval, even though the medieval picture is

Trampling the Lion Underfoot

a thousand years closer to us. Perhaps the overpowering religiosity of the Middle Ages, combined with, from our point of view, the appalling ignorance and confusion of the period, alienates us today. Yet the brilliance of the high moments of medieval art and philosophy still inspires many, as does the dedication to the idea of work—both intellectual and manual—as having personal, social, and religious value. (One of the buildings at my former college was condemned because of dry rot only 12 years after its construction. Yet, last summer, I visited several 700-year-old medieval structures that appeared prepared to last another 700 years.) In fact, for better or for worse, we in modern America and Europe all stand in the

shadows of the great medieval cathedrals of Europe. We do this in each of our cases either by inheritance or by adoption. Some people regret this; others do not. Many find a kind of beauty in the medieval prescription, looking back longingly either at the religious conviction and devotion of the age or at the richness of meaning offered by their semiotic system to the people of the Middle Ages but not to us.

Ironically, a new interest in medieval theory of signs (semiology) has been provoked by the writings of certain "postmodern" philosophers, especially in France. The works of Michel Foucault, Roland Barthes, Jacques Derrida, Julia Kristeva, and Jean Baudrillard, among others, have led some to embrace Adso's conclusion in the last sentence of *The Name of the Rose*: "*Stat rosa pristina nomine, nomina nuda tenemus*" ("The rose exists by virtue of its name; we have only names"). Suppose it is true (and I'm not suggesting for a moment that it is) that "we have only names"—that is, that humans are trapped in a circular system of signs, each of which refers either to other signs or to itself. In other words, suppose that if beyond language there is no reality to which we have access except in some inexplicable moment of transcendence, and there is still no solution to the problem of authority, no key to enable us to decipher and justify the meaning of the system of signs into which we are born and that dominates and dictates our lives. Then our case is, after all, not so different from that of medieval people.

Trapped in a Circular System of Signs

Summary

The dominant medieval conception of human nature was, then, a thoroughly religious one. Despite being influenced by the Platonic and Aristotelian theories we have already studied, it differed greatly from those Greek conceptions of human nature because, in one important sense, it was much more pessimistic than they were. The Greeks believed not only that human blessedness was possible in this world but that it could be achieved by oneself on one's own. Through a process of philosophizing correctly and acting virtuously, one could achieve excellence. The medieval Christian conception of human nature denies exactly this. One cannot do it by oneself. One needs help; indeed, one needs divine help. We can paraphrase Socrates as having said, "If I knew the good, I would be good; therefore, I must dedicate my life to the quest for knowledge of the good." Four hundred years later, Saint Paul said, "I know the good but do the evil; Lord have mercy on me." When the Western world identified with Paul's anxiety, the Classical Age was over and the Middle Ages had begun.

But there is some optimism even in this pessimism. If medieval men and women conceive of themselves as thoroughly *dependent* creatures, they are also *important* creatures, because their lives are intimately bound up with God's plan for the universe and with the drama of Christ's passion. Furthermore, everyone is linked to these related histories both as cipher in the story and as decipherer of the story, for everyone is part of a semiotic system of meaning ultimately grounded in the power and glory of God. Though the real rewards for faithful service in this life are to be reaped in the next life, this life is not to be disdained. Even the lowest entity in this world is a sign of what is higher, and hence has its worth as part of the great system of signs that is creation. If one is no longer, with Aristotle, *Homo philosophicus*, one is at least *Homo semioticus*.

Nevertheless, anxiety attaches even to the happy side of this picture, for the signs that must be deciphered are confusing. Often a sign is merely the sign of another sign, and almost always, signs are ambiguous. They have multiple meanings and are easily misunderstood, sometimes with deadly consequences in this world and horrible ones in the next world. What is needed is an authority to guide one in deciphering these signs. The Church offers itself as just such an authority. During the most stable periods of the Middle Ages, one could easily trust oneself to that authority; but often the authorities fought with one another for power over these signs. Then the demons in the tympana held sway. Pogroms, peasant uprisings, inquisitional trials, burnings at the stake, outbreaks of **St. Vitus's dance,** and other frenzies would sweep over the land. A misreading of a sign could unleash Satan. And even terrors whose source was beyond the mysterious system of signs were read semiotically. For 300 years, the Vikings pillaged and murdered seemingly at will, as people prayed at bedtime, "Lord, save us from the wrath of the Norsemen." In the thirteenth century, perhaps a third of the population of Europe succumbed to the Black Death. We now know that the immediate culprits were the fleas on rats carrying the bubonic plague, but medieval peoples, ignorant of this diagnosis, could not tell if these horrors were signs of God's wrath or of some terrible temporary triumph of the Antichrist.

Topics for Consideration

1. Explain what it means to say that Anselm's ontological argument for God's existence presupposes the truth of a Platonic worldview. (You may want to review Plato's metaphysics in Chapter 1.)

2. Both Greek philosophy and modern philosophy generally make the assumption that logic is its own authority, but the medieval mind often

seems to believe that *authority* is at least as important as logic. Discuss this assertion.

3. Make a list of what you take to be confusions and errors made by medieval thinkers that influenced the medieval worldview (for example, the misidentification of Saint John, the supposed author of the Book of John, as the same person as Saint John the Divine, the supposed author of the Book of Revelation). Try to arrive at some conclusion concerning the overall effect that all this misinformation had on the medieval conception of human nature.

4. What effect on the medieval conception of human nature results from the period's interest in semiology (the study of "signs")?

5. What are your thoughts concerning the claim that, during most of the Middle Ages, there was virtually no atheism?

6. Discuss the similarities and the differences between Anselm's and Thomas's proofs of God's existence.

7. Write a short essay in which you either defend or attack Thomas Aquinas's argument attempting to prove God's existence.

Suggestions for Further Reading

I. Main Medieval Philosophical Works Anthologized

Hyman, Arthur, and James J. Walsh. *Philosophy in the Middle Ages: The Christian, Islamic, and Jewish Traditions,* 2nd ed. Indianapolis, Ind.: Hackett, 1983.

II. Secondary Sources on Medieval Philosophy and Culture

Cahill, Thomas. *How the Irish Saved Civilization.* New York and London: Anchor Books/Doubleday, 1996.

Eco, Umberto. *The Name of the Rose.* Trans. William Weaver. New York: Warner Books, 1984.

Fremantle, Anne. *The Age of Belief.* New York: New American Library, 1954.

Kenny, Anthony, *Aquinas. Past Master Series.* New York: Hill & Wang, 1980.

Lewis, C. S. *The Discarded Image: An Introduction to Medieval and Renaissance Literacy.* Cambridge: Cambridge University Press, 1970.

Luscombe, David. *Medieval Thought.* Oxford and New York: Oxford University Press, 1997.

Mâle, Emile. *The Gothic Image: Religious Art in France in the Thirteenth Century.* Trans. Dora Nussen. New York: Harper & Row, 1972.

Price, Betsy. *Medieval Thought: An Introduction.* Cambridge, Mass.: Blackwell, 1992.

Notes

1. C. S. Lewis, *The Discarded Image: An Introduction to Medieval and Renaissance Literacy* (Cambridge: Cambridge University Press, 1970), p. 11.

2. Thomas Aquinas, *Summa Theologiae, iii, Supplementum,* Q. 94, Art. 1.

3. Saint Patrick, quoted in Thomas Cahill, *How the Irish Saved Civilization* (New York and London: Anchor Books/Doubleday, 1996), p. 132.

4. Anselm of Canterbury, *Prologium,* in Anne Fremantle, *The Age of Belief* (New York: New American Library, 1954), pp. 88–89.

5. Thomas Aquinas, *Summa theologica,* in Fremantle, *The Age of Belief,* p. 153.

6. Quoted in Stephen Nichols, *Romanesque Signs: Early Medieval Narrative and Iconography* (New Haven, Conn.: Yale University Press, 1983), p. 13.

7. Quoted in Emile Mâle, *The Gothic Image: Religious Art in France in the Thirteenth Century,* trans. Dora Nussen (New York: Harper & Row, 1972), p. 30.

8. Umberto Eco, *The Name of the Rose,* trans. William Weaver (New York: Warner Books, 1984), pp. 44–45.

9. Eco, *Name of the Rose,* p. 285.

5

The Cartesian Conception
of Human Nature

Historical Backdrop

The 150-year period that followed the collapse of the Middle Ages (approximately from 1450 to 1600) is called "the Renaissance," after the French word for "rebirth." Spearheaded by developments in Italy, the Renaissance reflected a recovery of classical Greek and Roman ways of looking at the world. In the arts, innovative and highly talented artists flourished, including painters (for example, Fra Angelico, Raphael, Michelangelo, and Leonardo da Vinci), sculptors (Donatello and Verrocchio), and architects (Giotto and Brunelleschi). In politics, the erosion of papal power opened channels for ambitious monarchs (for example, Charles I of Spain, Francis I of France, and Henry IV of England) and for influential religious

Look! You can get a genuine copy of a Titian!

I'm waiting until they invent Elvis on velvet.

reformers (such as Martin Luther, John Calvin, John Knox, and Jonathan Wycliff). The works of the artists and writers of the period, as well as translations of the Bible into local languages, were made available for mass consumption for the first time because of the invention of the printing press and of engraving procedures. New wealth, materials, and ideas derived from the exploratory voyages to the West (the so-called discovery of the New World) and the opening of trade routes to India and China. Throughout the Renaissance and into the era of the "hero" of this chapter, René Descartes (1596–1650), the budding of the arts and literature was accompanied by the emergence of the "new sciences." Nicolas Copernicus discovered the double movements of the planets (orbiting their own axes and orbiting the sun); William Harvey explained the circulation of blood; Galileo Galilei laid the foundations for modern physics and astronomy; and Johannes Kepler identified the laws of planetary motion.

Copernicus's Dizzying Discovery

The period that followed the Renaissance is sometimes called the Baroque (approximately 1600–1680), named after the exuberant art style that emerged after the more geometrical Renaissance style.[1] This period, too, was rich in the arts and letters (for example, Rubens, Rembrandt, Vermeer, Velázquez, Bernini, Shakespeare, and Cervantes). But some of the destructive forces engendered and let loose by the Reformation—the attack by revolutionary religious leaders on what they perceived as the corruption and dissolution of the Church—produced various forms of militant Protestantism, and the Catholic Counterreformation—the Church's counterattack against the reformers—created an equally militant form of Catholicism. These forces clashed in the disastrous Thirty Years War (1618–1648), which started out as a conflict between princes and kings supporting one religious movement or the other but soon became a testing ground for the ambitions of various royal houses—Austrian, Bohemian, Danish, French, and Dutch. The war disrupted the general processes of civilization, destroyed the sense of optimism accompanying the Renaissance, and devastated whole nations. (The population of Germany was reduced by half during these thirty years, not from battle-

field casualties but from starvation and disease produced by the collapse of agriculture and the general economy.) Several years into the hostilities,

the war had lost almost all semblance of being a religious conflict. René Descartes, himself a Catholic, was a "gentleman soldier" for a time in the army of the Protestant Prince Maurice of Nassau; later he played the same role in the army of the Catholic Maximilian of Bavaria. A telltale sign of the times was Descartes's long stay in the Protestant Netherlands where, he asserted, the great number of soldiers assured him of the safety and peace he needed for his studies.

Biography

René Descartes was born in 1596 at La Haye, a small town in central France near the city of Tours. (The name of "La Haye" has since been changed to "Descartes" in honor of its most famous native son.) His mother died when he was only a year old, and he was raised by his maternal grandmother. At ten years of age, he was sent to La Flèche, a Jesuit school excelling in mathematics but still dominated philosophically by medieval ideas, where he studied for eight years. After leaving La Flèche, he apparently suffered a nervous breakdown; when he recovered, he entered the University of Poitiers, and earned a degree in law.

Descartes's father was a minor nobleman who hoped for a military career for his son, who, in fact, served in Holland, Germany, and Hungary during different periods of the Thirty Years War. In 1619, in Ulm, Germany, he experienced a second nervous breakdown. But he also had three now-famous

René Descartes (1596–1650)

inspirational dreams, which he interpreted as obligating him to lay the foundations of the new sciences. He had already spent much of his spare time—of which he had plenty during the long winters of the war—attempting to solve various scientific problems, and, from this point on, he gave himself over to such studies and their intellectual justification. To this end, he sold all the property he had inherited, which guaranteed him a lifetime income of modest proportions.

The most scientifically significant of his endeavors was his development of analytic geometry—roughly, the proof that the totality of Euclidean geometry can be translated into pure arithmetic. He then turned to physics and wrote a manuscript called *Treatise on the World*, which he was about to publish in 1633 when he heard of Galileo's condemnation by an inquisitional tribunal. Knowing that his own theory corresponded in many ways with Galileo's, he prudently withdrew his manuscript from publication. Galileo had been arrested and tried for impiety because he had published a paper claiming that the planet Jupiter had four orbiting moons. (Why would the Church care, you ask? Because if Jupiter had moons that orbited it, then the fact that the earth also had an orbiting moon was no longer evidence for the earth's being the center of the universe. In that case, the sense of primacy bestowed upon humans by virtue of being right in the middle of everything was suddenly chal-

lenged.) To pave the way for the vindication of views like Galileo's and the eventual publication of his own book on physics, Descartes turned to writing philosophy, publishing *Discourse on Method* in 1637 as an introduction to a book about certain of his scientific experiments and *Meditations on First Philosophy* in 1641. It is from these books that we can derive not only his ideas about religion, science, and philosophy but his views on the nature of the self.

In 1635, the maid in the house in Amsterdam where Descartes resided gave birth to his daughter, Francine. Descartes came to cherish the girl, but she died of fever when she was five years old, leaving him alone. He soon began a useful correspondence first with Princess Elizabeth of Bohemia and then with Queen Christina of Sweden, who invited him to her court in Stockholm in 1649. The rigors of the Scandinavian winter were more than he could deal with, and he died of pneumonia in February of 1650.

Descartes's Theory

Descartes records in the autobiographical sections of his writings his disappointment with all that passed for knowledge in his time and his belief that confusion reigned in almost all fields of endeavor. This included religion, as was proved by the horrors of the Thirty Years War. Descartes was a

practicing Catholic, but he believed that religion as it was conceived and followed by some of his fellow Catholics—including some powerful ones—was riddled with contradiction and superstition. He disapproved of what he saw as the Church's reactionary stance in its confrontation with the newly emerging sciences, including Galileo's astronomical writings, and he thought that a correct picture of humans would include both spiritual values and the capacity for rigorous scientific investigation.

He hoped that his philosophical books would prove this view to the religious authorities and to the general populace. He believed that the only way to construct such a picture would be to sweep away all the confusions and misconceptions that plagued human thinking about the basic issues of facts and values, self and world, and religious domain and scientific domain.

Radical Doubt

Descartes believed that he would have to tear down the old "house of knowledge," riddled as it was with rotten beams and unsupported planks, and rebuild it from the foundations. Intellectually, he would have to start all over again from ground zero. To carry out this plan, Descartes locks himself alone in a room in the dead of winter, sits at a desk before a fireplace (in his "PJs," as he tells us in the Meditations), and engages in an amazing philosophical project.[2]

I thought it was necessary for me to reject as absolutely false everything as to which I could imagine the least grounds of doubt, in order to see if afterwards there remained anything in my belief that was entirely certain.

I was convinced that I must once for all seriously undertake to rid myself of all the opinions which I had formerly accepted, and commence to build anew from the foundation if I wanted to establish any firm and permanent structure in the sciences.

To execute this project, Descartes invents a method, since called "methodological doubt" or "radical doubt"—which is like a philosophical game, but a *serious* game. The primary rule of this "game" is that the player must doubt everything that can be doubted (*"de omnibus dubitandum est"*); the goal of the game is to find something indubitable, something that is impossible to doubt. Having once found such an absolute certainty—if such certainty can be found—it will serve as the *foundation* for the new house of knowledge he plans to construct.

You wanna play philosophy?

I doubt it.

Based on this program, Descartes finds that the everyday data provided by the senses do not produce certainty. Rather, each of the five senses is capable of generating misleading or even delusive information. "Thus," says Descartes, following the rules of his new game, "because our senses sometimes deceive us, I wished to suppose that nothing is just as they cause us to imagine it to be."[3] But, Descartes asks himself, is it really possible to stare at one's hand and wonder if, in fact, it is one's hand? Is it truly possible to be deceived in making such a simple judgment?[4]

And how could I deny that these hands and this body are mine, were it not perhaps that I compare myself to certain persons, devoid of sense, whose cerebella are so troubled and clouded by the violent vapours of black bile, that they constantly assure us that they think they are kings when they are really quite poor, ... or who imagine that they have an earthenware head or are nothing but pumpkins, or are made of glass. But they are mad, and I should not be any the less insane were I to follow examples so extravagant.

If you can cut through the wonderfully Baroque language here, you'll see that Descartes is saying that anyone who can stare at his hand and wonder if it is his hand is not a philosopher, but a madman. Radical doubt has suddenly become insanity.

Then maybe the only way to keep Descartes from leading us into folly is to acknowledge that simple commonsense judgments like "This is my hand" are legitimate foundations of knowledge. But remember, the philo-sophical game we are playing ("radical" or "methodological doubt") requires that the slightest ground for doubt be accepted as canceling out any claim of certainty. Therefore, Descartes goes on to scrutinize his thoughts to see if he can detect a weakness in them; he discovers one in his considera-tion of the dream-state:

I am in the habit of sleeping, and in my dreams representing to myself the same things or sometimes even less probable things, than do those who are insane in their waking moments. How often has it happened to me that in the night I dreamt that I found myself in this particular place, that I was dressed and seated near the fire, whilst in reality I was lying undressed in bed!

He comes to what he calls an "astonishing" conclusion:

[I]n thinking over this I remind myself that on many occasions I have in sleep been deceived by similar illusions, and in dwelling carefully on this reflection I see so manifestly that there are no certain indications by which we may clearly distinguish wakefulness from sleep that I am lost in astonishment. And my astonishment is such that it is almost capable of persuading me that I now dream.[5]

Descartes is unable to prove that he is not dreaming at that moment. There is no test that will resolve the issue, because any test he can conceive of could be dreamt. (Anything it is possible to *think*, it is possible to dream.) Therefore, after all, he cannot be certain that he is staring at his hand, because he cannot eliminate the possibility that he is only dreaming that he is staring at his hand. And if the sense experience of looking at your own hand cannot be considered to be certain, none can.

Either I'm asleep or I'm a philosopher, . . . or I'm dreaming that I'm a philosopher, . . . or that I'm a philosopher dreaming that I'm a philosopher, . . . or . . .

As an important aside, let me ask you to take special note of the way Descartes characterizes the state of dreaming in the previous quotation: "In my dreams [I represent] to myself the same things or sometimes even less probable things, than do those who are insane in their waking moments." In other words, dreams are *madder* than madness. And when you attach that idea to another of Descartes's ideas (surely an erroneous one)—that we dream throughout the whole time that we sleep—then it follows that every human being spends almost one-third of his or her life insane. Each night we fall into a state of temporary insanity; with luck, we

come to our senses in the morning. This odd view will surely matter in considering Descartes's conception of selfhood.

But what if someone dreams of a square? Isn't one's definition of a square correct even in a dream? Descartes writes: "For whether I am awake or asleep, . . . the square can never have more than four sides."[6] Does mathematics perhaps escape sense delusions and the dream problem, and prove to be the foundation of knowledge? (Surely René Descartes, a mathematician himself, would find this conclusion convenient.) But radical doubt requires that math, too, be challenged. Is there any possible doubt concerning the simplest of mathematical judgments, such as 3 + 2 = 5? Well, what if "reality" (including mathematical reality) was created not by the perfectly good God preached by Descartes's Catholicism, but by an all-powerful evil demon who had only one goal—the total deception of René Descartes? Suppose that such a malevolent genius could cause even the simplest of Descartes's judgments (such as 3 + 2 = 5) to be erroneous. Does Descartes know that such a demonic genie does not exist? No! Then radical doubt requires Descartes to assume that this demon may indeed exist. He writes:

> I shall then suppose [that] . . . some evil genius not less powerful than deceitful, has employed his whole energies in deceiving me; I shall consider that the heavens, the earth, colours, figures, sound, and all other external things are nought but the illusions and dreams of which this genius has availed himself in order to lay traps for my credulity; I shall consider myself as having no hands, no eyes, no flesh, no blood, nor any senses, yet falsely believing myself to possess all these things. . . .[7]

One more important aside: Note that Descartes's "evil genius hypothesis" is surely the most paranoid thought ever conceived by any human being, sane or insane—the thought that the whole of "reality" is nothing but a massive plot designed to deceive him, René

Descartes. Once again, Descartes's pursuit of philosophical truth has brought him to the frontier of insanity.

The Necessary Existence of the Self

Well then, is there any thought that would be certain to Descartes even if his senses are deceiving him, even if he is dreaming, even if an all-powerful evil demon is exercising its full might to deceive him? Is there any truth that is correct and certain even to a madman? Yes, there is one, and only one, such truth: "I THINK, THEREFORE I AM."[8] Even if his senses deceive him, even if he is dreaming, even if he is mad, even if an evil genie is set on deceiving him, this proposition is true for as long as he asserts it or holds it in consciousness. It and it alone cannot be doubted under any circumstances.

Perhaps we can see why Descartes thinks this is so if we compare these two sentences:

(A) "I doubt that I have a body."
(B) "I doubt that I have a mind."

Descartes's Trump Card

Doubt (A) is a very *odd* doubt, but it is only odd (and is one that Descartes indeed entertains in the "evil genius hypothesis"). But doubt (B) is an *impossible* doubt. To doubt that you have a mind is to prove you have a mind, because doubting is a form of mental

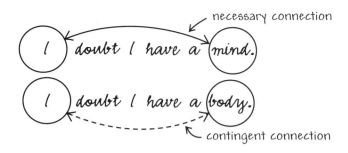

activity. From this exercise, Descartes deduces that there is a necessary connection between the self and the mind, but only a contingent (that is, nonessential) relation between the self and the body.

The Self as Mind

The self that I am, therefore, is my mind, my consciousness. If there is no necessary connection between myself and my body, perhaps my selfhood could survive the destruction of my body. (This view is, of course, compatible with Descartes's Catholicism, for he often uses the words *mind* and *soul* interchangeably. He is unable to prove the immortality of the soul, as he had hoped to do when he set out. But at least he has proved to his own satisfaction that the soul is the self, and as such, is only contingently related to the body.) Notice that Descartes is committed to the view that there is a "stream of consciousness" that lasts throughout one's life,

because if the self *is* consciousness, and that consciousness were interrupted, then selfhood would be interrupted. That is why Descartes holds that we must dream all night. Otherwise, the person who goes to sleep at night will not be the person who wakes up the next morning.

Once Descartes has the certainty of selfhood as the foundation of knowledge, he builds upon it. First, he expands the central idea of his foundation, "I think" ("*Cogito*" in the Latin in which Descartes is writing). What is it to think? Descartes answers this question by cataloguing a list of verbs naming mental acts—for example, "to affirm, to deny, to intend, to plan, to know, to hope, to will." (Note that doubting is a mental act, so if Descartes tries to apply radical doubt to thinking itself—that is, if he *doubts* that he is thinking—then he has in fact *proved* that he is thinking by virtue of doubting it. A very clever move in Descartes's philosophical game!)

A Clever Move

Another mental verb Descartes lists is "to sense," by which he means the act of registering **sense data**: colors, sounds, odors, and so forth. These sensations are objects of *conscious-*ness—I am mentally aware of the colors red, orange, and yellow as I look into the fire in the fireplace. The warmth that I experience from the fire also is a conscious sensation. Therefore, sensing for Descartes is a mental act, not merely a physical one. (Remember, Descartes has not yet proved that he has a body, but he knows that he is seeing colors and feeling warmth. That warmth may be coming from the fireplace, but before he can know that, he'll have to prove that fireplaces exist.)

Finally, in his attempt to catalogue the contents of his mind, Descartes claims to discover a number of **innate**

ideas (as did Plato before him). In particular, he focuses on the idea of *identity* (the foundation of mathematics, as in A = A, or 2 + 1 = 3), the idea of *thingness* (what Descartes calls "substance"), and the idea of *God*.

The Necessary Existence of God

Fortunately, for our purposes, we can skip Descartes's complicated argument showing that these ideas are innate and not learned. Suffice it to say that he tries to show that they are a priori (that is, present *before* sense experience). But even if you accept Descartes's conclusion that we do have innate ideas, that does not prove that these ideas are true. (The evil demon may have placed them in your mind at birth merely to fool you again.) So Descartes sets out to prove the truth of his innate ideas, beginning with the idea of God, defined as a "supremely perfect being."

Again, luckily for our purposes, we do not need to

The Evil Genius Introduces Innate Ideas into the Mind of the Fetus of René Descartes

inspect carefully Descartes's arguments proving God's existence. Let us simply say that the strongest of his arguments virtually duplicates Anselm's ontological proof, which we studied in Chapter 4. Like Anselm, Descartes tries to demonstrate that the very idea of a supremely perfect being logically entails his existence, because a supremely perfect being that lacks "existence" is not supremely perfect. In other words, Descartes wants to show that the very denial of God's existence leads to a self-contradiction, so that denial is logically impossible.

You don't exist!

Yeah, but in every other way, I'm perfect.

Here, as in Chapter 4, we will ignore what is held by various philosophers to be the weaknesses of the ontological argument in order to see where that argument takes Descartes. That is, we will grant Descartes's claim to have proved that, besides his own existence, he has established the existence of a supremely perfect being. There are now two certain things in Descartes's universe: he himself and God. This move, if legitimate, has significant consequences for Descartes's general argument, because the existence of an all-powerful, benevolent being is incompatible with the existence of an evil demon. Descartes has effectively eliminated from his universe the threat of any inherently malevolent power. That is, Descartes has recovered the use of mathematics as a valid analytical tool, for the only purchase radical doubt had on math was the possibility of such a demon.

So then, Descartes's universe is no longer **solipsistic,** strictly speaking. (A "solipsist" is someone who believes that he or she is the only

BEGONE

person in existence, or, more precisely, that he or she cannot know anything other than the existence of his or her own mental states.) Three things are certain now: Descartes himself, God, and the truth of mathematics. Can Descartes build a bridge between his own consciousness and the existence of other things in the universe? He knows that God is no deceiver. He also knows that he has a God-given faculty of understanding that will not fail him if he uses it correctly—if he accepts as certain only those ideas that are indubitable or that can be logically deduced from indubitable ideas. From the fact that

Descartes Drifting Alone in the Universe

he has an innate idea of "body" (a version of his idea of "substance") and a compelling idea of the existence of external bodies derived from his sometimes not-so-happy experiences, an idea that he cannot refute no matter how hard he tries, he concludes that such bodies do indeed exist. (If they don't, and if God has given him no way of proving that they don't, then God is a deceiver, which is impossible.)

So now Descartes knows for sure that there is a physical world that surrounds him. But radical doubt forces him to admit that the bodies in the newly recovered physical world "are perhaps not exactly what we perceive by the senses"[9]—senses that still have not been rehabilitated into Descartes's epistemology. Sense data are certain ("I sense red, here now"), but there is no

The Compelling Idea of the Existence of Material Substance

guarantee that they correctly report real facts in the external world ("The object on the table is red"). Indeed, in the final analysis, Descartes is willing to concede to the senses only those portions of their data that he can grasp "clearly and distinctly"—that is, whatever in them lends itself to measurement and mathematical analysis.

Therefore, physical bodies in the world turn out to exhibit the following characteristics: extension (that is, three-dimensionality),

Descartes Now Knows with Certainty That a Physical World Surrounds Him

size, shape, location, divisibility, and movement, but nothing else. They are, in a phrase, masses in motion or at rest. They are quantitative (they can be measured) but not qualitative (they have none of the perceived qualities we mistakenly attribute to them). There are no colors in the physical world. There are *light waves*, but these are not colored—they are "achromatic." "Color" is the result of the impact of these light waves on the senses, the mind's receptors. Similarly, in the physical world, there are no tastes, no odors, no sounds—though, again, there are sound waves. Sound waves and light waves are physical and can be mathematically analyzed. They are part of the public world, yet only scientists (like Galileo and Descartes) have true knowledge of them. But *perceived sounds*

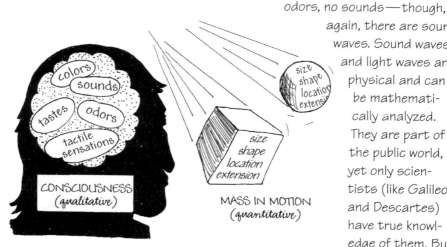

The Subjective World   **The Objective World**

and colors cannot be mathematically analyzed. They exist in private worlds—individual minds—and science has no access to them.

Radical Dualism

René Descartes, as a "thinking thing"—a mind—was particularly closely attached to one of these bodies in the physical world—his own body. But how? In what way? The problem is, he has already identified his true self with his mind; his relation to his body is only contingent. He addresses the issue with an analogy:[10]

I am not only lodged in my body as a pilot in a vessel, but...I am very closely united to it. And so to speak so intermingled with it that I seem to compose with it one whole. For if that were not the case, when my body is hurt, I, who am merely a thinking thing, should not feel pain, for I should perceive this wound by the understanding only, just as the sailor perceives by sight when something is damaged in his vessel.

Descartes is surely right here, isn't he? If your relationship to your body were the same as the relationship between a ship's captain and the ship, you would only know you'd broken a bone when you heard a snap or know that your flesh was on fire when you smelled the smoke. (This may indeed be your relation to *other* bodies in the world, but not to your own body.) Well then, again, exactly how is the mind connected to the body?

What was that? Did you just hear something?

SNAP!

Descartes's final answer is that the mind meets the body at the pineal gland. He says, "[T]he part of the body in which the soul exercises its functions immediately is in nowise the heart, nor the whole of the brain, but merely in the most inward of all its parts, to wit, a certain very small gland which is situated in the middle of its substance. . . ."[11]

As you can imagine, *nobody* has been satisfied with this answer, because it is self-contradictory. If the mind *meets* the body at the pineal gland, then the mind is *located there*. But if it is located anywhere, then it is not mind; rather, it is body and has all the characteristics of body—extension, size, shape, location, and so on. No, the truth seems to be that Descartes has been so scrupulous in depicting the difference between mind and body that he has made it logically impossible for them ever to meet. Most students of Descartes think that he can never resolve the problem of his **dualism** within the confines of his own system. (Conveniently, Descartes died of complications from the common cold before he was pushed hard on the issue.)

TODAY'S LECTURE:
Everything you always wanted to know about the pineal gland

Still, let us forge ahead to see what conclusions Descartes draws from his radical dualism. The mind, then, meets the body at the pineal gland and controls it there. The body itself is only a mindless mechanical object, "a sort of machine so built up and composed of nerves, muscles, veins, blood and skin, that though there were no mind in it at all, it would not cease to have those same motions as at present, exception being made of those movements which are due to the mind."[12]

Spirit Meets Body in a Brain Cavity

Recall that one of the mental acts of the mind is "willing," and it is this mode of mental effort that activates the body in other than purely mechanical ways. (I *want* my thumb to move, and—behold!—it *does* move.) Bodies (including Descartes's body) obey the laws of physics, but minds,

being nonspatial, spiritual things, are not bound by those same laws. Therefore, the human will is free, and though the will cannot overturn the deterministic laws of physics, it can intervene in existing causal chains, creating new causal chains. (The key will fall if I drop it, unless I choose to reach out and catch it.) Indeed, not only is the will not susceptible to natural laws, and not analyzable by science, but no part of the mind (equals the self) is approachable by science, for the method of science is measurement, yet only that which has extension, location, size, shape, and motion is measurable. Bodies can be analyzed by mathematical physics. (Galileo was right about that, and Descartes consigns bodies to the physicists, with an implied reproach to the Church for having tried in scientific ignorance to impose its authority on science.) But minds cannot be the object of scientific investigation. Physics is possible, but psychology is not. Minds are unmeasurable, and only the individual has access to his or her mind and is the sole authority over its contents. You alone know what you are thinking or feeling. I can observe behavioral evidence of your thoughts or emotions, but I can never experience them. Because each individual is the sovereign authority over his or her own free mind, the individual who has followed Descartes's arguments and knows the role of God in all knowledge may well choose to turn to ecclesiastical authorities for moral and spiritual guidance. Descartes has delivered bodies to scientists and souls to individuals, and by extension to the Church.

Summary

Let us take stock of the picture of human nature being painted by René Descartes. The memory of the medieval world, a world whose loss was still being lamented in Descartes's time, was the memory of a unified social and natural world. Through a tradition of symbolic interpretation, most medieval citizens had found their place in that world, and there was a seamless transition from the personal space that each individual subjectively occupied to the various realms of the hierarchy of reality. But in the political, social, and religious upheavals following the Middle Ages, the sense of certainty was lost, and the center of the universe on whose main stage the human drama had been acted out seemed to slide away into an infinitely expanding space.

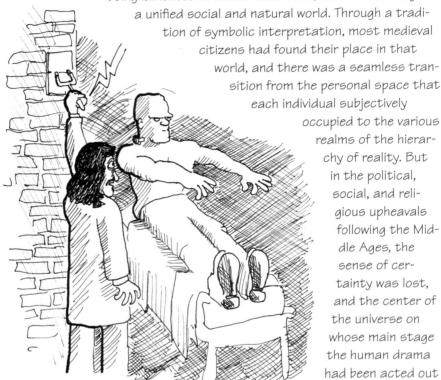

René Descartes Creates the Modern Self

Descartes's philosophy reestablishes certainty, recenters the universe, and makes each individual the ground zero of that centering. In a sense, Descartes single-handedly created the modern autonomous self. This is a staggering accomplishment. But the self he created is one that is alienated from nature, because Descartes's "nature" contains only extended bodies (*res extensa*) with no qualities, only math-friendly quantities. This includes that part of nature that is one's own body, which, for a purely spiritual being like Descartes (*res cogitans*, or "thinking thing") must be at best a nuisance and at worst an embarrassment. (Descartes would surely have been upset to hear that, despite the many unanswered questions about the function of the pineal gland, there is evidence that it controls the size of the sexual organs.) At least at the end of his meditation,

When I prioritized the pineal gland, I certainly didn't know it would lead to this.

Descartes is *certain* of the existence of the physical world and of its nature. Yet the reach of that certainty beyond the *cogito* (Latin for "I think") is only as strong as Descartes's precarious arguments for God's existence, arguments that most critics have deemed insufficiently strong to bear the tremendous weight that he places upon them.

The self to which Descartes gives birth in his moment of certainty is a peculiarly *male* self. (The Cartesian scholar Susan Bordo says, "The soul that Descartes drained from the world was a *female* soul."[13]) As the poet Tom Leonard has Descartes say:

(male) I think therefore I am
I (male) think therefore I am
I think (male) therefore I am
I think therefore (male) I am
I think therefore I (male) am
I think therefore I am (male)

What the World Is Like

What the World Would Be Like If
You Were Surrounded by Robots

    It is a self that is alienated from all other selves. Descartes never satisfactorily proves that any self beyond his own exists. Early in the *Meditations*, he had raised the possibility that what seemed to be other human beings were in fact only sophisticated robots. All observable data are consistent with the hypothesis that these other beings are automatons. (Ask yourself this question: How do I know for certain that the people sitting nearest me are not highly sophisticated [meaty] robots?) An act of judgment tells Descartes that they are indeed humans and not automated dolls. He peers from his chamber window to people passing in the street below and asks: "What do I see from the window but hats and coats which may be covering automatic machines? Yet I judge these to be men. . . . [S]olely by the faculty of judgment which rests in my mind, I comprehend that which I believed I saw with my eyes."[14] Either this act of judgment is, for Descartes, based on another God-given innate idea (in which case the belief in the existence of other humans is again only as good as the proofs for God's existence), or Descartes means that we judge from the behavior of others, which we find similar to our own behavior, that they have minds like our own. (In the latter case, there is no certainty of other minds, but only a shaky inferential probability—shaky because our inference is based on explaining thousands of cases by generalizing one case—our own.) Finally, the self that Descartes creates is always at risk of madness. It spends a third of its embodied life in a state of temporary lunacy (dreams); it can find certainty only by adopting a systematic paranoia (radical doubt); its logic takes it to the most extravagant flirtations with insanity (the evil demon hypothesis); and its central truth ("I think, therefore I am") is perfectly compatible with madness, for even the inmates of a mental asylum can know that truth.

So, in conclusion, René Descartes has given birth to the modern, autonomous self. However, this self is alienated from its own body and from nature, and it believes itself to be based on the certainty of divine approval and the

possibility of eternal happiness, but it is, in fact, precariously close to eternal uncertainty, solitude, and madness.

Topics for Consideration

1. Defend one of these views:

   a. The reason Descartes inserts God into his philosophy is to get past religious censorship. His real goal is to present his scientific picture of the world to the general public without interference from the Church. In fact, one must omit God from Descartes's philosophy to get his true message.

   b. The inclusion of God in Descartes's philosophy is very sincere on his part. Too much of the burden of his theory is placed on God's existence for God to be merely a deception to escape censorship.

2. "Radical doubt" prevents the information provided by the five senses from being a candidate for the foundation of knowledge. How? Give an example from each of the five senses to show that all the senses are capable of delivering deceptive information.

3. Descartes argues that it is impossible to know for certain at any given moment that one is not dreaming at that moment. Write an essay entitled "The Dream Problem" in which you defend or attack his claim.

4. Write an essay entitled "Methodological Doubt and Madness" in which you discuss the way Descartes's philosophy constantly threatens to slide into insanity.

5. Defend or attack Descartes's claim concerning the certainty of the assertion "I think, therefore I am."

6. Write a critique of Descartes's dualism.

7. At the beginning of his philosophy, Descartes "doubts away" the physical world (the world that we seem to perceive daily with its colors, odors, sounds, tastes, and so on). At the end of his philosophy, he "gets back" the physical world (a world of extended bodies with size, shape, dimensionality, and so on). Is the world that he recovers in the end the same world that he lost in the beginning? If they differ, which world do you think is the "real" physical world?

8. Give a detailed depiction of the "self" that Descartes's philosophy claims to reveal.

Suggestions for Further Reading

I. Descartes's Main Philosophical Works

The Essential Descartes. Ed. Margaret D. Wilson, trans. Elizabeth S. Haldane and G. R. T. Ross. New York: New American Library/Mentor, 1969. (Contains *Discourse on Method, Meditations on First Philosophy,* and *The Passions of the Soul.*)

A Guided Tour of René Descartes's Meditations on First Philosophy, 2nd ed. Ed. Christopher Biffle, trans. Ronald Rubin. Mountain View, Calif: Mayfield, 1996.

II. Secondary Sources on Descartes

Bordo, Susan R. *The Flight to Objectivity: On Cartesianism and Culture.* Albany: State University of New York Press, 1987.

Frankfurt, Harry G. *Demons, Dreamers, and Madmen: The Defense of Reason in Descartes's Meditations.* New York: Bobbs-Merrill, 1970.

Gaukroger, Stephen. *Descartes: An Intellectual Biography.* Oxford: Clarendon Press, 1995.

Williams, Bernard. *Descartes: The Project of Pure Inquiry.* New York: Penguin Books, 1978.

Notes

1. In using these dates, I am following the lead of José Antonio Maravall (*The Culture of the Baroque: Analysis of a Historical Structure,* trans. Terry Cochran [Minneapolis: University of Minnesota Press, 1986]). It should be mentioned that the application of the term *Baroque* to cover these dates is complicated by the later appearance of Baroque music, recognizable until about 1760.

2. René Descartes, *Meditations on First Philosophy*, in *The Essential Descartes*, ed. Margaret D. Wilson, trans. Elizabeth S. Haldane and G. R. T. Ross (New York: New American Library, 1969), p. 165.

3. René Descartes, *Discourse on Method*, in *The Essential Descartes*, p. 127.

4. Descartes, *Meditations*, p. 166.

5. Descartes, *Meditations*, pp. 166–167.

6. Descartes, *Meditations*, p. 168.

7. Descartes, *Meditations*, pp. 169–170.

8. Descartes, *Discourse*, p. 128.

9. Descartes, *Meditations*, p. 215.

10. Descartes, *Meditations*, p. 216.

11. René Descartes, *The Passions of the Soul*, in *The Essential Descartes*, p. 362.

12. Descartes, *Meditations*, pp. 218–219.

13. Susan R. Bordo, *The Flight to Objectivity: On Cartesianism and Culture* (Albany: State University of New York Press, 1987), p. 101.

14. Descartes, *Meditations*, p. 177.

6

The Religious Existential Conception of Human Nature
Kierkegaard

Historical Backdrop

Denmark is a small nation. In the early nineteenth century, it had a population of only two million souls. Despite its bustling capital, Copenhagen, with its banking centers and stock market benefiting from international trade in Denmark's agricultural, fishing, and wool industries, Denmark had a provincial air about it. (*Copenhagen comes from a Danish word meaning "shopping haven."*) Even its well-educated, prosperous, politically dominant bourgeois class provided only a small readership for books published in Danish. Denmark's larger and louder neighbor to the south, Germany (actually, a loose confederation of German states at that time), managed to dominate Denmark culturally— dictating, for example, much of the nature of its artistic production and the form and content of studies pursued at the University of Copenhagen. The most powerful intellectual force from the south was the philosophy of the Swabian thinker Georg Wilhelm Friedrich Hegel (1770–1831), whose massive, dense,

Kierkegaard at the Shopping Mall

and often obscure volumes provided food for thought—indeed, whole banquets—for a generation of intellectuals following in his wake. The star of this chapter, Søren Kierkegaard, was deeply influenced by Hegel's thought and, at the same time, quite annoyed by it.

Hegelianism

It is impossible to describe Hegel's philosophy without offending some of his interpreters, because there is still much contention over what he was actually saying. Therefore, we will limit ourselves to describing it from what appears to be Kierkegaard's perspective. From that point of view, these were the salient features of Hegel's metaphysics (that is, his overall worldview):

1. Its **systematization:** a completely structured depiction of the totality of reality, claiming to give an account of virtually everything in existence and to show how each feature of reality and history was systematically linked to every other feature.
2. Its **rationalism:** an equation of Reason with reality, asserting that everything real is rational (and vice versa) and that everything irrational is unreal (and vice versa).
3. Its **idealism:** an equation of consciousness with reality (hence, an equation of consciousness with Reason).
4. Its **dialecticism:** a claim that all thought processes are structurally linked with a teleological (that is, goal-oriented) historical movement that operates "dialectically." Dialectical, as used by Hegel, refers to the fact that history involves perpetual conflict

and resolution of opposites that will eventually lead the world (and particularly Europe, and especially the German principality of Prussia) to a state of total knowledge and total being that Hegel called "Absolute Spirit."

In Hegel's philosophical system, all differences were eventually abolished, all individuality overcome, and all apparent accidents and choices seen as actually being rational and necessary moments in the great parade of world history marching toward Absolute Spirit.

The March Toward Absolute Spirit

Religiosity

Another remarkable aspect of Danish social life in the early nineteenth century was the domination of "Churchism" over all features of everyday life. The official state religion of Denmark was Lutheranism. Every Danish citizen was automatically born into the Danish church unless a petition to the contrary was filed—a rare event! Lutheranism was based on the doctrines set forth by the German Protestant reformer Martin Luther in the early sixteenth century. Luther, who spent his youth as a Dominican monk, eventually turned against the Catholic Church, accusing it of theological error and worldly corruption and ultimately denouncing the pope as the Antichrist and all Catholics who would not convert to his views as "agents of Satan."[1] In Kierkegaard's time, much of the "fire and brimstone" of Luther's message still existed in the rural fundamentalist version of Lutheranism known as Pietism. But it had cooled off considerably in the sophisticated urban circles of priests, pastors, and deacons surrounding the bishop of Zealand, Denmark's powerful religious leader. According to Kierkegaard, under the auspices of the official Church of Denmark, Christianity had been watered down to the point of being nothing but a justification for bourgeois morality, social privilege, and capitalist entrepreneurship—it had a stranglehold on the whole of Danish society.

Kierkegaard's life in both its intellectual and mundane aspects should be thought of in terms of this social, economic, religious, and philosophical context: (1) the conservative, complacent provincial middle-class life of Copenhagen, (2) the "churchified" character of all social and economic activity, and (3) German cultural hegemony—particularly the dominance of the philosophy of Hegel.

Biography

Søren Kierkegaard's Pietist father, Michael Kierkegaard, who even after his death was an overwhelming influence in his son, spent his childhood tending sheep in western Denmark under conditions of extreme poverty. He came to Copenhagen as a youth and managed to parlay a few balls of wool into a sizable fortune. By the time Søren was born in 1813, the last of seven children from his father's second marriage, the Kierkegaard family was firmly established and well respected in Copenhagen's small social, commercial, and intellectual world. Early on, Kierkegaard's father recognized his son's genius and personally guided his education. Unfortunately, the old man was given to moods of deep depression, derived from some perceived sin in his earlier days (perhaps a sexual sin, perhaps the sin of cursing God, perhaps both), and his melancholy oppressed his whole family, especially his youngest son.

At school, Kierkegaard was taught Greek, Latin, philosophy, and all the worldly arts and sciences. At home, however, he was brought up in a strict religious environment dominated by a stark and severe version of Christianity stressing guilt and particularly concerned with the idea of "sin against God." Kierkegaard was twenty-five years old and a student of theology at the University of Copenhagen when his father died in 1838, liberating him from the morbid belief that his father would outlive all his children (five had already died) and also liberating him "for the world"—at least, temporarily. Kierkegaard obtained his theology degree, became engaged to a young woman named Regine Olsen, the object of his love for the previous three years, and seemed headed for a normal life as a husband, father, and perhaps country pastor. But in 1841,

Søren Kierkegaard (1813–1855

Kierkegaard broke off his engagement to Regine in an abrupt and mysterious manner, leaving her heart-broken and ashamed. Kierkegaard wrote in his diary that God had "vetoed" the marriage. Kierkegaard left Copenhagen for Berlin, where he studied Hegelian philosophy at the university and, in a period of five months, wrote two books that contained a hidden communication to Regine.

But Regine did not "get" the cryptic message and married her former boyfriend, leaving Kierkegaard lovesick for the rest of his life. He settled into a rather pampered if solitary routine, writing a steady stream of philosophical and religious books while living off his inheritance from his father. Several of the books he wrote were motivated by his feelings for his dead father and for the lost Regine. But this is not surprising in an "existentialist" author, according to whom all philosophy is necessarily subjective. (Don't worry! We'll say more about existentialism in a moment.)

In 1846, Kierkegaard managed to insult the editor of the local muckraking newspaper, *The Corsair*. A former admirer of Kierkegaard, the editor turned on him, mocking and caricaturing him almost daily in his newspaper, making Kierkegaard's figure so notorious that schoolboys and ruffians taunted him in the streets of his own neighborhood. By this point in his life, because of a childhood injury or some form of calcium deficiency, Kierkegaard's spine had become deformed, causing him to

If you are having trouble in your romantic life, study Hegelian metaphysics. It gets your mind off things.

walk with a stoop and to require a cane. *The Corsair* even made fun of this handicap in its cartoon illustrations. An embittered Kierkegaard continued writing, and in 1854, he turned his bitterness into a vitriolic attack on "official Christianity" as it was being preached in the churches of Denmark, and particularly in the main house of worship in Copenhagen by the bishop of Zealand—an attack that further alienated him from most of Copenhagen's citizenry.

In October 1855, Kierkegaard collapsed in the street, paralyzed. He told the doctors at the hospital where he was transported that there was nothing that they could do for him, as his disease was of the spirit and not of the body; six weeks later, he died. At his funeral, radical theology students incited a small riot, angered that the same Church of Denmark that Kierkegaard had attacked in his final year was performing the funerary rites. Although Kierkegaard had lived only forty-two years, he left almost as many volumes of books and journals for scholars to puzzle over.

Kierkegaard's Theory

The philosophy of Søren Kierkegaard is peculiarly Christian. And "peculiar" is the right word here, for his is in many ways an idiosyncratic view exhibiting particularities of Kierkegaard's own life and his struggle with his father's religion. He is often thought of as the founder of existentialism (a term actually coined by the twentieth-century French philosopher Jean-Paul Sartre, as we will see in Chapter 10).

I invented the term!

Yeah, but I did all the hard work.

Existentialism

As the attribution of the label "existentialist" to Kierkegaard perhaps indicates, Kierkegaard was not interested in universal truths, generalizations, and abstractions about the "essence" of humankind. He was interested in concrete existence—something that seemed to him to have been absorbed and dispensed with in Hegel's universal abstractions—and he was especially concerned about his own concrete existence. He was concerned with the anguish or dread that seems to be the natural consequence of the freedom that he believed was the condition of every human being. (All of these themes were picked up by the twentieth-century philoso-

Let me clarify this for you. I am principally interested in ME.

phers who came to be known as existentialists—especially Sartre, as we will see at the end of this book.)

For Kierkegaard, philosophy becomes autobiography. Paradoxically, most of his philosophical works were written under pseudonyms, thereby alienating those books from his own life, perhaps so they could be appropriated by his readers. (As an author, Kierkegaard employed a strategy he called "indirect communication," which was inspired by Socrates and Jesus. Here, the reader learns from irony—that is, one learns from overstatement, understatement, misstatement, humor, paradox, and shock. All of this, of course, makes it particularly difficult for commentators to say with certainty exactly what Kierkegaard [or Socrates, or Jesus] meant.)

> I am ignorant.

> The Kingdom of Heaven is like a mustard seed.

> Never take either of them literally.

Doubt, the Uncertainty of All Things, and Faith

Let us begin our investigation of Kierkegaard's theory of the self by inspecting a short and curious passage from a rather unsung book of his called *Johannes Climacus, Or, "De omnibus dubitandum est"* (which means, "everything is to be doubted," and you will recognize it as the motto of Descartes's method of radical doubt). Under the pseudonym Johannes Climacus (John Climax or John the Ladder), Kierkegaard writes:

Cannot consciousness then remain in immediacy? This is a foolish question, for if it could, no consciousness would exist. If this immediacy be identical with that of an animal, then the problem of consciousness is done away. But what would be the result of this? Man would be an animal, or in other words, he would be *dumb*. That which annuls immediacy therefore is speech. If a man could not speak, then he would remain in immediacy. . . . [T]his might be expressed by saying that immediacy is reality and speech is ideality. For when I speak, I introduce opposition. If, for example, I want to express the actual world which I perceive with my senses, the opposition is present. For what I say is quite other than what I want to express. Reality I cannot express in speech, for to indicate it I use Ideality, which is a contradiction, an untruth. . . .

The possibility of doubt then lies in consciousness whose very essence is a kind of contradiction or opposition.[2]

According to Kierkegaard, only in the minds of animals (or human infants) is there direct contact with "reality" as it is at any particular moment. Kierkegaard calls such contact "immediacy." But once a language has been acquired, experience of reality is counteracted by words. Language *mediates* between reality and consciousness as a third term. Linguistic signs denote not individual objects for Kierkegaard but concepts, abstractions, and ideal classes (as they did for Plato). Therefore, reality is counteracted by ideality, and that which *is* (reality) is opposed to that which

Immediate Contact
with Nature

Mediated Contact
with Nature

could be (possibility). To call something a "door" is to designate it as something that, by definition, is possibly open, possibly closed, possibly either a barrier to freedom or a route of escape. Possibility enters consciousness with the advent of language. Hence, in consciousness, there is always opposition and therefore never certainty, but rather doubt. (Both in English and in Danish, the word for "doubt" derives from a root meaning "double.") Recall that Descartes claimed to discover certainty in consciousness, but Kierkegaard denies it, for the elements of ideality and possibility in one's consciousness mean that there is always an incongruity between one's thought process and one's actual thoughts. Consciousness can never capture a unity as Descartes hoped with his "*sum*" (Latin for "I am"). There is no certainty in consciousness, and none in selfhood; both the self and the world are experienced as uncertain. Contrary to Descartes, thinking "I am" or "I think, therefore I am" does not constitute experiencing selfhood, which is always presented as fragmented, uncertain, and incomplete, as continually being constructed and reconstructed.

What holds together the contradiction in consciousness for Kierkegaard? What holds the self together, and what holds together self and
world? What overcomes doubt? The opposite of doubt is not knowledge and
certainty, as in Plato and Descartes; rather, it is belief—a special kind
of faith in the world and in the self, and for Kierkegaard, that most radical
and dangerous belief, faith in God. Descartes claimed to know
that God exists. Kierkegaard does not know. He believes,
realizing full well that he may be wrong. The self and
the world are at risk, for Kierkegaard, and he calls
on a certain kind of heroism to face that risk
without fleeing from it.

Thus, the self must be constructed out of our freedom. How
will that construction be performed?
Kierkegaard sees three basic possibilities open to him, three possible selves,
which he calls "the aesthetic," "the ethical," and "the religious." (There are
numerous variations and gradations
within each of these frameworks,
but we will concentrate on the
broad outlines of each possibility.)

Super-Søren

The Three Spheres of Existence

THE AESTHETIC SELF The aesthetic self is the self that, one way or another, is governed by the quest for pleasure. The word *aesthetic* comes from a Greek word referring to the senses. The "aesthete," then, is a sensualist. He (I say "he" because all of Kierkegaard's examples are males) pursues sensual gratification. Now, a number of lifestyles could be based on this motivation, ranging in sophistication (or lack thereof) from the Homer

Simpson type, to the workaholic businessman whose idea of a thrill is making another difficult sale, to the sophisticated snob who pursues only the most refined of pleasures: the finest wines, the "hautest" cuisine, or the intellectually-laced flirtations with an exquisitely beautiful and refined object of sexual desire. Yet, what they all have in common, from the crudest to the most cultivated, is that their lives are governed by the external contingencies of what Freud would later call "the pleasure principle"—the same motivation that governs the behavior of worms, dickey birds, and human babies.

Kierkegaard is clearly something of an elitist, and he has nothing but scorn for those far down on the aesthetic ladder. Nevertheless, he would admit that if the aesthete on the lowest rung is lucky enough to be stupid, then he may never conceive of his life as existentially problematical, because here, as everywhere in Kierkegaard, the higher the consciousness, the greater the anxiety. Therefore, the aesthete who is aware of his plight comes to realize that the very logic of the pursuit of pleasure is self-defeating. For one thing,

the pleasure is never, or hardly ever, as good as one anticipates it will be, so disappointment is built into it. In this sense, desire is never satiated; it never gets what it wants. But in another sense, it does get what it wants and finds it boring. We don't want to repeat the same pleasure, so we seek ever more exotic titillation, and we are caught up in a spiraling attempt to escape boredom. Furthermore, Kierkegaard links the desire for pleasure with the desire for death (as Freud would do some eighty years later). One of Kierkegaard's pseudonymous authors is a young aesthete who is

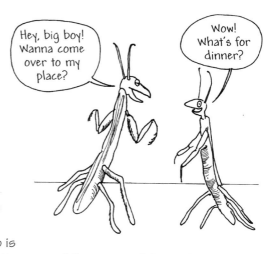

already world-weary and cynical. He writes: "There are well-known insects that die in the moment of fecundation. So it is with all joy; life's supreme and richest moment of pleasure is coupled with death."[3]

The problem with aestheticism—at least, sophisticated aestheticism—is that the desire for pleasure leads to the desire for nothingness. Kierkegaard's pseudonymous aesthete (actually, anonymous aesthete, because he is referred to only as "A" in *Either/Or*) tries to solve the problem of boredom from within the sphere of aestheticism, recommending what he calls the "rotation method." Here, you create your own surprise pleasures. You arrive late at the theater and leave early, seeing only the middle of the show. (Kierkegaard actually did this!) You read only one section of your novel, picking it at random. You provoke righteous people to anger. You pursue love affairs but abandon them just at the moment of success, making certain in the first place not to fall in love with the woman, but only with the *idea* of her. In these ways, pleasure is not externally dictated by others or by nature; rather, it is generated by one's own self.

Provoking Righteous Indignation

But Kierkegaard (under another pseudonym, Judge William) denies that the aesthete has a true self. The aesthetic "self" is disjointed and fragmented, and it is determined by otherness, for the aesthete cannot disguise from himself that he is still reacting to others rather than being the true agency of action. This life, for Kierkegaard, can only lead to despair and, taken to its extreme, to suicide. (And, again, Kierkegaard knew whereof he spoke, having been brought close to suicide himself.)

THE ETHICAL SELF Kierkegaard's exposition of the aesthetic sphere is found in Volume 1 of his book *Either/Or*. The second volume is dedicated to the ethical sphere, so the suggestion seems to be that we are to choose *either* the aesthetic *or* the ethical. However, strictly speaking, the aesthete cannot choose at all, because he does not have enough of a centered self-hood to be the author of any true action. Hence, we are told by Judge William, the "author" of Volume 2:[4]

My either/or does not in the first instance denote the choice between good and evil; it denotes the choice whereby one chooses good and evil or excludes them.... For the aesthetical is not evil but neutrality, and that is the reason why I affirmed that it is the ethical which constitutes the choice. It is, therefore, not so much a question of choosing between willing the good or the evil, as of choosing to will, but by this in turn the good and evil are posited.

How is it possible that an aesthete can make this choice, if there is no true freedom in aestheticism, if the schizoid aesthete has no self? It is because the despair of the aesthete forces him to an extreme position that puts him—even if only briefly—in possession of the ability to make a negative judgment about his old, sick self. He can at that moment choose to choose, so to speak. He can *choose himself.*[5] What is required is that the individual place himself under a law according to which he will judge himself. This law must point inward so that the individual can judge his (impossible) attempt to achieve self-perfection ("Thou shalt become perfected as is thy Father in Heaven"). And it must point outward in that it must relate the individual to other human beings.

The new self crystallizes around this choice, which unifies all features of the personality. If the individual chooses the Christian ethic (as surely Kierkegaard hoped his readers would), then the law to which one submits might be something like, "Let love be served." Perhaps if one chooses a Communist ethic, the law would be, "Let the revolution be served." In either case (or in any of several other possible cases compatible with Kierkegaard's account of the ethical sphere), the law that one chooses transforms one's world, for after "the choice," there are very few neutral situations. Almost every new context requires a new decision and an action, and in each new case, the individual is either "guilty" or "not guilty" under the law that he has chosen for himself. This law is absolute, but its application is not always obvious. (How shall love be served? Do I demonstrate love for my students by grading gently or harshly?)

Kierkegaard's own version of the ethical life—a life that he finally rejected—was the apparently conservative one that found its paradigm in the relationship of marriage. A man and a woman publicly commit themselves to each other forever. They mutually agree that they will find their happiness in the happiness of the other. This will be a "defining relationship."[6] The individual defines himself in his relation to another human being. If Søren had married Regine, this would have been his relation to her, he believed.

At the philosophical level, Kierkegaard's critique of the aesthetic mode of life also constitutes a critique of Hegelian metaphysics, for in

Kierkegaard's interpretation of that philosophy, Hegel has eliminated the possibility of individual freedom by eliminating the "either/or" and replacing it with a "both/and." In Hegel's dialectical philosophy, as Kierkegaard sees it, all apparently decisive moments in the life of individuals or communities are in reality parts of historical organic wholes that are not in the control of the individual or the community. Recall that, for Hegel, there is a universal teleology leading to the absorption of all oppositions into the Absolute Spirit that is history's goal. This historical force cannot be resisted. Even rebellious attempts to oppose it play into its hands and become what Hegel calls "the cunning of Reason." As Kierkegaard's aesthete says, at the end of a little essay titled "Either/Or," in the book of the same title:

The Cunning of Reason

> Hang yourself, you will regret it; do not hang yourself, and you will also regret that; hang yourself or do not hang yourself, you will regret both; whether you hang yourself or do not hang yourself, you will regret both. This, gentlemen, is the sum and substance of all philosophy.[7]

Well, it may not be the sum and substance of *all* philosophy, but it is the sum and substance of Hegelian philosophy, according to Kierkegaard.

In some interpretations of Kierkegaard's work, the ethical realm, with its commitment to self-perfection and to another human soul, constitutes a legitimate form of selfhood—one against which Kierkegaard could have

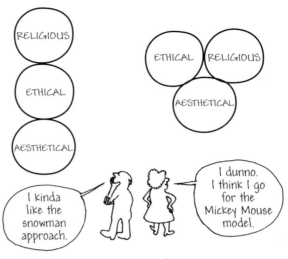

Either / Or

no valid objection, even if he personally rejected the ethical realm and chose the third realm, the religious realm. In other interpretations, the religious sphere transcends the ethical, and true selfhood can only be achieved in the religious realm. In other words, the question is, Which of these diagrams is correct? Here, we will avoid the debate (there is evidence supporting each interpretation) and peer into the religious realm.

Søren's Engagement

THE RELIGIOUS SELF If the ethical sphere requires a "defining relation-ship" in the form of an unqualified commitment to one or more per-sons, the religious realm involves a defining relation to God— again, in the form of an unqualified commitment. (In his diary at the time of his renunciation of Regine Olsen, Kierkegaard wrote, "My engagement to her and the break are really my relation to God; they are, if I may say so, divinely speaking, my engage-ment with God."[8])

We have already seen that, for Kierkegaard, all relationships between consciousness and the object of consciousness require an element of faith in order to be sustained. Therefore, although faith is involved in an ethical relationship, the role of faith in a religious relationship is obviously much more critical—especially for Kierkegaard, who says there can be no talk of God as the object of knowledge, but only as the object of belief. We saw in Chapter 4 that medieval Catholicism provided a type of *knowledge* of God derived not only from the various proofs of his existence but also from a chain of analogies

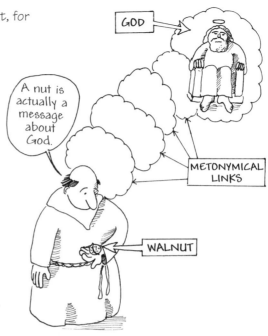

The Medieval Catholic Analogical Ladder to Knowledge of God

that can become a ladder between the human being and God—a series of **metonymical** and metaphorical links that allows us to move from knowledge of the finite world to knowledge of the infinite. But for Kierkegaard's radical Lutheranism, there is an absolute qualitative abyss between the human and God, and no analogical or logical bridge can be built across the chasm. The believer must exist suspended "above 40,000 fathoms." Everything is at extreme risk. To be a Christian is to gamble all: "If He [Christ] is a delusion, my life is lost."[9]

Lutheran Protestantism's Difficult Path to God

Divine Madness

Perhaps the most intriguing of all of Kierkegaard's accounts of the religious self is found in his little masterpiece of 1843, *Fear and Trembling*. Purportedly, this was written by one Johannes de silentio (John the Silent), who is obsessed with the Biblical story of Abraham and Isaac and chagrined at his inability to understand the story.

Here are the amazing events told in the Book of Genesis in the Old Testament of the Bible: Abraham, patriarch of his tribe, makes a covenant with God agreeing to follow God's will in all things. God, for his part, promises Abraham a son who will, in turn, become the father of a great new nation. Years pass, but Abraham's wife, Sarah, does not become pregnant; still, Abraham believes. Finally, when Abraham is ninety-nine and Sarah is ninety, she conceives and gives birth to a son, whom they call Isaac. The child is deeply loved by Abraham and Sarah, and his great destiny seems assured until the horrible night recounted in Genesis 22:1–2. Abraham is

awakened by the voice of God and told to take Isaac to a mountain in the desert of Moriah, which God will indicate to him, and to sacrifice his son there on an altar as a gift to God. Abraham, telling no one, takes young Isaac to the appointed spot, places him on the stone altar, and lifts his knife to take his life, but he is stopped in the nick of time by an angel who informs him that he has passed the divine test. Abraham is allowed to sacrifice a ram in place of Isaac. Father and son return to their village, where Abraham lives out his days in honor and esteem, and Isaac indeed becomes father to a great new nation.

Now, the problem for Johannes de silentio is that he can make no sense of this story. To him, Abraham's acts seem to be those of a lunatic. (A man hears a voice in the night, and acting on its orders, he takes his long-awaited, beloved son into the desert to kill him.) Moreover, Johannes cannot understand how, based on his horrifying willingness to kill his son, Abraham could become a great man and even be referred to as "the father of us all." At one point, Johannes writes in exasperation, "Abraham enjoys honor and glory as the father of faith, whereas he ought to be prosecuted and convicted of murder."[10]

Johannes's scrutiny of Abraham's act detects in it a "double movement"—a "movement of infinite resignation" and a "movement of faith." In the movement of infinite resignation, Abraham gives up everything. In losing his son, he loses the world and even his old self. But in losing his old self, a new, hardened, autonomous self is forged: "What I gain is myself . . ." (p. 59) ". . . and only then can there be any question of grasping existence by virtue of faith" (p. 57). Indeed, in the second movement, Abraham's unintelligible faith recovers everything that was lost. All that is taken away is restored, but to a new self.

Johannes de silentio comes to admire Abraham, but he never comprehends him. He can understand the act of resignation—giving up everything in order to gain his self—but he cannot understand Abraham's faith, which for Johannes is a state of "divine madness." Abraham acts "by virtue of the absurd" (p. 69). Kierkegaard has Johannes say: "Abraham was greater than all, great by reason of his power whose strength is impotence, great by reason of his wisdom whose secret is foolishness,
great by reason of his hope whose form is madness" (p. 31). But this madness has allowed Abraham to take a "blessed leap into eternity" (p. 53). Kierkegaard is probably best known for advocating this "leap of faith."

What we get here is a rather harsh account of the religious life—very different from what we saw in Descartes's rationalized Catholicism or Buddhism's unification with the cosmos. Kierkegaard's effect is perhaps reminiscent of the terror inspired by the scenes of damna-

The Leap of Faith

tion in the medieval tympana. There is no community of the religious in Kierkegaard's vision. Each person is alone before God and must choose him- or herself in the "absolute isolation" (p. 89) of the desert of Moriah. Despite being perpetually a potential madman, Kierkegaard's "knight of faith," as he calls his religious hero, is indistinguishable from others in society. "He" may be the postman, the

Hell (detail), Tympanum, Saint Foy, Conques, France

adolescent girl next door, or the tax collector. The difference between him and you, however, is that he is prepared to kill his son if it is required of him: "Faith is a paradox which is capable of transforming a murder into a holy act well-pleasing to God" (p. 64).

But a word of caution! We do not really know what Kierkegaard "meant" by this story. He admitted that his books were often "correctives"—by which I suppose he meant exaggerations to counter exaggerations heading in the opposite direction. Kierkegaard could write that churches are places of horror because they dwell on the fact that the human race murdered God. But he could also write a book called Works of Love and talk about Christ's open arms beckoning those who are weak, weary, and burdened, saying that Christians needed to become as little children. He wrote most of his philosophical works under pseudonyms but then backed away from those works, claiming that not a single word written by the pseudonymous authors represented his own ideas. In his journal, he delighted in thinking that he would go to his grave knowing that no one had understood anything he had written. He also claimed to agonize over the thought that, after his death, professors would massacre his ideas trying

HEE HEE

SK

to interpret them. But he hoped as well that someday his lover would come—that someday an audience, or at least a single individual, would understand him. Or did he mean that someday Regine would be restored to him, as Isaac was restored to Abraham?

Summary

It has become common to hear sociologists and philosophers talk about the self as "constructed," but almost always this construction will have been carried out in deterministic fashion by external forces—economic, political, social, linguistic, or biological. What Kierkegaard provides is a picture of a self that is constructed by the self. For him, the emergence of selfhood is not automatic. It is not granted simply by virtue of having had humans as parents. Rather, achieving selfhood is the culmination of a hard-won and perpetually ongoing battle

I sure wish they'd included instructions.

Self-Construction of the Self

in which there is no support from others and no court of appeal. Kierkegaard sees himself as a Socrates who cannot bestow selfhood but who can help others bestow it on themselves by pushing them to the brink of meaning, of possibility, and of sanity itself—alienating them from all that is familiar and comforting, placing them in a space of "absolute isolation" from which they can make a fundamental decision to "choose themselves." Of the two possibilities he suggests—the ethical self and the religious self—the second is clearly the most radical and disturbing, though its structure is similar to the first, the ethical self. A negative action—"infinite resignation"—disposes of all external objects in whose terms one had previously defined oneself. This move is like

Kierkegaard Pushes His Readers to the Brink

a passionate version of Descartes's radical doubt. Then, "suspended over 40,000 fathoms," one makes a decision "by virtue of the absurd," according to which one determines one's own reality based on values one has created by choosing them.

Some of Kierkegaard's critics argue that, in committing himself totally to God, the knight of faith loses his selfhood rather than gains it, as he subjugates himself to God's will and becomes merely an instrument of it. Kierkegaard denies this accusation. On that terrible night when Abraham heard the voice of God ordering him to sacrifice his son, Abraham had to determine the meaning of the commandment for himself.

Søren Kierkegaard: God's Lackey?

Kierkegaard catalogues all the possibilities: Abraham can say to himself, "This must be the voice of the devil, and I will not obey it"; or he can say, "This voice comes from an evil deep inside myself, and I will not obey it"; or he can say, "I have misunderstood the commandment, for the God of my fathers would not ask of me this thing"; or he can say, "This is indeed the voice of God, but such a God is a monster, and I will not obey." Or, he can do as, in fact, he did. He can say, "I will do this thing." In any case, it is Abraham, not God, who is the source of his action, and it is he who is responsible for it. In fact, in Kierkegaard's account, Abraham's freedom authorizes God's command. Abraham has in a sense created God in his world by choosing him. Abraham obeys God absolutely because he has chosen to bestow authority on God, authority deriving from his own freedom. According to Kierkegaard and his erstwhile disciple Jean-Paul Sartre, every authority we obey derives its authority from our decision to obey it. Abraham's freedom is its own authority, and so is ours. It derives from itself, and selfhood is its manifestation. Kierkegaard asks, "What is this self of mine? . . . it is freedom."[11] No pair of philosophers in this book—and perhaps in the history of philosophy—has placed as much of the burden of selfhood on freedom as have Kierkegaard and Sartre, for better or for worse.

Topics for Consideration

1. Contrast the Kierkegaardian categories of "the leap," "the absurd," "the choice" (either/or) and "the individual" with the key notions in the metaphysics of Hegel.

2. Try to reconstruct imaginatively Kierkegaard's account of the story of Abraham and Isaac as they apply to Kierkegaard's own life and his relations with his father, Michael Kierkegaard, and his fiancée, Regine Olsen. (For example, who is sacrificing whom, for what cause? Who is Abraham in this story—Michael or Søren? Who is Isaac—Søren or Regine?)

3. Compare some instances of Jesus' use of parables in Matthew, Mark, and Luke with Kierkegaard's use of "indirect communication."

4. Write an imaginary debate on the topic of "certainty" between René Descartes and Søren Kierkegaard.

5. If Kierkegaard's "aesthete" has no self, how can he arrive at the moment when he "chooses himself"?

6. How is it possible that the radical "knight of faith" could prove to be the postman, the tax collector, or the adolescent girl next door? And why would it be impossible for us ever to know if they were?

Suggestions for Further Reading

I. Kierkegaard's Main Philosophical Works in English (Danish publication dates in brackets)

Either/Or, Vols. I and II. Trans. David F. Swenson and Lillian Marvin Swenson. Garden City, N.Y.: Doubleday/Anchor Books, 1959 [1843].

also

Either/Or. Trans. Howard V. Hong and Edna H. Hong. Princeton, N.J.: Princeton University Press, 1987.

Fear and Trembling (with *The Sickness unto Death*). Trans. Walter Lowrie. Garden City, N.Y.: Doubleday/Anchor Books, 1954 [1843].

also

Fear and Trembling (with *Repetition*). Trans. Howard V. Hong and Edna H. Hong. Princeton, N.J.: Princeton University Press, 1983 [1843].

also

The Concept of Dread. Trans. Walter Lowrie. Princeton, N.J.: Princeton University Press, 1957 [1844].

Fear and Trembling. Trans. Alastair Hannay. New York: Penguin Books, 1985.

Johannes Climacus, Or, "De omnibus dubitandum est." Trans. T. H. Croxall. London: Adam & Charles Black, 1958 [written 1842–43; published posthumously].

Philosophical Fragments. Trans. David Swenson, Howard V. Hong, and Edna H. Hong. Princeton, N.J.: Princeton University Press, 1967 [1844].

Repetition (with *Fear and Trembling*). Trans. Howard V. Hong and Edna H. Hong. Princeton, N.J.: Princeton University Press, 1983 [1843].

also translated as

The Concept of Anxiety. Trans. Reider Thomte and Albert B. Anderson. Princeton, N.J.: Princeton University Press, 1980.

Concluding Unscientific Postscript. Trans. David F. Swenson and Walter Lowrie. Princeton, N.J.: Princeton University Press, 1960 [1846].

The Point of View for My Work as an Author. Trans. Walter Lowrie. Ed. Benjamin Nelson. New York: Harper Torchbooks, 1962 [written in 1848; published posthumously].

The Present Age. Trans. Alexander Dru. New York: Harper Torchbooks, 1962 [1846].

Stages on Life's Way. Trans. Walter Lowrie. New York: Schocken Books, 1967 [1845].

The Sickness unto Death (with *Fear and Trembling*). Trans. Walter Lowrie. Garden City, N.Y.: Doubleday/Anchor Books, 1954 [1849].

also

The Sickness unto Death. Trans. Howard V. Hong and Edna H. Hong. Princeton, N.J.: Princeton University Press, 1980.

II. Kierkegaard's Philosophy Anthologized

Bretall, Robert, ed. *A Kierkegaard Anthology.* Princeton, N.J.: Princeton University Press, 1973.

III. Secondary Sources on Kierkegaard

Collins, James. *The Mind of Kierkegaard*. Princeton, N.J.: Princeton University Press, 1983.

Gardiner, Patrick. *Kierkegaard*. Oxford: Oxford University Press, 1988.

Hannay, Alastair. *Kierkegaard*. London: Routledge & Kegan Paul, 1982.

Lowrie, Walter. *A Short Life of Kierkegaard*. Garden City, N.Y.: Doubleday/Anchor Books, 1961.

Mackey, Louis. *Kierkegaard: A Kind of Poet*. Philadelphia: University of Pennsylvania Press, 1971.

Mooney, Edward F. *Knights of Faith and Resignation: Reading Kierkegaard's "Fear and Trembling."* Albany: State University of New York Press, 1991.

Palmer, Donald. *Kierkegaard for Beginners*. New York: Writers & Readers, 1996.

Thompson, Josiah. *The Lonely Labyrinth: Kierkegaard's Pseudonymous Works*. Carbondale: Southern Illinois University Press, 1967.

Notes

1. Elaine Pagels, *The Origin of Satan* (New York: Random House, 1995), p. 180.
2. Søren Kierkegaard, *Johannes Climacus, Or, "De omnibus dubitandum est,"* trans. T. H. Croxall (London: Adam & Charles Black, 1958), pp. 148–149.
3. Søren Kierkegaard, *Either/Or*, I (Garden City, N.Y.: Doubleday/Anchor Books, 1959), p. 20.
4. Kierkegaard, *Either/Or*, II, p. 173.
5. Kierkegaard, *Either/Or*, II, p. 226.
6. "Defining relationship" is a phrase coined by Prof. Hubert Dreyfus of the University of California at Berkeley in his lectures on Kierkegaard.
7. Kierkegaard, *Either/Or*, I, p. 37.
8. Søren Kierkegaard, *The Journals of Kierkegaard: 1834–1854*, trans. and ed. Alexander Dru (London and Glasgow: Collins Fontana, 1969), p. 224.
9. Søren Kierkegaard, *Christian Discourses*, trans. Walter Lowrie (New York: Oxford University Press, 1961), p. 244.
10. Søren Kierkegaard, *Fear and Trembling* (with *The Sickness unto Death*), trans. Walter Lowrie (Garden City, N.Y.: Doubleday/Anchor Books, 1954), p. 65. The page numbers of future quotations from this book will be included in the body of the text, in parentheses.
11. Kierkegaard, *Either/Or*, II, p. 218.

7

The Darwinian Conception of Human Nature

Historical Backdrop

Queen Victoria was one of Britain's longest-reigning monarchs, coming to the throne in 1837 when she was barely eighteen years old and leaving it upon her death in 1901. She oversaw an empire based on the wealth generated by the Industrial Revolution and on the raw materials and cheap labor of a vast colonial system that stretched literally around the globe. The British victory over Napoleonic France (the Battle of Waterloo had been fought in 1815) had somewhat compensated for the loss of the American colonies at the end of the eighteenth century and seemed to dampen the fiery spirit of the French Revolution, whose ideas had been viewed by the British ruling class as a threat to the public order. The victory over the French also undercut the reach of one of Britain's primary imperialist competitors.

Though a venerable aristocracy whose wealth was based on land and agriculture still existed in Britain, its prerogatives were being whittled away by emergent middle classes led by powerful industrialists and financiers. The gradual collapse of the old agrarian economy drove thousands of unskilled laborers to migrate to the cities and form the ever-growing and ever-more-restless working classes, with the worst-off inhabiting large slums.

Queen Victoria (1819–1901)

175

In nineteenth-century Britain, great technological advances were made in industry, transportation, and medicine. In the arts, poetry, the novel, and landscape painting reached new heights of excellence. Despite dramatic challenges to the status quo by the **Romantic** poets, socialist political clubs, the **pre-Raphaelites** in art, abolitionists, and marchers for women's suffrage, the spiritual and social values of the century were largely determined by organized religion. The Church of England, established after Henry VIII broke with the pope in the sixteenth century over the latter's refusal to grant Henry a divorce from his first wife, Catherine of Aragon, had gained tremendous power, and its bishopric had close ties with the aristocratic class. The Church's faithful constituency, however, was thoroughly middle class—though they generally shared a conservative view of the world with their aristocratic "betters." Even if the High Church seemed to flirt with Catholic-like ritual, pageantry, and pomp, the Church of England, along with other Protestant sects, made the Bible and not religious

authorities the source of social and spiritual values. In addition to this religious commitment, the Victorian middle classes gained a reputation—justified or not—of stuffiness, snobbery, and sexual repression. This era also was characterized by the violence required to keep order at home and in the colonies—to wage the disastrous Crimean War of 1854–56, to suppress bloody rebellions in India, and to control the riots and raucous demonstrations that periodically rocked the cities. Furthermore, there seemed to be a cultural fascination with figures of horror—real, imagined, and fictitious—what we could perhaps call "Victoria's secrets." Perhaps Mary Shelley's *Frankenstein* was the first in the century's cycle of terror, but it was only the first. As a Victorian scholar has recently written in an essay on Bram Stoker's *Dracula*,

> The specter whose sighting was announced in London in 1848 by Karl Marx and Friedrich Engels ["A specter is haunting Europe—the specter of communism"] would not be the only phantom to haunt the Victorian imagination in that century. Among the fictitious, semifictitious, or real apparitions

would also be counted Darwin's man-ape, Stevenson's Mr. Hyde, Conan Doyle's Dr. Moriarty, Jack the Ripper, and Dickens's spontaneously combusting bodies. Lewis Carroll would even create several just for children, including the Jabberwock and the frumious bandersnatch.[1]

The "specter" we will review here, of course, is the "man-ape" discovered by Darwin—or, as most people apparently hoped, concocted by Darwin—for this specter turns out to be ourselves.

Biography

Charles Darwin was born in Shrewsbury, Shropshire, in 1809. His father was a physician, and he sent sixteen-year-old Charles to Edinburgh University to continue the family tradition. However, the squeamish lad was horrified by the idea of performing surgery, so his disappointed father decided that Charles should become an Anglican clergyman instead. To that end he sent his son to Christ's College at Cambridge to study for the ministry. Looking back on his three years there, Darwin concluded that it was a waste of time; he was more interested in his hobby of natural studies. In his twenty-first year, while hunting rare beetles in Wales, he caught two

Charles Darwin (1809–1882)

lovely specimens. With a beetle cupped in each hand, he found a third and excitedly freed up his hand to catch it by popping one beetle in his mouth for safe-keeping. He quickly discovered that he didn't like beetles quite as much as he thought, losing the specimen when he spit it out.

Darn! There goes the missing link.

PA-TOOEY

The next year was a turning point in Darwin's life. He was invited to join the crew of the HMS *Beagle* on its surveying expedition into the Atlantic and Pacific oceans as the unpaid conversationalist companion of the twenty-six-year-old captain. But Darwin soon upstaged the official naturalist hired by Her Majesty's government and for all practical purposes became the *Beagle*'s acting naturalist on its five-year journey. Darwin collected some 900 pages of notes based on his observations, and in the three-year period after his return to England in 1837, he worked out his theory of evolution. The organization of his data was guided by two theoretical models of recent vintage. First, while sailing on the *Beagle*, Darwin read Sir Charles Lyell's *Principles of Geology* (1830–33), which argued that the same natural forces that were at work in the nineteenth century had been at work in the remote past. The slow but inevitable process of these forces (heat, cold, wind, water, ice, and lava) meant that the earth was much older than the 5834 years ascribed to it by Bishop Ussher, who, counting the generations mentioned in the Bible, concluded that the earth had been created in seven days in the year 4004 B.C.E. (His more fastidious disciple located the exact moment of creation as 9 A.M. on October 23 of that year.)

ADAM — EVE

ABEL   CAIN   ?

GRAMPS   GRAMMY

DAD   MA

ME

Bishop Ussher's Family Tree

Second, Darwin read Thomas Malthus's *Essay on Population* (1798), which argued that all species multiply at a rate beyond the environment's capacity to support them, leading to the notorious principle of the struggle for survival.

During the period in which Darwin was developing his theory of evolution, he married his first cousin, Emma Wedgwood (just as in the next year Queen Victoria would marry her first cousin, Prince Albert). Three of their ten children died, provoking deep grief on Darwin's part, and his own health began a slow, mysterious deterioration after 1840. Fortunately, he had inherited enough wealth to allow him to work in peace, and he slowly compiled his notes in preparation for the eventual publication of his bombshell.

In 1858, Darwin was shocked to receive correspondence from an unknown admirer living in Borneo, Alfred Russel Wallace; his letter included an essay that summarized concisely the complete theory of evolution on which Darwin was laboring. Fearing that he would be upstaged if Wallace published his views before he had completed his study, Darwin hurriedly pared down his massive work and published a truncated version as *On the Origin of Species by Means of Natural Selection* (1859). It immediately provoked both enthusiasm and hostility in the scientific community and among the lay public. Darwin stayed aloof from the raging controversy, but the debate came to a head in Oxford in 1860 in a confrontation between the rhetorically gifted Bishop Samuel Wilberforce and the biologist Thomas Huxley (who became known as "Darwin's Bulldog"). During a meeting of the British Association for the Advancement of Science, the bishop, carried away by his own eloquence,

Darwin's Bulldog

attacked the theory of evolution by asking Huxley whether he was related to an ape on his grandfather's or his grandmother's side. Huxley's triumphant rejoinder has been recorded:[2]

A man has no reason to be ashamed of having an ape for his grandfather. If there were an ancestor whom I should feel shame in recalling, it would be a man, a man of restless and versatile intellect, who, not content with an equivocal success in his own sphere of activity, plunges into scientific questions with which he has no real acquaintance, only to obscure them by an aimless rhetoric, and distract the attention of his hearers from the real point at issue by eloquent digressions, and skilled appeals to religious prejudice.

By the end of his life, Darwin had become very rich as a result of royalties from his books and his astute investments. He died in 1882 and was buried with honors in Westminster Abbey.

Darwin's Theory

The Game of "Invent-a-Bird"

Let me begin with an anecdote. Several years ago I reluctantly agreed to be a substitute instructor at San Quentin Prison in California for an anthropologist friend of mine who had fallen ill. Not wishing to let him down, I spent several hours "boning up" on the theory of evolution, the topic for the class I would be teaching. Once in the classroom, I soon realized that I had overprepared. Although a handful of students had read everything about Darwin available to them in the prison library, most of them had never heard of him and had no inkling of the meaning of the word *evolution*.

But I had never seen such eagerness to learn (so much so that I volunteered shortly after to teach philosophy at San Quentin). To achieve the goal, I devised on the spot a game I called "Invent-a-Bird." I cut paper into

small, card-shaped pieces
and drew on each of the
seven cards a different bird
head (for example, one with
a long, pointed bill; another,
a strong, nut-cracking beak;
a third, a wide, flat, "duck-
ish" bill; a fourth, a sharp,

hooked beak for tearing flesh; a fifth, a cavernous, fish-holding bill; and so
on). On another seven cards, I drew different legs and feet (for example,
webbed feet; feet with sharp talons; short, strong legs; long, thin legs; and
so on). Then I made a series of cards with similarly discrepant bodies,
another with a variety of wings, and another with various tails. Finally, I
made a series of environmental cards: marsh, snow scene, desert, ocean,
prairie, and forest. I shuffled each group of cards and stacked them in a
row along the front of my desk. Next I had each student—these convicted
murderers, arsonists, rapists, and thieves—march one by one past the
desk, picking up one card from each "bird part" pile. Each student then went
to the blackboard and drew the bird he had randomly invented. Most drawings produced monsters: a pathetic creature with long, dainty legs on huge
feet, with a gigantic, hawklike beak; or a bird
with a huge body and tiny feet and head; a
duck with talons; a hummingbird with big
webbed feet. The students laughed
uproariously at each natural disaster
produced. At last, after scores of fail-
ures, a bird was drawn that seemed to
"work": long, thin legs on webbed feet,
with a large, round body, small tail,
graceful long neck, and long, sharp
bill—surely a proto-ibis or flamingo.
But there was one more pile from which
to choose—the environmental stack. There
was absolute silence as the husky, heavily tattooed inmate picked the card
. . . a desert! This bird was doomed.

I tried to restate our game in terms of Darwin's theory of "natural
selection," "survival of the fittest," Mendelian genetic theory, and what little I could explain of DNA (deoxyribonucleic acid)—less than I hoped, as
it turned out. Upon his recuperation, my friend pointed out to me that
there is no one-to-one relationship between DNA and body parts. That is, a
single gene may affect not merely a single trait, but a whole "trait complex,"

because the protein produced by DNA may be simultaneously the basis of a number of otherwise unrelated bodily features. My only defense is that even Darwin could not have known this, because these discoveries were made after his death. Nevertheless, I felt that my class had been a pedagogical

Mother Nature Selects

success, allowing me to introduce in a plausible way the various themes of Darwinian evolution—the combination of randomness and natural laws that produced new forms, the ideas of **adaptation** and speciation—to intellectually eager people of a skeptical mindset. (My own enthusiasm had caused me to press the alarm buzzer in my pocket accidentally against the desk, causing heavily armed guards to charge into the classroom with weapons drawn, much to my embarrassment and to the pleasure of my already wired students.)

Teaching Darwin

"Natural Selection": Continuity and Variation

What, then, is Darwin's theory? It is deceptively easy to state. The theory can be divided into two parts: (1) All life is related—all living species have descended from earlier species as a consequence of branching out from those ancestral forms—and (2) the fundamental mechanism of these developments is **natural selection.** *Now the theory gets complicated. The first aspect of natural selection is* continuity: *Life-forms duplicate themselves; they reproduce. This process of reproduction generates many more duplicates than can survive in the host environment, so there is a constant struggle for survival, either among members of the same species or among species themselves. Another aspect of natural selection is that of* variation, *which, ironically, is the result of breakdowns in the process of continuity. These breakdowns result in imperfect copies of the originals.*

These "flaws" are either the product of novel combinations of genes that were individually already present in the combined gene pools of the parental generation or the product of genetic mutations (chemical breakdowns in the gene). The flaws manifest themselves as new body traits. Most of these new characteristics will be damaging, resulting in the death of the offspring that carries them. But some of these new traits will, relative to the environment in which the individual organism finds itself, be advantageous, allowing it to reproduce more successfully. This can lead to a new species that is in some way an improvement on the parental species. The new species gives the appearance of having been intentionally designed for its environment, but in fact it is the accidental product of the process just described.

> You see? I'm a perfect fit. The competition doesn't stand a chance.

Religious Objections

The first half of this two-part theory (namely, that current species are descended from ancestral species) is, strictly speaking, *the* theory of evolution. It had first been suggested in ancient Greece by the philosopher Empedocles, and by Darwin's time, it was accepted by many scientists and philosophers. Darwin's true originality rests in the second half of the theory, in the assertion that the *cause* of speciation (the emergence of new species) is natural selection in the context of the struggle for survival. But both halves of the theory encountered opposition from various religious camps, and the second half was also opposed by some scientists.

Concerning the general theory of evolution, many religious-minded people objected to its obliteration of the distinction between humans and ani-mals. They claimed that because humans have an immortal soul, there must have been a special cre-ation of that soul by God that made humans indepen-dent of evolution.

Literal-minded read-ers of the Bible went even further and denied that evolution was true of any level of nature. They believed that when, in Gene-sis 1:24, God says, "Let the earth bring forth the living creature after his kind, cat-tle and creeping thing, and beast of the earth after his kind: and it was so," this ruled out evolu-tion of any sort. Some of these literal readers of the Bible explained the already voluminous fossil record as the result of Noah's flood; a few, even more dramati-cally, saw it as the work of the devil.

The Fossil Record as the Work of the Devil

The Attack on Teleology

Other more liberal theologians believed that the fossil record could not be so easily dismissed. They felt that the general theory of evolution was compatible with the idea of an all-seeing, all-powerful God who had simply used evolution to achieve his overall goal. But even this compromise was spoiled by the publication in 1859 of Darwin's *Origin of Species*, for his book had the effect of removing teleology (literally, the study of purposes, intentions, and goals) from nature. There were no "natural purposes" of the type described by Aristotle, and no references to divine purpose were needed to account for the process of evolution.

Let me explain this by relating one more personal anecdote. My freshman year in college, I enrolled in a botany class. Each student had to perform an experiment and report it to the class. I planted a bean in some soil in a milk carton whose top I had removed. (This was my "control unit.") Then I planted another bean in an identical carton; on top of this carton, I taped a column of milk cartons about four feet high, leaving an opening of about two square inches at the top of the column. (This was the "experiment unit.") I placed both items—control unit and experiment unit—in my backyard exposed to the sunny California sky. The "control bean" received about five hours of direct sunlight a day, while the "experiment bean" received sunlight only at high noon. Luckily, beans grow fast, so after a few weeks I was able to bring my experiment to the

My Brilliant Experiment

lab for exhibition. The control bean had grown into a bushy, healthy, deep-green plant protruding about eight inches out of its carton and laden with succulent pods. The experiment bean was a pale, stringy stem that had wound its way torturously up the inside of the four-foot column of milk cartons, hung a scraggly stem and a pale, flaccid leaf out through the hole in the top of the column; and then it stopped growing, apparently too pooped to produce even one pod.

My experiment was visually provocative, and I was proud of it. In my report, I wrote that the bean plant encased in the column had used up all of its energy striving to reach the light. At the next class meeting, the professor returned my report. I eagerly anticipated a high grade for the ingenuity of my experiment, so I was shocked to see a large, red "F" scribbled across the top of my paper. The professor had written only three short sentences at the bottom of my page: "This bean is not 'striving to reach the light.' No bean has ever 'striven' to do anything. (See Charles Darwin.)" Luckily, we were allowed to rewrite our reports. Then the *real* work began, because I had to research the chemical composition of bean seeds, discovering which chemicals were activated by dark, damp soil with the effect of a growth hormone and which chemicals were activated by sunlight to commence photosynthesis, terminating massive growth and effecting flowerage. That is, I had replaced a *teleological* account of my experiment with a purely *mechanical* one. (I got a "B" on my rewrite.)

Bean Plants Striving to Reach the Light

"Darwin's Dangerous Idea"

Many of Darwin's contemporaries were horrified by precisely this mechanical feature of his theory—what Daniel Dennett has called "Darwin's Dangerous Idea" in his book of the same title.[3] In the eighteenth century, the favorite proof of God's existence had been what was called "the teleological argument" or "the argument from design." This proof compared the intricacies of natural entities such as eyeballs with the intricacies of designed artifacts like watches. It concluded that just as the subtlety of the watch entails an intelligent and purposeful master designer—namely, a watchmaker—so does the subtlety and perfection of the eyeball entail a master designer, an eyeball maker—namely, God. Yet Darwin's theory purported to show that even a phenomenon as complicated as the eyeball could be the product of natural selection

Master Eyeball Designer

(that is, of the laws of physics and chemistry), along with the laws of probability and randomness applied to the components of organic matter within the context of the struggle for survival. (Remember that Darwin could not actually present a complete account of natural selection because that turns out to involve the science of genetics and even an explanation of deoxyribonucleic acid [DNA]. Though Gregor Mendel published the first account of genetics in 1866, his book was ignored until the turn of the century, and DNA was not discovered until 1953 by Francis Crick and James Watson. Also, the completed theory of natural selection needs statistics, another science unavailable to Darwin.)

Isn't anybody listening?!

Father Gregor Mendel, the Founder of the Science of Genetics

Despite the technical complications of the theory, certain examples illustrate different ways in which natural selection works to favor one strain of "phenotype" (the physical creature that is the result of the interaction between genetic heredity and environmental conditions) over another. A well-known case involves a species of moth, *Biston betularia*, that inhabits the English Midlands. There are white and black varieties of this moth. Before the nineteenth century, the white variety was predominant and the black was scarce. The latter was too easily spotted by birds, the moth's natural enemy, against the white bark and lichen that covered the trees of the Midlands. In the 1800s, the heavy industrialization of the region produced smoke and soot that killed the pale lichen and stained the bark, and both trees and buildings were left covered by a layer of black grime. As a consequence, the black moths began to find themselves safer from predators than their white cousins. The frequencies of the genes determining color in these moths rapidly changed, and now the black moths predominate. The white moths suddenly found themselves being "selected out" (or "selected in" . . . as bird dinners). There are no "intentions"—no teleology—involved in this process. It is purely mechanical.

Darwinism and the Human Being

But enough about moths. What implications does Darwin's theory of evolution have for our quest for a philosophical theory of human nature? Oddly enough, the answer to this question is unclear. Darwin himself was certainly not anxious to answer it in *On the Origin of Species*, where, speaking of the application of his theory to human beings, he says only, "Much light will be thrown on the origins of man and his history."[4] Though his early notes show his interest in human evolution, he did not find the courage to publish *The Descent of Man* until 1871, twelve years after *Origin*. There he concludes that the facts compel us to believe "that man is descended from some lower form, notwithstanding that connecting-links have not hitherto been discovered" and that the human being "is but one of several exceptional forms of Primates."[5]

Exceptional Primates

So then, "human nature" is not so different from the nature of certain other animals. What are the moral implications of this aspect of "Darwin's Dangerous Idea"? Darwin is seen by many as one of the great revolutionaries of intellectual history and by some as having dealt one of the three great blows to human self-importance. (The first: Galileo's proof that we are not at the center of the universe; the second: Darwin's discovery that we are mere animals; the third: Freud's demonstration that we are sick animals.) But did Darwin himself draw revolutionary conclusions about human nature and morality from his theory of evolution, as would many of his self-proclaimed disciples? Apparently not. For Darwin, the gradation between our nearest primate relatives and ourselves is so smooth that hardly a ripple is caused. Rather than looking at our animal cousins and ancestors to discover the worst about them and then projecting that "bruteness" into ourselves, Darwin does the reverse.

The First Blow

He looks first at us humans and then at simians, finding in them the same things that (or sometimes even better things than) he finds in us. He summarizes his analysis in *The Descent of Man:*

> It has, I think, now been shown that man and the higher animals, especially the Primates, have some few instincts in common. All have the same senses, intuitions and sensations—similar passions, affections and emotions, even the more complex ones, such as jealousy, suspicion, emulation, gratitude and magnanimity; they practice deceit and are revengeful; they are sometimes susceptible to ridicule, and even have a sense of humor; they feel wonder and curiosity; they possess the same faculties of imitation, attention, deliberation, choice, memory, imagination, the association of ideas and reason, though in very different degrees. The individuals of the same species graduate in intellect from absolute imbecility to high excellence. They are also liable to insanity, though far less often than in the case of man. (p. 67)

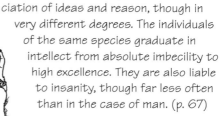

Darwin admits that animals are not self-conscious, nor do they have "the habitual use of articulate language . . . peculiar to man" (p. 72). Nor do they have a belief in God; but neither are they plagued with the superstitions that terrify such a great part of humankind. They *do* have a sense of beauty and moral capacities. In fact, after describing various acts of heroism on the part of monkeys and baboons, Darwin concludes that he would prefer to think of himself as descended from a brave, heroic little monkey than from a superstitious human savage who treats his wives like slaves, delights in torturing his enemies, and offers up bloody sacrifices to imaginary gods.

But according to Darwin, human beings in a civilized state need not worry that their culture is the mere product of mechanical forces of natural selection. "For the moral qualities are advanced, either directly or indirectly, much more through the effects of habit, the reasoning powers, instruction, religion, etc., than through natural selection, though to this latter agency may be safely attributed the social instincts which afforded the basis for the development of the moral sense" (pp. 327–328). In fact, for Darwin, the process of natural selection—"the struggle for existence" and "the survival of the fittest"—seems to apply to humans within society only in times of population crises, and at those times, the human being "is occasionally subjected to a severe struggle for existence, and natural selection will have effected whatever lies within its scope" (p. 316).

Darwin distinguishes between natural selection and "sexual selection," which involves the conscious choice of the "selector," and he claims that, in the case of humans, sexual selection plays a larger role than does natural selection.[6] In fact, civilization assumes so much of the role that evolution plays in nature and in precivilized society that it preserves "a considerable number of individuals, weak in mind and body, who would have been promptly eliminated in the savage state" (p. 45). (Indeed, Darwin suspects that this explains why the Neanderthal's skull was larger than our own.) Nevertheless, even civilized society has its method of "elimination of the worst dispositions." Darwin writes confidently that executions, imprisonment, confinement, suicide, bloody

Unnatural Selection

fights, liver diseases, and infertility dispose of "malefactors," "melancholic and insane persons," "violent and quarrelsome men," and the "profligate" as well, preventing them from transmitting their "bad qualities" (p. 120). Furthermore, "although civilization . . . checks in many ways the action of natural selection, it apparently favors the better development of the body, by means of good food and the freedom from occasional hardships" (p. 119).

Mother Nature Cleaning Up

Darwinism and Morality

Still, society does not need to depend on these substitutes for natural selection, for based on its moral development, humanity has risen "to the very summit of the organic scale" (p. 328). Moral development is not a heroic, voluntary choice, of course. The foundations of morality are built into our biology as the result of natural selection.

Our predecessors experienced both selfishness and sympathy for others, and these opposing values synthesized into a desire to help others along with the hope that others would reciprocate. This combination of selfishness and sympathy would be open to natural selection, "for those communities, which included the greatest number of the most sympathetic members, would flourish best and rear the greatest number of offspring" (p. 92). According to Darwin, this would lead members of such communities to state with the German philosopher Immanuel Kant, "I will not in my own person violate the dignity of humanity" (p. 95).

Kant (1724–1804) had argued that reason imposes upon all rational creatures a moral duty (which Kant called the **Categorical Imperative**) to respect the dignity of all other rational creatures. In the nineteenth century, the main philosophical competition with Kant's moral rationalism was **utilitarianism,** based on the writings of Jeremy Bentham (1748–1832) and John Stuart Mill (1808–1873). The utilitarians argued that morality was grounded not in reason but in

Polite People Reproduce More Efficiently

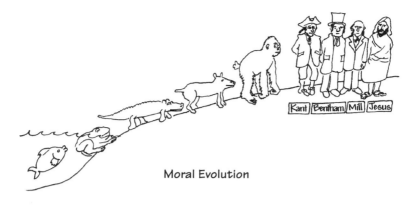

Moral Evolution

feeling and passion, in the desire for happiness. From this, they deduced their primary principle of moral philosophy—that each act should be motivated by a desire for "the greatest amount of happiness for the greatest number of people." Darwin astutely disagrees with Bentham's claim that all actions are, in fact, motivated by a desire for happiness. Some are motivated by "instinct, or long habit, without any consciousness of pleasure" (p. 104). But he agrees that the "greatest happiness principle" has justifiably become civilization's goal. So, in Darwin's mind, not only have natural selection and the general processes of civilization led to the Categorical Imperative and the Principle of Utility, but they also "naturally lead to the golden rule" (pp. 109–110), yet another block in the foundation of morality.

If Darwin believes that the agency of natural selection has advanced the human race inexorably to embody a form of civilized morality that synthesizes Kantianism, utilitarianism and Christian morality, then it must be said that the moral picture that Darwin believes follows from his theory of evolution is not a very radical one after all and should not be one that evoked horror in his audi-

The Final Judgment: God (as Christ) in Consultation with Saint Matthew (as Angel) and Saint John (as Eagle) [Tympanum, Saint Pierre, Moissac, France]

ence. Yet so it did. Some of his opponents believed that morality could be justified only if there was an immortal soul and a final judgment at the hands of an all-wise, wrathful God. Without belief in the eventual triumph of Good over Evil in eternity, or, in some cases, without the fear of eternal punishment for moral transgression, people would become either too dispirited to be willing to make the sacrifices required by morality or so emboldened as to pursue selfish and immoral acts. Clearly, Darwin was not so pessimistic about the human race. A theological grounding was no more needed for morality than it was needed for the natural sciences.

The Darwinian Legacy: Uses and Abuses of Darwinian Theory

There is another reason for the revulsion that the theory of evolution provoked among some of its critics, both in Darwin's day and later. A number of Darwin's followers deduced moral precepts from the theory of natural selection very different from those of Darwin himself.

Social Darwinism

The most famous moral interpretation in the second half of the nineteenth century was **social Darwinism,** "a peculiarly beastly form of social climbing."[7] According to this doctrine, the laws of evolution meant that social progress could come about only if the "strong" were unhindered by governmental and moral restrictions in their inevitable climb to the top of the social heap.

Social Darwinism was derived from the interpretation of Darwin's theories by his younger English contemporary, Herbert Spencer (1820–1903), about whose work Darwin had mixed feelings.

The Climb to the Top of the Heap

Spencer created a sociology analogous to Darwin's biological theory. Spencer was interested in survival value for *social* units rather than biological individuals and species. Nevertheless, Darwin and Spencer influenced each other. It was from Spencer that, for better or for worse, Darwin had borrowed the phrase, "survival of the fittest." Spencer, in his enthusiastic misinterpretation of Darwin's views, concluded that, in "the struggle for existence," those who survive are superior to those over whom they triumph. This superiority is not merely in terms of the ability to reproduce more efficiently, nor is it merely in relation to a particular natural environment (in the way that longer-necked giraffes on the African savannas were superior to their forebears in that they were able to reach more leaves). Rather, this superiority existed in some *absolute* sense, one with moral overtones. Spencer's appropriation of Darwin's views equated evolution with progress toward some absolute, inevitable goal. Especially in America, social Darwinism coincided with the prevailing political conservatism and enthusiasm for capitalist and industrial expansion. Thus, it supported the doctrine of laissez-faire, according to which government should keep its hands off the developing economic forces, allowing the economy's victors to be handsomely rewarded and treating its victims as necessary casualties. Social Darwinism confirmed the "naturalness" of hardship for most and the "unnaturalness" of governmental interference in economic matters. It railed against any effort at reform or relief. For instance, Spencer opposed all government aid to the poor, who, by their poverty, proved their unfitness:[8]

Mother Nature Guarantees Progress

Spencer Speaks

Spencer's "gospel of progress" could also mollify those who were offended by the atheistic overtones of Darwin's theory, for social Darwinism was a kind of substitute religion. Spencer included in his theory a "Doctrine of the Unknowable," and readers who chose to do so could interpret this vagueness as a space for God. One such follower was the American oil magnate John D. Rockefeller, who in a Sunday-school lesson said:[9]

Racism and Imperialism

Darwin's theory was also used in the nineteenth and early twentieth centuries to promote racism and imperialism. The ideas of natural selection and survival of the fittest were called upon to vindicate a jingoistic militarism, imperialism, and suppression of the "savage races." Darwin may be partly at fault here. He had given *On The Origin of Species* the unfortunate subtitle *The Preservation of Favoured Races in the Struggle for Life.* He was not thinking here about human races, of course, but, despite Darwin's opposition to slavery, many of his statements have racist overtones. There are numerous references to "the higher races" in *The Descent of Man,* and Darwin finds similarities among "monkeys, . . . microcephalous idiots, and . . . the barbarous races of mankind" (p. 75). He claims that the anthropomorphous apes occupy a space "between the Negro or Australian [aborigine] and the gorilla," and in the same passage, he anticipates "some future period, not very distant

as measured by centuries, [when] the civilized races of man will almost certainly exterminate and replace the savage races throughout the world" (p. 139).

So we can blame Darwin for remarks to which racists and imperialists could appeal for "scientific" justification of their bigotry, but we cannot suppose that Darwin caused them to hold the views they did. It was convenient for them to find a leading scientist whose musings might lend legitimacy to projects that were otherwise morally repugnant.

T. Roosevelt

Eugenics

Darwin's name was also used to justify a program of **eugenics**—a term coined by his cousin, Frances Galton, to designate the belief that human (or, in some cases, national) improvement should be brought about by selective breeding of superior types and that biological deterioration should be arrested by intervention in the breeding patterns of inferior types. This philosophy, which enjoyed great popularity in the early twentieth century, differed from social Darwinism in that it required state intervention. By 1915, twelve American states had passed sterilization laws, and anti-immigration sentiment was swelling. But eugenics found perhaps its most loathsome manifestation in the doctrines of the Nazi party in Germany in the 1930s and 1940s.

Once again, it must be acknowledged that some of Darwin's own remarks helped fuel the eugenics movement. For example, he wrote: "Excepting in the case of man himself, hardly anyone is so ignorant as to allow his worst animals to breed" (p. 117) and "Both sexes ought to refrain from marriage if they are in any marked degree inferior in body or mind" (p. 327).

"Ultra-Darwinism"

Is Darwin responsible for what Ashley Montagu calls "the tendentious, the stupid, and the really vicious misuses" of his ideas?[10] Daniel Dennett observes that "Darwinism has always had an unfortunate power to attract the most unwelcome enthusiasts—demagogues and psychopaths and misanthropes and other abusers of Darwin's dangerous idea" (p. 264). Dennett makes this observation in the context of an accusation against himself by Stephen Jay Gould, one of America's foremost biologists, that Dennett is a "hyper-Darwinist" or an "ultra-Darwinist"—that is, Dennett, too, is an abuser of "Darwin's dangerous idea." The source of the accusation is Dennett's defense of the thesis that natural selection is the exclusive mechanism of evolutionary change. Dennett's view seems to be that almost everything significant about human existence can be explained by the theory of evolution, and especially by the theory of natural selection. And the purely mechanical nature of the process of natural selection sets up Dennett's view that the Darwinian theory of evolution leads directly to the theory of artificial intelligence and to computer-based models of the brain. This results in the virtual disappearance of the idea of consciousness as an explanatory concept. In short, Dennett apparently wants to swathe these computer theories in the authority of Darwin's theory of evolution. (Not only does Dennett disagree with Stephen Jay Gould in this matter, but he seems horri-

Daniel Dennett as Tattletale

fied that "Gould is not fond of computers, and to this day he does not even use a computer for word processing"[!] [p. 306].)

Sociobiology

Dennett's commitment to the efficacy of natural selection as the primary explanatory force in the biological and social sciences leads him to defend

Genes at Work

a modified version of sociobiology, which Jonathan Howard has called "a neo-Darwinian cult."[11] It is the product of the eminent American biologist, Edward O. Wilson, in his *Sociobiology: The New Synthesis* (1975). According to Wilson, many social and moral phenomena that were previously attributed to cultural inculcation or individual choice were now to be explained (and therefore justified) as biological phenomena that had been naturally selected for their survival value. Sociobiology has at one time or another explained and justified aggression, property ownership, hatred of foreigners, conformity, confinement of women to the kitchen, homosexuality, and rape. Dennett himself is critical of what he takes to be excesses in Wilson's views and those of his followers, claiming that they are "greedy reductionists." Dennett calls for a less greedy form of **reductionism.**

Summary

It is, then, very difficult to be sure what the implications of Darwin's theory of evolution are for our purposes—namely, our attempt to construct a theory of human nature and of selfhood. Darwin's personal views on this topic proved to be amazingly conventional, if somewhat ethnocentric. Natural selection, he claimed, had given the higher primates social instincts, which, in the case of humans, has led to a form of civilization superior to some of its competitors due to its elevated moral capacity. This moral capacity is a synthesis of all strands of the moral tradition in the West: egoism, altruism, Kantianism, utilitarianism and the Sermon on the Mount. Darwin's views also were quite conveniently compatible with the British policies of imperialism and colonialism and very comfortable with Victorian family values. Yet many members of the Victorian gentrified classes that his moral theory complimented took deep umbrage at the atheistic tone of Darwin's theory and believed that the "man-ape" undermines human dignity and would be a model of the brutishness that the theory of evolution would unleash.

Bully for the Empire

But his disciples seemed no more prepared to accept Darwin's own moderate moral conclusions than were his detractors. They could agree only that the theory of evolution supported their own individual radical social programs. Both capitalists (John D. Rockefeller and J. Pierpont Morgan) and Communists (Karl Marx and Friedrich Engels) found in Darwin's theory confirmation of their deepest sentiments. The German and Austrian general staff in World War I and pacifists during the same war flew Darwin's flag. Darwin has been hero both to racists and to those who deny the validity of the concept of race (such as anthropologist Ashley Montagu and biologist Stephen Jay Gould). Today, deeply committed Darwinians such as Daniel Dennett and Steven Pinker, on the one side, and Gould and Richard Lewontin, on the other, lash out at their antagonists' misappropriation of "Darwin's dangerous idea" for their own political or scientific agenda. As historian Richard Hofstadter has pointed out, Darwin's theory seems to have an uncanny ability to support opposing ideologies. Therefore, the few conclusions drawn here will be very ten- tative, and it will be more obvious than in other chapters that these conclusions are my own.

John D. Rockefeller, J. Pierpont Morgan, Karl Marx, and Friedrich Engels

First, we should take seriously Dar- win's assertion that in human society natural selection has produced agencies that in some ways transcend their origins. The evolutionary anthropologist Alexander Alland says, "Man is . . . the only animal in which breeding is regulated through the operation of social rules."[12] Culture is the result of adaptation, but social rules and intentionality function differently than the mechanism of adaptation. Thus, contrary to the sociobiologists and to philosopher Daniel Dennett, sociology and anthropology do not have to be reducible to biology, or even analogous to it.

Nevertheless, evolution, if true, puts certain limitations on all other theories. They must be **naturalistic** (no dualism of mind and body as in Descartes; no supernatural or "spiritual" forces as in medieval philosophy; no purposes in nature as in Aristotle). Moreover, the theory of natural selection tells us that, even if culture can override the environment, culture must always respond to environment. This fact commits us to a kind of environmental ethics. (There is a type of practical "ought" [value] that can be derived from this "is" [fact]—what Kant called a "hypothetical imperative"—if you want to survive, then you must care for environmental balances.)

Let us turn now to the implications that a commitment to evolution- ary theory has for a philosophical outlook on the world in general. First, let us address the issue of Darwinism and religion. Clearly, the theory of evolution, like all other scientific theories, can have in itself no theological component. So-called creationism and creation science are not science. To the extent that any science appeals to supernatural intervention, it stops being science. Recall my statement in the Introduction that no claim about God's existence can be either proved or refuted by scientific procedures. Any "science" that has a supernatural being as a component has abandoned science and become religion or, at best, metaphysics. This does *not* mean that acceptance of Darwin's theory of evolution is incompatible with religious belief. As one religious writer has recently expressed it:

> Religion is getting real about evolution. Some fundamentalists and creationists continue to fulminate against Charles Darwin. But mainstream faith draws ever closer to admitting that evolutionary mechanics must be correct. In 1996, Pope John Paul II called evolution "more than just a hypothesis." Some mainstream denominations, such as Episcopalianism and Reform Judaism, no longer contest natural-selection theory, seeing nothing in it that contradicts the existence of the divine. Stick-in-the-mud views about evolution have long made many of the religious seem, to scientists, simply not worth talking to. Now that mainstream faith is beginning to accept evolution, dialogue between science and religion becomes possible.[13]

So in one sense, Darwinism is indifferent to religion. The theory of evolution cannot include religion, but it cannot exclude it either.

Beyond that, a Darwinian worldview must be pragmatic and **anti-essentialist.** The American pragmatist John Dewey (1859–1952) derived much of his philosophy from Darwin. A great debate has been raging in philosophy ever since the clash in ancient Greece between Heraclitus (c. 540–c. 470 B.C.E.), who claimed that nothing ever remains the same, that all things are in constant motion, and Parmenides (c. 515–c. 440 B.C.E.), who argued that nothing ever changes, that everything that is real is permanent, that apparent change is an illusion. In Plato, Parmenides found a champion. True reality is composed of unchanging essences, immutable natures, which the human mind can grasp as mathematical equations or eternal laws. This is **essentialism,** and it influenced all of science in one way or another until Darwin, in whom Heraclitus found *his* champion. Plato's word for "Forms" or "essences" was *Eidos*, which was translated by the medieval philosophers into "species."

One of the great ironies of Darwin's *On The Origin of Species* is his proof that there are no species. Well, I exaggerate, . . . but that is roughly the effect of his work. Darwin declares that the term *species* is "arbitrary" (p. 157), like the definitions that "decide whether a certain number of houses should be called a village, town or city" (156). The only "natural order" around which species could be defined is genealogical. Yet Darwin warns that one "might with justice argue that fertility and sterility are not safe criterions of specific distinctions" (p. 152). As Dennett points out, dogs, coyotes, and wolves do interbreed though they are categorized as different species, and Chihuahuas and Saint Bernards can't mate except with extraordinary intervention. In addition, Dennett

shows that a declaration of speciation can only be made retrospectively; that is, we can only designate something to be a new species with hindsight. This produces the oxymoronic idea of "nominal essences" (p. 95), essences in name only, and threatens to put us strangely on the watershed side of **nominalism** (see Chapter 4) rather than realism.

If ideas, too, are the ultimate product of natural selection and adaptation, then both ideas and values are open to the same sort of pragmatic analysis. **Pragmatism** is a kind of instrumentalism in which ideas and actions are viewed as instruments or tools for solving practical problems. And morality is viewed as a specific class of problems to be solved—problems determined and solved contextually, not in terms of so-called moral absolutes of Good and Evil, which, even though they are spelled with capital letters (or perhaps *because* they are), are simplistic and can easily become invitations to demagoguery. In this respect, perhaps Dennett, who associates his views with Dewey, is right to say that what is needed is a "Moral First Aid Manual" rather than absolutist rules or abstract hypothetical cases to test our moral logic.

Topics for Consideration

1. What would you say is peculiarly "Victorian" about the horror inspired by Darwin's theory of evolution in his own day?

2. What do you take to be the role of "randomness" in the theory of evolution? What is the role of "laws of nature"?

3. What is "natural selection," according to Darwin? (Does nature really "select"?)

4. What is the difference between a "teleological" explanation and a "mechanical" one? When do you think the first type of explanation is in order? What about the second type?

5. In what way does Darwin's theory of natural selection counter the proof of God's existence known as "the argument from design"?

6. Is Darwin's theory compatible with theism? Give the reasons for your positive or negative response.

7. Explain why Darwin believed that morality did not need a theological grounding.

8. Would Darwin agree with "social Darwinism"? Why or why not?

9. What is Darwin's main objection to Plato's philosophy?

Suggestions for Further Reading

I. Darwin's Main Works
(original publication dates in brackets)

The Descent of Man and Selection in Relation to Sex. Norwalk, Ct.: Heritage Press, 1972 [1871].

On the Origin of Species. New York: Random House, 1993 [1859].

The Voyage of the Beagle. Garden City, N.Y.: Doubleday, 1962.

II. Secondary Sources on Darwin

Alland, Alexander, Jr. Evolution and Human Behavior: An Introduction to Darwinian Anthropology, 2nd ed. Garden City, N.Y.: Anchor Press/Doubleday, 1973.

Dennett, Daniel. Darwin's Dangerous Idea: Evolution and the Meanings of Life. New York: Simon & Schuster, 1995.

Desmond, Adrian, and James Moore. Darwin: The Life of a Tormented Evolutionist. New York: Norton, 1992.

Dewey, John. *The Influence of Darwin on Philosophy, and Other Essays.* Amherst, N.Y.: Prometheus Books, 1997.

Gould, Stephen Jay. *Bully for Brontosaurus.* New York: Norton, 1991.

——. "Darwinian Fundamentalism." *New York Review of Books,* June 12, 1997, pp. 34–37.

——. *Ever Since Darwin: Reflections in Natural History.* New York: Norton, 1979.

——. "Evolution: The Pleasures of Pluralism." *New York Review of Books,* June 26, 1997, pp. 47–52.

Hofstadter, Richard. *Social Darwinism in American Thought.* Boston: Beacon Press, 1967.

Wilson, Edward O. *Sociobiology: The New Synthesis.* Cambridge, Mass.: Harvard University Press, 1975.

Notes

1. Leila S. May, "'Foul Things of the Night': Dread in the Victorian Body," *Modern Language Review,* vol. 93, no. 1 (Jan. 1998), p. 16.

2. Jonathan Howard, *Darwin* (New York: Oxford University Press, 1982), p. 7.

3. Daniel Dennett, *Darwin's Dangerous Idea* (New York: Simon & Schuster, 1995). Page references to this work will be included in the body of the text in parentheses.

4. Charles Darwin, *On the Origin of Species* (New York: Random House, 1993), p. 647.

5. Charles Darwin, *The Descent of Man* (Norwalk, Ct.: Heritage Press, 1972), pp. 128, 137. Future page references to this work will be included in the body of the text in parentheses.

6. The anthropologist Ashley Montagu believes that Darwin has overestimated the role of sexual selection throughout the total history of human societies. He writes: "It has become increasingly evident that in most non-literate societies there is very little opportunity for the operation of sexual selection, for the simple reason that most individuals are not free to choose their mates." Ashley Montagu, "Preface" to Darwin, *The Descent of Man,* p. x.

7. Howard, *Darwin,* p. 89.

8. Herbert Spencer, *Social Statistics* (New York: Appleton, 1874), pp. 414–415.

9. John D. Rockefeller, quoted in Richard Hofstadter, *Social Darwinism in American Thought* (Boston: Beacon Press, 1967), p. 45.

10. Montagu, "Preface," p. viii.

11. Howard, *Darwin,* pp. 75–76.

12. Alexander Alland, *Evolution and Human Behavior: An Introduction to Darwinian Anthropology,* 2nd ed. (Garden City, N.Y.: Anchor Press/Doubleday, 1973), p. 141.

13. Gregg Easterbrook, columnist, in *The News and Observer,* March 21, 1999, p. A27. Easterbrook is the author of *Beside Still Waters: Searching for Meaning in an Age of Doubt* (New York: Morrow, 1998).

8

The Marxian Conception of Human Nature

Historical Backdrop

The French Revolution of 1789 signaled an auspicious ending to the eighteenth century. It swept the royal family of France off the throne and onto the platform of the guillotine. It also represented the final chapter in the

history of the feudal economy, sounded the death knell for the politics of absolutism and the divine right of kings that had governed European politics, and discovered a universal theme in the new "holy trinity"—*liberté, fraternité, egalité*—before it degenerated into The Terror. King Louis XVI was condemned to the guillotine (he who had earlier signed the law legalizing execution by the guillotine) followed by his wife, Marie Antoinette, as were hundreds of nobles and priests. In addition, numerous heroes of the Revolution were condemned by the Committee of Public Safety, under the direction of Citizen Maximilien de Robespierre, leader of the Jacobins—the most radical revolutionary party. Eventually, Robespierre himself was put to death by that same terrible machine.

In the power vacuum that existed following The Terror, there emerged a military hero, Napoleon Bonaparte, who had defeated the Austrian army that had tried to take advantage of the political confusion in France. Napoleon went on to challenge all of the Revolution's enemies—Austrian, German, Spanish, Russian, and British—aided greatly by the enthusiasm of the world's first citizen army and by the new technology of canned food rations. His amazing military feats vaulted him to power and pushed him ever closer to the role of dictator. Indeed, he eventually had himself declared Emperor Napoleon I. Yet in every country he attacked, he claimed to be acting in the name of freedom—*liberté, fraternité,* and *egalité*. His victories did, in fact, sweep away old absolutist monarchies in the countries he occupied, infusing many individuals even in the lands he conquered with a burning desire for the new freedoms. Napoleon died in exile in 1821 after having been soundly defeated by the British at the Battle of Waterloo in Belgium in 1815.

I actually do look a bit like Marlon Brando.

The rest of the nineteenth century on the European continent was dominated by a series of seesawlike political movements. The new forces of liberalism (calling for representative governments, free markets, and the dismantling of police states) and radicalism (demanding workers' rights and redistribution of wealth) fought to maintain the momentum toward constitutional guarantees of freedom, while the old forces of absolutism fought to restore the pre-1789 regimes based on authoritarianism and class privilege. On the grand scale, it looked as though the conservative powers would triumph. The monarchy was restored in Spain under Ferdinand VII and in France under Louis XVIII; and it was strengthened in Germany, as the Prussian Friedrich Wilhelm IV extended his domain over formerly independent German-speaking duchies and baronetcies. The governments of Russia, Austro-Hungary, and Germany formed the reactionary "Holy Alliance" to douse the flames of revolution and even to cork the hot-water bottles of liberalism.

But many of the new monarchies were weak, and some rulers were quite feeble-minded. (Look carefully into the eyes of Ferdinand VII in his

Ferdinand VII (1784–1833)
(After Goya)

portrait by Francisco Goya.) Most of them were forced to grant more power to their parliaments than would ever have happened in the old days of absolutism. Gradually, liberal democracy was undermining the old regimes of Europe. And where popular sentiment was flouted or repressed, radicalism found a fertile field. In 1830, the moderate "July Revolution" turned France into a constitutional monarchy, and, in the dramatic year of 1848, spontaneous revolts broke out in many countries. In France and Germany, for instance, middle-class and workers' parties suddenly emerged victorious. Reactionary forces eventually launched bloody reprisals, but these revolutions left their permanent marks. Spain would suffer two civil wars in that century, and France would experience yet another revolution in 1870, this time after Napoleon III, Bonaparte's nephew, was captured by the Germans in the Franco-Prussian War. The year 1871 even saw the first significant attempt at modern communism in the form of the "Paris Commune," which took over the city for several months before being brutally suppressed by the French army.

A naïve historian in the spring of 1914 might well have looked back over the hundred-year period since the defeat of Napoleon and perceived it as a "march of progress," because constitutional parliamentary government had succeeded, or at least had planted its seeds, in most countries in Europe. This historian might even have viewed the century as the advance of Reason that the philosopher Georg Wilhelm Friedrich Hegel, at the beginning of that epoch, had predicted would emerge from the social turbulence. Scientific, social, and political progress had been so dramatic in the previous one hundred years that our imagined historian might have expected that a new age of perfection was dawning in Europe. A walk through the streets of Paris, London, or Berlin in the spring of 1914 might have strengthened that sentiment, for these cities teemed with excitement, prosperity, and beauty (but only if one walked in the right parts of town). But by August of 1914, the bubble had burst, as Europe was plunged into the first of two world wars that would scar the first half of the twentieth century and litter the landscape with millions of corpses. As a more pessimistic historian had it, old Europe bled to death in a few hundred yards of muddy trenches in the fields of Flanders and Ypres, in what came to be known first as the Great War and eventually as World

War I. It was this war that also provoked the first successful Marxist revolution, in czarist Russia, which was soon to become the USSR (Union of Soviet Socialist Republics).

The troubles and triumphs of nineteenth-century Europe can also be illuminated by looking at the socioeconomic scene. Not only were the old political regimes toppling, but the economic landscape was rapidly being transformed by the Industrial Revolution, as what had been a rural, agricultural world became an urban, industrial one. With the invention of the steam engine and all its related technologies, such as mills, factories, sewing machines, pumps, cutting and stamping tools, and cotton gins, as well as great networks of trains that transported the products of the new mercantilism across the vast reaches of Europe, Russia, and America, the economy changed radically. A "middle class" of entrepreneurs, businessmen, and industrialists emerged, achieving various levels of success, wealth, and power on the new capitalist pyramid that was being constructed. This middle class appropriated much of the power of the old landed gentry and of the aristocracy—holdovers from the Middle Ages. One reason for the failure of the restoration of the monarchies was this loss of power and wealth by supporters of the old monarchies.

But it was not simply the nobles and the gentry who were displaced. Much more literal was the displacement of hundreds of thousands of farmers and peasants who could no longer earn a

living off the land. They were flocking into the newly burgeoning cities, forced into slums with abominable living conditions, working fourteen hours a day, six days a week, for bare subsistence wages—if they were lucky. There was not always enough work for all. Or sometimes there was only work for specialized members of the family, such as small boys, who were especially sought after as chimney sweeps. It was into these turbulent times that Karl Marx, the "hero" (or "demon," depending on your perspective) of this chapter was born.

Biography

On May 8, 1818, Karl Marx was born in the old German city of Trier, near the French border. His ancestry was Jewish and included numerous rabbis, but his parents had converted to Protestantism so that the official anti-Semitism of the period would not hinder his father's legal career. At seventeen, Marx became engaged to his childhood sweetheart, Jenny von Westphalen. That same year he enrolled in the University of Bonn to study law, but he seems not to have been an entirely dedicated student. During his first semesters, he was wounded in a sword duel (and remained proud of his scar throughout his life) and was jailed for drunkenness. His angry father had him transferred to the University of Berlin, considered less of a "party school." There, Marx's interest in philosophy supplanted his interest

Karl Marx on Spring Break

in law, and he received his doctorate in 1841 by defending a dissertation on ancient Greek philosophy. He hoped for a university career, but because of his reputation for radical ideas and his association with certain professors who had been fired on political grounds, no university job was offered to him. Marx turned to journalism, rising within a year to the editorship of the new liberal newspaper *Die Rheinische Zeitung*.

When the Prussian government took a conservative swing in 1843, the censors closed down Marx's newspaper. He left Germany to take a coediting job in Paris with a new journal, *German-French Annals*, giving him an income that would finally allow him and his fiancée to marry. Jenny von Westphalen was of German and Scottish aristocratic background, being a direct descendant of the dukes of Argyll, but she renounced all the advantages these family connections might have given her when she married Marx. She agreed with his philosophical and political ideas, contributed to the development of his work, and was willing to share some of the extreme poverty that lay ahead of them. When the new journal folded, Marx was out of work again. Warrants for his arrest had been issued by the Prussian government based on the charge that the

Friedrich Engels (1820–1895)
and Karl Marx (1818–1883)

Annals was seditious, so Karl and Jenny could not return to Germany. Fortunately, Marx had been paid a sizable amount before the journal crashed, so in 1844, he began writing out his own philosophical thoughts in what was eventually published as *Philosophical and Economic Manuscripts*. That year he met Friedrich Engels, the son of a wealthy German industrialist who owned a factory in northern England. Unlike his father, Engels was a political and economic radical who soon began a writing collaboration with Marx that was to last a lifetime. They published their first book together in 1845.

However, Karl and Jenny Marx, along with their new baby girl, had to leave Paris when the French government succumbed to Prussian pressure to clamp down on German radicals living in France. The Marxes moved to Belgium, settling in Brussels for three years. Because Marx had virtually no income during this time, Engels helped him out financially. In 1848, a new revolution in France ushered in a left-wing government, and the Marxes were free to return to Paris and even to Berlin, where revolutionary fervor had also produced a leftist government. But these radical regimes were short-lived, and the Marxes (now with two daughters and a son) soon found themselves in London, where they hoped to wait out the political turmoil in Germany. As it turned out, they spent the rest of their lives there.

Despite occasional generous gifts from Engels, during their London exile the Marxes lived in poverty. Their fourth and fifth children died in infancy of diseases associated with malnutrition, and their only son died at age eight of tuberculosis. Finally, in 1852, Marx got a job as a European correspondent for the *New York Tribune*, which brought in a steady income. And in 1856, Jenny Marx received an inheritance that improved their financial condition considerably.

During this period, Marx continued to associate with revolutionaries and workers' groups, including the Communist Correspondence Committee, The Communist League, and the International Workingmen's Association— later called the First International, of which he became a leader. Marx also worked hard on various manuscripts from the 1840s until his death, but he allowed himself to be distracted by squabbles with rival left-wing thinkers, and much of his writing is directed against them.

Karl Marx and Other Radicals Duke It Out

Between 1844 and 1856, Marx wrote a number of important works that were not published until after his death. Some of these were not even available to the Bolshevik leaders of the Russian Revolution in 1917, so their versions of communism and Marxism were formulated without the advantage of some of these early, seminal works. (Not surprisingly, the official Soviet line came to be that those early works were insignificant, containing ideas that the mature Marx abandoned.) Nevertheless, he and Engels had made a name for themselves in radical circles by 1848 when they wrote *The Manifesto of the Communist Party*. In 1867, Marx finally published the first volume of *Capital*; the other two volumes would only appear after his death. Volume 1 was officially dubbed "The Bible of the working class" in 1868 by the Congress of the International. In fact, Marx's reputation as a writer among the general public was based more on his 1871 book *The Civil War in France*, about the Paris Commune and its suppression, than on his economic and philosophical writings.

Workers of the world, buy low, sell high!

By the time of the publication of that book, Marx was fifty-three, and his life was a mix of blessings and tragedies. On the positive side, his poverty was definitely over, as he actually earned some royalties from his books, and the legacies both to him and to Jenny left them relatively well off. (Marx even invested money in the stock market and bragged about the killing he made.) His fame among some circles and his infamy in others was growing as well. He had a comfortable new home and the undying love of his wife and three daughters. On the negative side, Marx was in poor health, he had lost control of the Congress of the International, three of his seven children were dead, and four of his grandchildren would die during this period. Also, with the family maid, Marx had fathered an illegitimate son who had been whisked off to live with foster parents.

In 1881, Jenny Marx died, leaving Karl alone and distraught. Then, eighteen months later, his beloved first daughter, Jenny, also died. This was the final blow. Within months, he had contracted bronchitis; he succumbed at his desk on March 14, 1883. He was sixty-four years old.

Marx's Theory

When Peter Singer wrote his little book called *Marx* for the Oxford University Press "Past Masters" series in 1979, he began by saying:

> Nearly four out of every ten people alive today live under governments which consider themselves Marxist and claim—however implausibly—to use Marxist principles to decide how the nation shall be run. In these countries Marx is a kind of secular Jesus: his writings are the ultimate source of truth and authority; his image is everywhere reverently displayed. The lives of hundreds of millions of people have been deeply affected by Marx's legacy.[1]

In fact, had India gone Communist, as it threatened to do at one point, more than half of the world's population would then have been living in so-called Marxist societies, and all within a hundred years of the publication of Marx's main works. Yet suddenly this Marxist monolith has toppled. Now only a handful of countries call themselves Marxist—most notably, Cuba,

North Korea, and China. China is the most populous nation in the world, has one of the largest armies in history, sits on some of the most expansive oil fields on the planet, and has potentially one of the major economies of the globe, so its Marxist orientation is no insignificant thing. Yet even China's Marxism seems so distant from that of its first Communist leader, Mao Tsetung, that the connection

between Marxism and China is decidedly tangential. At a minimum, China seems to be moving toward a market form of socialism that Marx did not foresee and of which he may not have approved.

All of these dramatic historical and political facts will be hard to ignore as we consider Karl Marx's theory of human nature. However, we must ignore them to the extent we can, because Marx's theory of human nature would remain what it is regardless of how history appropriated that theory after his death. (This is not to say, of course, that the rise and fall of communism will be treated with indifference in our evaluation of his theory, nor that theories remain static over time. Nor may it even be possible to recover in any absolute sense, the "original theory" of a thinker from the past.) Nevertheless, we will be aided in our attempt to concentrate on Marx's philosophical theory as distinct from the political history of Marxism when

we realize just how far actual Marxist states were and are from implementing Marx's theory as it will be laid out here.

Hegel

With Marx, as with Kierkegaard in Chapter 6, we must begin our story with the German metaphysician Hegel (1770–1831), whose wide-ranging philosophical writing influenced an entire generation of European intellectuals (or corrupted them, as Hegel's young contemporary, Arthur Schopenhauer, claimed). As you were warned in Chapter 6, Hegel's language is so dense and cryptic that there are many different interpretations of his meaning, with each interpreter defending passionately his or her version against forceful attacks by other interpreters. For instance, is Hegel a Christian, a **pantheist** (according to which reality itself is God), or an atheist? There are nimble defenses of each of these stances. All of this is Hegel's fault, for his writing is turgid, opaque, and deceptive, littered with brilliant but ambiguous metaphors and puzzling allusions. Therefore, here, as with the chapter on Kierkegaard, we will not try to locate the "real" Hegel; rather, we will attempt to set forth a few of Hegel's main ideas as Marx himself seems to have understood them.

...and what do you think of freedom, Herr Professor Hegel?

I'm all for it. In fact, I am it.

In Marx's view, Hegel is primarily a philosopher of freedom. (You'll remember that Kierkegaard specifically rejected this interpretation.) In fact, for Hegel, the goal of history is the final revelation of Freedom, which Hegel equates with Reason.

= Mutual dependency

= Opposition, contradiction

= Transcendence, overcoming ("Aufhebung")

The Dialectic

Freedom is the realization of Reason because Reason penetrates the dark forces of ignorance and contingency that bind us. Reason frees us from our fetters. History moves *dialectically* from unreason and unfreedom to Reason and Freedom. That is, society at any given moment is a cluster of contradictions (theses and antitheses) whose resolution (synthesis) results in the overthrow (*Aufhebung*) of the old contradictory conditions by bringing together certain positive features from each side of the opposition and eliminating others.

Each new historical moment produces an advance of Freedom, even if it is not always obvious that this is so. For example, ancient Athens and ancient Rome were democracies that advocated liberty and autonomy for their citizens, yet both were slave-holding societies. This latter fact shows that "freedom" was misunderstood in Greece and Rome even by those that advocated it—as it always is by all "masters" and "slaves." The collapse of the classical world (ancient Greece and Rome) led, after the Dark Ages, to a feudal system of rule. This medieval political arrangement may not seem on the surface to be an "advance of Freedom." But for Hegel, it is indeed progress, because in the Middle Ages universal law was promoted under the influ-

Hey! At least I'm free!

Me too.

It's all the work of the cunning of reason.

ence of Christianity, and labor was performed not by slaves but by serfs who had rights under that law. The fact that this progress is hidden was due to what Hegel calls "the cunning of Reason."

So, once again, history is the history of the emergence of freedom— or, more accurately, of the *idea* of freedom, for Hegel is an *idealist*. That means he believes that ideas and the whole mental world are ontologically most important—that is, they have a higher status in reality than do matter and the whole physical world. Even if matter in some sense came before mind, matter is *potentially* mind. In other words, mind, or spirit (the German word *Geist* means both of these) evolved out of matter, so matter is *potential* spirit, and indeed spirit (= reason = freedom) is the meaning of matter.

Hegel and Marx

The radical philosophy students of Karl Marx's generation were known as the "Young Hegelians." They disliked what they took to be the conservative political implications of Hegel's philosophy. (Hegel, who as a German university professor was paid by the German government, had gone so far as to say that the repressive Prussian state of Emperor Friedrich Wilhelm was the epitome of Reason and Freedom.) These Young Hegelians blamed much of Hegel's error on his idealism, which they believed minimized and even justified real human suffering as an "idea" that was in the service of the cunning of Reason.

But the Young Hegelians, including Marx, were still captivated by Hegel's theory of the dialectic, so they turned Hegel's dialectic against itself. The dialectic, after all, was not only the account of the laws of history and of thought, and not only a theory of progress, but also a *method* of analyzing and philosophizing according to which we are advised to see all things in terms of their opposites. (For example, in his famous analysis of the master–slave relationship, Hegel had argued that the masters' freedom is really a form of slavery and that slavery is really a form of [future] freedom, because the masters are dependent on the slaves for both their identity and their well-being, while the slaves are dependent on the masters only for their unhappiness. By opposing the masters, the slaves have everything to gain.) In a certain sense, Hegel claimed, everything is its opposite. So the

Turning Hegel Upside Down

Young Hegelians turned Hegel upside down and derived a new Hegelianism from the *Aufhebung*, or "overturning," of Hegel. **Materialism** (the view that the material world has priority over the "spiritual" world) became the now-revealed secret of Hegel's idealism, and radical politics—or even revolutionary politics—became the now-exposed secret of Hegel's conservatism. According to these wayward disciples, this little dialectical inversion clears up the confusion in Hegel's dialectic. As Marx wrote in 1873:

> The mystification which dialectic suffers in Hegel's hands by no means prevents him from being the first to present its general form of working in a comprehensive and conscious manner. With him it is standing on its head. It must be turned right side up again if you would discover the rational kernel within the mystical shell.[2]

Besides the dialectic, another Hegelian theme that excited the Young Hegelians was that of "alienation," which was Hegel's term for the loss of self-identity. Human beings as self-conscious beings are, in fact, manifestations of spirit, and hence of freedom. But, as we have seen, throughout history humans have failed to understand their own freedom (reason); therefore, they have failed to grasp their own selfhood. They have confronted themselves as alien beings; they are self-alienated. (Hegel even goes so far as to talk of the self-alienation of God, who confronts his own

Satan—God's Dialectical "Other"

negative self in Satan.) Hegel's great masterpiece, *The Phenomenology of Spirit* (1807) theorizes about this self-alienation, showing how it necessarily came about and how it will necessarily be aufgehoben—"overcome." (Unfortunately, Hegel seems to say that the publication of *The Phenomenology of Spirit* itself signals the end of alienation.)

To what extent is Marx's theory Hegelian? There is much debate over this question. Some argue that the mature Marx totally escaped the dreamy Hegelianism of his youthful writings; others claim that there is a clear dedication to Hegelian themes throughout the various developments of Marx's theory. Certainly, Marx increasingly abandoned Hegelian terminology as his career progressed, and he became less interested in being thought of as a philosopher and more interested in being seen as both a scientist and a political activist. As

READ ALL ABOUT IT! History ends with me!

Do you take credit cards?

Marx wrote in 1845, remonstrating against both Hegel and the Young Hegelians (notably, Ludwig Feuerbach):[3]

The philosophers have only interpreted the world in various ways; the point, however, is to change it.

As Marx says, he stood Hegel on his head—or he stood him upright, if we, like Marx, assume that Hegel already was standing on his head from the beginning. As with the young Hegelians, Hegel's idealism becomes materialism, and his conservatism becomes revolutionary. Marx moves away from Hegelian metaphysical speculation (philosophy) and toward empirically testable hypotheses (science). Just as Aristotle tried to bring Platonism "down to earth," Marx tries to ground the dialectic in real, everyday activity. He writes in 1846, "In direct contrast to German philosophy, which descends from heaven to earth, here we ascend from earth to heaven."[4]

Alienation

"Alienation" proves to be one of the Hegelian themes developed throughout Marx's career. Although the term (*Verfremdung*) appears much more often in his early writings, it still shows up in significant passages of *Capital*, his most mature work. As we have seen, Hegel claims that the mind is alienated from itself. It fails to grasp itself as Absolute Idea, which is to say, as pure freedom. Marx, contrary to Hegel, sees human life not as primarily a mental process, but as *action*. The human is not *Homo sapiens* (man the knower), but *Homo faber* (man the maker or doer). Humans are natural producers, natural creators. So, of course, are animals like ants, bees, and beavers, but these creatures produce "in the realm of necessity" and not in "the realm of freedom." These animals, Marx says, "produce only under the compulsion of direct physical need, while man produces when he is free from physical need and only produces in freedom from such need."[5] This was written in 1844, yet even in the book that he was writing when he died almost forty years later, Volume 3 of *Capital*, Marx repeats this Hegelian idea:

When Mother Nature Speaks, Brother Beaver Listens

"In fact, the realm of freedom does not commence until the point is passed where labor under the compulsion of necessity and of external utility is required. In the very nature of things it lies beyond the sphere of material production in the strict meaning of the term."[6] Indeed, the human being "constructs also in accordance with the laws of beauty."[7] Therefore, when human beings are alienated from themselves, it is their powers of production and their artistic creativity from which they are alienated; they confront their own works as alien beings and as enemies. This is what Marx calls "alienated labor."

Of all the systems of production in the social history of the world, only slavery creates greater alienation of labor than does capitalism. Here is how Marx describes this alienation:

The Human Being Constructs in Accordance with the Laws of Beauty

What constitutes the alienation of labor? First, that the work is *external* to the worker, that it is not part of his nature; and that, consequently, he does not fulfill himself in his work but denies himself, has a feeling of misery rather than well being, does not develop freely his mental and physical energies but is physically exhausted and mentally debased. The worker therefore feels himself at home only during his leisure time, whereas at work he feels homeless. His work is not voluntary but imposed, *forced labor*. It is not the satisfaction of a need, but only a *means* for satisfying other needs. Its alien character is clearly shown by the fact that as soon as there is no physical or other compulsion it is avoided like the plague. External labor, labor in which man alienates himself, is a labor of self-sacrifice, of mortification. Finally, the external character of work for the worker is shown by the fact that it is not his own work but work for someone else, that in work he does not belong to himself but to another person.[8]

Clearly, Marx believes himself to be describing the conditions in the factories of Britain and the rest of Europe in the middle of the nineteenth century. Even the classical economists of early capitalism (Adam Smith, David Ricardo, Thomas Malthus, whom Marx calls "political economists") know that these conditions found in the urban factories of mid-nineteenth-century Europe are part of the essence of capitalism according to Marx:

> The alienation of the worker in his object is expressed as follows in the laws of political economy: the more the worker produces the less he has to consume; the more value he creates the more worthless he becomes; the more refined his product the more crude and misshapen the worker; the more civilized the product the more barbarous the worker; the more powerful the work the more feeble the worker; the more the work manifests intelligence the more the worker declines in intelligence and becomes a slave of nature.[9]

And finally:

> The *alien* being to whom labor and the product of labor belong, to whose service labor is devoted, and to whose enjoyment the product of labor goes, can only be *man* himself. If the product of labor does not belong to the worker, but confronts him as an alien power, this can only be because it belongs to a *man other than the worker*. If his activity is a torment to him it must be a source of enjoyment and pleasure to another. Not the gods, nor nature, but only man himself can be this alien power over men.[10]

History and Human Desire

So we have now seen a large chunk of Marx's theory of human nature: We humans are *Homo faber*—creators, producers, artists—and yet it is possible to alienate ourselves from this essential feature of our existence. Our productive powers can be systematically stolen from us and even turned against us.

Besides our always endangered natural creativity, what other features of human nature does Marx list? He draws a distinction between

"human nature in general" and "human nature as modified in each historical epoch."[11] This distinction would apply to the concept of *Homo faber*
(humans are producers in general, but historical conditions determine what
and how they produce), as well as to the other categories that are natural
to us, such as Marx's idea
(borrowed from Ludwig
Feuerbach) of humans as
species-beings. That is,
humans are conscious of
being members of the human
race and of having interests
in common with other hu-
mans, of being dependent
upon others. Humans, then,
are essentially *social* beings
—though, once again, not in
the way that ants and bees
are. In fact, Marx goes so
far as to say, "The human
essence is no abstraction
inherent in each single individual. In its reality it is the ensemble of the
social relations."[12] (This is another lesson Marx learned from Hegel, and
it provides ammunition for those critics who charge Hegel and Marx with
believing that individuals as such do not exist; they exist only in societies.)
So our social nature is a fixed part of our universal essence, but historical
conditions determine the nature of the social relations at any particular
historical moment and geographical point. In that sense, human nature
changes from one historical period to another.

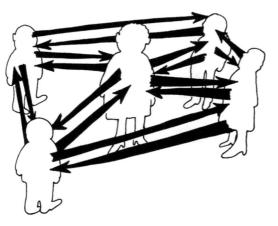

**Human Nature: A Concatenation
of Social Relationships**

Marx gives the same kind of relativistic analysis to what we might
call our basic biological needs. Hunger, thirst, and the need for warmth, for
exercise, and for companionship—social and sexual—are constant biological features, and these needs produce desires. But the actual form that
these desires take is determined by relations to other humans (another
Hegelian idea). In this sense, desires are not fixed, but are social in nature.
Somewhat paradoxically, we create society as a response to our needs and
desires, but then society takes over those needs and desires, restructuring
them; "history" is the result of this social hegemony over needs ("as soon
as a need is satisfied, . . . new needs are made, and this production of new
needs is the first historical act"[13]). As one Marxist scholar writes, "Society
continually alters human nature, and it may become part of man's nature
to want a deodorant."[14]

This last point brings up a tricky issue for Marx, because despite his commitment to the historical relativity of needs and desires, he also draws a distinction between "true needs"[15] and "false needs." He characterizes **false needs** as "inhuman, depraved, unnatural, and *imaginary* appetites."[16] He uses this distinction to arrive at one of his most powerful critiques of capitalism, for it is the essence of capitalism to create false needs. In capitalism,

> Every man speculates upon creating a *new* need in another in order to force him to a new sacrifice, to place him in a new dependence, and to entice him into a new kind of pleasure and thereby into economic ruin. Everyone tries to establish over others an *alien* power in order to find there the satisfaction of his own egoistic need. With the mass of objects, therefore, there also increases the realm of alien entities to which man is subjected. Every new product is a new *potentiality* of mutual deceit and robbery.[17]

The very product that entices one's desire therefore becomes a "useful" product, but the capitalists forget that "the production of too many useful things results in too many useless people."[18]

There seems to be an inconsistency between Marx's category of false needs and his insistence on the historicity of needs. It is as if Marx should have said that the needs created and fulfilled by capitalist production are not "false" needs but are the "true" needs of people in capitalist societies. Perhaps the tension here can be alleviated by appealing to Marx's idea of species-being. The need to be able to choose among three breakfast cereals each morning is a false need if most people in the world are underfed. When there is plenty for all, such needs are no longer false. The need for a home with many rooms and a view over the valley is a false need when many people have no home at all; but when all are well housed, such needs are no longer unnatural.

Right now, I would say that the need to read Marx is not a "true need" for me.

Materialism

If a society is no more than the sum total of the relationships within it, how is it that a social structure can take on a life of its own, and can produce, for example, whole cultures of "useless people"? To answer this question, we will now turn to Marx's "materialism." Let us examine a few key passages in which Marx sets forth his materialist theory of the structure of society:

> In the social production which men carry on they enter into definite relations that are indispensable and independent of their will; these relations of production correspond to a definite stage of development of their material powers of production. The sum total of these relations of production constitutes the economic structure of society—the real foundation, on which rise legal and political superstructures and to which correspond definite forms of social consciousness. The mode of production of material life determines

the general character of the social, political, and spiritual processes of life. It is not the consciousness of men that determines their existence, but, on the contrary, their social existence determines their consciousness.[19]

Rosie the Riveter

So the "foundation" of society[20] is composed of the "relations of production," the "material powers of production" and "the mode of production." The material powers of production comprise labor power (the productive force of workers—their strength, ability, and knowledge) and the modes of production (the raw materials, tools, and machines, and the locations where these are put into play).[21] These powers of production determine the "relations of production"—that is, the actual relations among workers. These, then, are the foundation of society on which is built a "superstructure"—legal and political agencies such as courts, prisons, police forces and armies, lawyers' offices, congresses, parliaments, "oval offices," and palaces.

We can now add another layer to our model—what might be called "higher culture." This would include art, religion, morality, literature, poetry, and philosophy. These Marx calls **ideology,** meaning that these forms of higher culture are really "echoes," "reflexes," and "sublimates" of the economic foundation. Thus, they provide a kind of political propaganda for a specific historical form of production, and, at the same time, a disguise, covering the dialectical contra-

dictions of that partic-
ular economic structure.
This propaganda is not
meant to convince oppo-
nents of the system and
win them over; rather, it
is meant to convince
members of the "in-
group" of the correct-
ness of their beliefs and
behavior. Ideology is the
intellectual story a cul-
ture tells to itself in
order to justify itself to
itself (as when Plato, the
aristocrat, discovers the
eternal truth that in perfect societies aristo-
crats rule; or when Aris-

Aristotle Explains Slavery

totle writes in a slave-holding society that gives no political rights to
women that slaves have incomplete human souls, and probably women do as well; or when Des-cartes, writing to a Catholic community, "proves" that the human being is essentially soul). Marx says that "morality, religion, metaphysics, all the rest of ideology and their corresponding forms of consciousness . . . no longer retain the sem-blance of independence; they have no history, no development."[22]

But the ideological sphere is not seamless. There are conflicts there, too, because the economic world that it represents is also in conflict. Nevertheless, as Marx says, "The ruling ideas of each age have ever been the ideas of the ruling class."[23]

The Proletariat

This account of ideology is yet another picture of alienation, as in it we are all trapped by propaganda and its "corresponding form of consciousness"—namely, **false consciousness.** We misunderstand our own motives and situation. For example, in a political "democracy," we will use our "freedom" to vote in politicians who are dedicated to defending the privileges of a wealthy minority who do not have our interests in mind. We will also commit our labor and our wealth to the production and consumption of useless products that are only "useful" relative to the values of a useless society. All of this is true, for Marx, except for the case of one group—the working class, the proletariat.

Marx believes that the "proletariat" ("the class of modern wage laborers who, having no means of production of their own, are reduced to selling their labor power in order to live") are, like the "bourgeoisie" ("the class of modern capitalists, owners of the means of social production and employers of wage labor"),[24] alienated people, but because of their physical misery, the proletarians recognize their alienation for what it is. They, and only they, do not live in a state of false consciousness and need no ideology to justify their political aspirations. These aspirations are revolutionary in nature. Therefore, without the proletariat's realizing it, these aspirations are motivated not merely by class interests but also in concordance with the laws of history, for "the dialectic" (the laws of history) is the story of revolution. (Reminder: "Thesis" and "antithesis" [for example, master and slave] are mutually dependent but also in contradiction with each other. They eventually clash, and there is a revolution [Aufhebung] in which features of both thesis and antithesis are combined [synthesis] and carried forward as a

I am in misery, therefore, I exist.

new thesis.) Indeed, the beginning of the *Manifesto of the Communist Party* tells us: "The history of all hitherto existing society is the history of class struggles."[25]

The Discovery of Private Property

Why will the revolution of the proletariat be the last revolution, according to Marx? First, all earlier revolutions were motivated by merely *class* interests. But for Marx, perhaps romanticizing the working class a bit, the proletariat now represents not only itself but also the interests of the whole of the human race. Therefore, whereas all other revolutions (slave revolts in Rome; peasant revolts in the Middle Ages; the British ("Glorious"), American, and French revolutions in the seventeenth and eighteenth centuries) still produced alienated individuals (for example, the revolutionary peasants of the medieval period who acted in the name of religion), the revolutionary proletarians have no ideology and are rebelling against alienation itself. Hence, they will not bring the seeds of alienation into the new world that their revolution creates—well, at least not in the *long* term. But because the revolutionary generation was raised in conditions of alienation, the victorious workers may tend to fall back into the old ways of greed, acquisitiveness, and status-mongering. This is why a "dictatorship of the proletariat" may be needed for a generation

The Victorious Workers Take Over the Factory

or two—but not to worry! This dictatorship will dissolve itself when it sees that its work is complete.

Furthermore, the virtue of capitalism, as opposed to all the other "ruling classes" in history, is that it actually produced the machinery that could meet the "true needs" of all humans—which had never happened before. Of course, the capitalists did not ask the question, "How shall we use these materials to end misery?" Rather, they asked, "How shall we use these materials to make a profit?" But now, when the revolutionaries seize the machinery, tools,

Yes. I believe I've done a good job here. I think I'll just step down now and give the power back to the people.

RIGHTTT.

COMRADE STALIN

and technology, they can use them to feed, house, clothe, and medically care for all present and future generations. Therefore, no former revolution could have been the revolution to end all revolutions.

The dialectic (the history of hitherto existing society) was the history of class conflict. But because there will be no social classes after this final revolution, there will be no class conflict, and the dialectic will end. Therefore, the revolution will be "the closing chapter of the prehistoric stage of human society."[26] True human history will have begun.

It is difficult not to notice the almost religious fervor in this account. Just as in the New Testament, "the first shall be last and the last shall be first." Marx's theory of history is even structured something like the Christian account. In the Bible, human history begins in a paradisiacal garden. In Marx, it begins with hunter-gatherer societies that he calls "primitive communism." In Christianity, something goes wrong (sin), and humans are expelled from their paradise. In Marxism, too, something goes wrong (the development of private property, alienation, and social classes of haves and have-nots), and humans are expelled from their primitive conditions.

In these two accounts, the bulk of human history "hitherto" has been the history of sin or of alienation, respectively. Then, in Christianity, a voice is heard, crying in the desert wilderness, "Prepare ye the way. Prepare ye the way" (John the Baptist). In Marxism, a voice is heard, crying in the urban

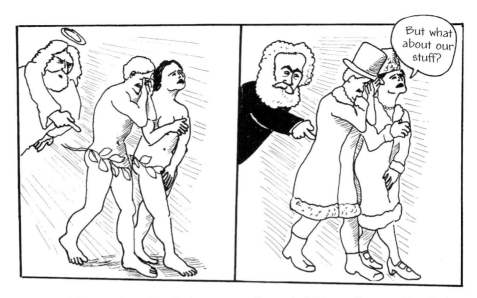

**Adam and Eve Expelled
from the Garden of Eden**

**Owners of Private Property Expelled
from Primitive Communism**

wilderness, "Workingmen of all countries, unite!"[27] These two voices each initiate a series of events, which in turn unleash a final apocalypse or a final revolution, respectively. (If Karl Marx is John the Baptist, who will play the role of Jesus? Vladimir Lenin? Joseph Stalin seems to have thought it was himself, but most Marxists today see him as a kind of Antichrist figure.) These history-ending events are followed by a reentry into paradise (heaven or communism, respectively), which in both cases is higher than the original paradise that was lost— higher because there is now *knowledge*, whereas in the earlier paradise there was ignorance, *happy* ignorance, but ignorance nonetheless. Marx himself seems to encourage such a speculative comparison between his theory and religious revelations by consciously

A Voice Crying in the Wilderness

using biblical quotations and metaphors as rhetorical devices throughout his works.

It should be added that Marx also gives a much more technical account of revolution than the somewhat romantic one we've examined. He says:

> At a certain stage of their development the material forces of production in society come into conflict with the existing relations of production, or—what is but a legal expression for the same thing—with the property relations within which they had been at work before. From forms of development of the forces of production these relations turn into their fetters. Then comes the period of social revolution. With the change of the economic foundation the entire immense superstructure is more or less rapidly transformed.[28]

Here, developments in the forces of production outstrip the old relations of production, which now fetter progress. (In other words, new inventions, technical breakthroughs, and realignments of workers result in productive possibilities that are prevented by prevailing property arrangements, such as ownership of the means of production by nonworking financial speculators.) In these cases, the potentialities themselves overwhelm the restrictions on them, and a social revolution (not necessarily a bloody one) takes place. This account of the causes of revolution is not the same as the one we examined

earlier, though it is in most ways compatible with it. However, this account seems to play down class conflict as the main vehicle of historical change.

Economics

Based on what you've already read, you might think that our chapter on Marx's theory of human nature could be subtitled "Human Nature As Determined by Economics." But, in fact, exactly the opposite is the case. For Marx, human nature can blossom only in "the realm of freedom," which actually is beyond the realm of economics. According to him, economic bondage is the chief form of alienation. The classical economists, like J-B Say, Malthus, Smith, and Ricardo, believed that they had discovered the absolute and objective laws of economics. They were the ones who showed that workers must prostitute their essence—their productive force—and sell it as a commodity, thereby turning themselves into commodities, subject to the laws of supply and

The Escape from the Prison of Economics

demand. According to these laws, there must be more workers than jobs, and the employed workers must compete with the unemployed for the available jobs, guaranteeing that wages will always be at bare subsistence level (that is, only enough to keep the worker and his family alive). The classical economists also correctly saw that the capitalists garnered their wealth from the labor of the workers by ignoring "use value" (the worth of an hour's labor to satisfy someone's need) and by insisting on "exchange value" (the amount of value deriving from the sales of the workers' product). Thus, capitalists can become wealthy by accumulating as "surplus value" the amount of profit earned by the workers' labor over and above the amount needed to pay them subsistence wages. For example, when capitalists invest in new machinery to raise productivity, *their* wealth increases, but not the wealth of the workers.

The classical economists knew all of these things. What they did not know, Marx tells us, is that their so-called universal economic laws were merely the laws of *capitalism,* an egregious but historically necessary form of human alienation. For instance, there is no such thing as the law of supply and demand; capitalism creates (false) needs in order to be able to fill the needs it just created by providing new products, and each new need leads to yet another, generating a world chock-a-block full of commodities, including people who have become mere objects for sale—workers and "consumers."

The classical economists also failed to realize, according to Marx, that the *real laws of history*—the dialectic—demonstrated that capitalism contained the seeds of its own destruction. The dialectic of inflation and unemployment (thesis: the cure to inflation is unemployment; antithesis: the cure to unemployment is inflation) would produce a series of ever greater economic crises, until finally reaching explosive critical mass. The need for ever cheaper labor and more and more natural resources to exploit would produce competition between capitalist states leading to disastrous wars of colonialism. The so-called natural laws of competition would lead to their own opposite, monopoly, as more and more business owners lost out in the commercial war of each against all and were thrown into the working class, whose ranks were ever swelling and whose eventual sheer mass would overwhelm the shrinking ranks of the monopolists. All of this, the dialectic predicted, would bring about the workers' revolution that would end prehistory and usher us into a social paradise—communism.

Communism

Given this inevitable historical outcome, you might expect that Marx would have written a lot about the nature of communism. He did not. Apparently, he felt that from within "prehuman history" he could not predict exactly what form "true human history" would take. We will inspect one or two of the few passages in which he discusses his future communist utopia. In the *Economic and Philosophical Manuscripts of 1844*, Marx wrote:

> Communism is the *positive* abolition of *private property*, of human self-alienation, and thus the real *appropriation* of *human* nature through and for man. It is, therefore, the return of man himself as a *social*, i.e., really

human, being, a complete and conscious return which assimilates all the wealth of previous development. Communism as a fully-developed naturalism is humanism and as a fully-developed humanism is naturalism. It is the definitive resolution of the antagonism between man and nature, and between man and man. It is the true solution of the conflict between existence and essence, between objectification and self-affirmation, between freedom and necessity, between individual and species. It is the solution of the riddle of history and knows itself to be this solution.[29]

Two years later, in *The German Ideology*, in the context of a discussion of the "division of labor" in historical societies, and especially in capitalism, where each person must truncate his or her naturally expansive creative powers by becoming exclusively a specialist in one detail or another of the world of commodities, Marx gives us a rather fascinating picture of life under future communism:

> In communist society, where nobody has one exclusive sphere of activity but each can become accomplished in any branch he wishes, society regulates the general production and thus makes it possible for me to do one thing today and another to-morrow, to hunt in the morning, fish in the afternoon, rear cattle in the evening, criticize after dinner, just as I have a mind, without ever becoming a hunter, fisherman, shepherd or critic.[30]

Notice first that, under communism, "society regulates the general production." This was always an important idea to Marx and Engels, who asserted that, under laissez-faire capitalism, economics created a world of its own and with it "useless" human beings. What was needed was for human beings to take control of economics rather than allowing economics to control them. This would be economics produced "with a collective will according to a collective plan," as Engels wrote in 1894.[31] There would still be onerous economic tasks to perform (somebody has to dig the wells and empty the septic tanks). But if everyone was expected to work for the social good only a few days a week, then with the help of the tools and technology left by the old capitalists, this would produce enough labor in "the realm of necessity" to feed, clothe, and care for all human beings. The rest of one's week would be spent in "the realm of freedom." Furthermore, human creativity is so expansive (Marx is primarily an *optimist*) that much of free productivity would have social use, reducing necessary labor even more. (Maybe some people *like* to dig holes.) By the way, Marx is not arguing here against specialization; even he does not want his brain operated on by a part-time shepherd. He is arguing against *exclusivity*, whereby a brain surgeon is *only* a brain surgeon and a shepherd *only* a shepherd.

Otherwise, this depiction by Marx of future communism is remarkable for its pastoral setting. Except for poetry criticism, all the other examples Marx gives are rural. Hunting, fishing, rearing cattle and sheep—is this a pastoral romanticism on Marx's part? Or should we understand this as hinting that future communists will abandon the cities and return to self-sufficient communes in the countryside, where the rule will be "From each according to his ability, to each according to his needs"![32]

Summary

Karl Marx's theory of human nature is in many ways one of the most optimistic visions to be set forth in this book. According to Marx, we humans are naturally social animals, and to realize the full potential of our species-being, we have only to tear down the artificial barriers that have impeded our return to ourselves—that is, our return to ourselves as *Homo faber,* "man the producer." Humans are naturally creators of abundance, and "in the fullness of time," this power of creativity will inevitably generate a fully human society in which each person finds his or her multiple forms of creative expression "according to the laws of beauty"—perhaps in a pastoral paradise in which we

Tearing Down the Barriers to Selfhood

tend our flocks, hunt, fish, fence, and critically analyze poetry.

Regarded in this light, Marx is definitely a man of his age. As we saw in the historical introduction to this chapter, the story of nineteenth-century Europe is the story—told in fits and starts—of something called *liberté,* which had been discovered at the end of the eighteenth century. Karl Marx wanted to be first the philosopher of this *liberté* and then its scientist. This desire to be *Homo scientificus* is fitting for Marx's age, which is an age of increasing positivism (the conviction that all knowledge is ultimately scientific knowledge). By standing Hegel on his head, Marx believed that he had discovered certain laws of history that would ineluctably lead to human liberation.

Yet Marx's optimism is paradoxical in several ways. First, there is the rather awkward, if not contradictory, position Marx chose for himself of both scientist (discovering the laws that determine history, describing them, and showing how to take advantage of their knowledge) and political

It's really all molecules.

That's the most beautiful sunset I've ever seen...

...and that's the greatest picture ever painted...

...and my sweetheart, whom I love deeply, is the artist.

activist (urging the workers of the world to unite and perform a heroic revolution whose success would require timely, urgent action and great personal sacrifice). It is difficult to reconcile these two roles.

Second, Marx's insight concerning the historicity of human nature, according to which human nature is not fixed because changing historical conditions modify it, seems somewhat at odds with his theory of alienation, according to which changing historical conditions can estrange us from our true human nature. Indeed, it is puzzling that a philosopher who claims that we must take history seriously if we are to understand human nature would also claim that human nature has been alienated from itself throughout the bulk of recorded history.

There is, of course, the very serious question of the extent to which actual Communist nations truly embodied "Marxism" as Marx would have understood it. It is difficult to imagine that he would have approved of most of the policies implemented in his name by countries such as the former Soviet Union, North Korea, and Cambodia. But Marx's optimism about human nature is so generous and his belief in the inevitability of justice is so strong that it has made him complicit in some of the serious abuses committed in his name. Marx was so convinced of the ultimate triumph of liberty and equality that he made few provisions addressing potential abuses of power in future Communist societies.

There is an unfortunate connection between this theoretical failure and the rise of Communist dictators like Joseph Stalin of the former Soviet Union and Pol Pot of Cambodia. Moreover, there are obvious errors in the factual predictions made by his theories. For example, successful Communist revolutions took place not in the most industrialized nations, where proletarian consciousness was the highest, but in the least industrialized

nations, such as Russia, China, and Cuba. Capitalism did not collapse internally; rather, it proved itself flexible enough to change in the face of some of its problems (which Marx correctly described). The living conditions of workers improved rather than deteriorated in most of the industrial world. It is international communism rather than international capitalism that seems to have collapsed, partly because of internal problems within Communist countries and among Communist alliances, and partly because of having been outspent by conservative capitalist political leaders in the Cold War.

Finally, then, it must be said that the many weaknesses in Marx's theory, and in those societies claiming to put that theory into practice, seriously damage his credibility. But these mistakes do not annul his many valuable insights. His understanding that societies take on a life of their own and operate according to laws that are invisible to most of their members makes him one of the founders of modern sociology. His insistence on the importance of economic motivations within fields that seem distant from economics (politics, art, medicine, education, and religion, among others) makes him thoroughly modern. His insistence (along with Hegel) that human nature must be understood historically breaks the Platonic mold of ahistorical essences holding sway over all things. His theory of creativity is refreshing and hopeful. And, despite his many errors about capitalism, his critique of its abuses and unintended effects deserves serious consideration.

Topics for Consideration

1. What features of nineteenth-century European history does Marx's theory address?

2. To what extent is Marx's philosophy Hegelian, and to what extent is it anti-Hegelian?

3. Explain the Hegelian "dialectic," using some examples from your own experience (for example, relations between parent and child, or teacher and student, or employer and employee).

4. Discuss the idea of "freedom" in the nineteenth century in general, in Hegel's philosophy, and in Marx's philosophy.

5. Discuss the idea of "alienation." Show how, in Marxian terms, it would be possible to become alienated from nature, from fellow human beings, and from oneself.

6. Humans, bees, and ants are all "social animals." In what ways do we differ from nonhuman social animals, according to Marx?

7. Explain how it is possible for Marx to say that there is something permanent in human nature, yet also to say that human nature changes over time.

8. Critically examine Marx's distinction between "true needs" and "false needs."

9. Compare Marx's vision of communist society with such historically existent societies calling themselves "Communist" as the former Soviet Union.

10. Explain what Marx means by "ideology," using examples from your own knowledge and experience.

Suggestions for Further Reading

I. Marx's Main Works

Capital: A Critique of Political Economy. New York: International, 1967.

Economic and Philosophical Manuscripts. Trans. T. B. Bottomore. In Erich Fromm, *Marx's Concept of Marx.* New York: Ungar, 1969.

Marx and Engels: Basic Writings on Politics and Philosophy. Ed. Lewis S. Feuer. Garden City, N.Y.: Doubleday/Anchor, 1959. (Contains, among other writings, *Theses on Feuerbach, The German Ideology, Manifesto of the Communist Party, A Contribution to the Critique of Political Economy.*)

II. Secondary Sources on Marx

Cohen, G. A. *Karl Marx's Theory of History: A Defense*. Oxford: Clarendon Press, 1978.

Fromm, Erich. *Marx's Concept of Man*. New York: Ungar, 1969, pp. 1–89.

McClellan, David. *Karl Marx: His Life and Thought*. New York and London: Macmillan, 1973.

Rader, Melvin. *Marx's Interpretation of History*. New York and Oxford: Oxford University Press, 1979.

Singer, Peter. *Marx*. New York and Oxford: Oxford University Press, 1983.

Tucker, Robert. *Philosophy and Myth in Karl Marx*. Cambridge: Cambridge University Press, 1961.

Notes

1. Peter Singer, *Marx* (Oxford: Oxford University Press, 1983), p. 2.
2. Karl Marx, *Capital: A Critique of Political Economy*, Vol. 1, in Lewis S. Feuer, ed., *Marx and Engels: Basic Writings on Politics and Philosophy* (Garden City, N.Y.: Doubleday/Anchor, 1959), p. 146.
3. Karl Marx, *Theses on Feuerbach*, in Feuer, ed., *Marx and Engels*, p. 245.
4. Karl Marx, *The German Ideology*, in Feuer, ed., *Marx and Engels*, p. 247.
5. Karl Marx, *Economic and Philosophical Manuscripts*, in Erich Fromm, *Marx's Concept of Man* (New York: Ungar, 1969), p. 102.
6. Karl Marx, *Capital*, Vol. 3, in Fromm, *Marx's Concept*, p. 59.
7. Marx, *Economic and Philosophical Fragments*, in Fromm, *Marx's Concept*, p. 103.
8. Marx, *Economic and Philosophical Fragments*, in Fromm, *Marx's Concept*, pp. 98–99.
9. Marx, *Economic and Philosophical Fragments*, in Fromm, *Marx's Concept*, p. 97.
10. Marx, *Economic and Philosophical Fragments*, in Fromm, *Marx's Concept*, p. 104.
11. Marx, *Capital*, in Fromm, *Marx's Concept*, p. 25.
12. Marx, *Theses on Feuerbach*, in Feuer, ed., *Marx and Engels*, p. 244.
13. Marx, *The German Ideology*, in Fromm, *Marx's Concept*, p. 201.
14. G. A. Cohen, *Karl Marx's Theory of History: A Defense* (Oxford: Clarendon Press, 1978), p. 103.
15. Karl Marx, *Introduction to the Critique of Hegel's Philosophy of Law. Critique of Religion*, in Fromm, *Marx's Concept*, p. 220.
16. Marx, *Economic and Philosophical Manuscripts*, in Fromm, *Marx's Concept*, p. 141.
17. Marx, *Economic and Philosophical Manuscripts*, in Fromm, *Marx's Concept*, pp. 140–141.
18. Marx, *Economic and Philosophical Manuscripts*, in Fromm, *Marx's Concept*, p. 145.
19. Karl Marx, *A Contribution to the Critique of Political Economy*, in Feuer, ed., *Marx and Engels*, p. 43.

20. Notice that just as Descartes viewed the "structure of knowledge" in terms of the metaphor of a building, so does Marx view the "structure of society" using the same metaphor.

21. Here I am following Cohen's account in *Karl Marx's Theory of History*, p. 85.

22. Marx, *The German Ideology*, in Fromm, *Marx's Concept*, p. 198.

23. Karl Marx and Friedrich Engels, *Manifesto of the Communist Party*, in Feuer, ed., *Marx and Engels*, p. 26.

24. These definitions are found in a note added to the *Manifesto of the Communist Party* by Friedrich Engels after Marx's death; in Feuer, ed., *Marx and Engels*, p. 7.

25. Feuer, ed., *Marx and Engels*, p. 7.

26. Marx, *Critique of Political Economy*, in Feuer, ed., *Marx and Engels*, p. 44.

27. Marx and Engels, *Manifesto*, in Feuer, ed., *Marx and Engels*, p. 41.

28. Marx, *Critique of Political Economy*, in Feuer, ed., *Marx and Engels*, pp. 43–44.

29. Karl Marx, *Economic and Philosophical Manuscripts*, in Fromm, *Marx's Concept*, p. 127 (emphases in original).

30. Marx, *The German Ideology*, in Fromm, *Marx's Concept*, p. 206.

31. Friedrich Engels, "Letter to Heinz Starkenburg," in Feuer, ed., *Marx and Engels*, p. 411.

32. Karl Marx, *Critique of the Gotha Program*, in Feuer, ed., *Marx and Engels*, p. 119.

9
The Psychoanalytic Conception of Human Nature
Freud

Historical Backdrop

Sigmund Freud was born in the middle of the nineteenth century in Freiburg, Moravia, which at the time was part of the Austro-Hungarian Empire. Except for spending a few months in Leipzig, Germany, when he was three years old, and passing the last three years before his death in London,

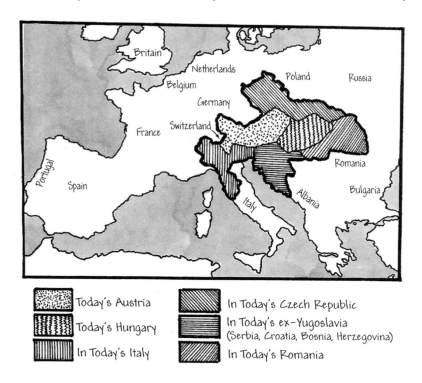

Today's Austria   In Today's Czech Republic

Today's Hungary   In Today's ex-Yugoslavia (Serbia, Croatia, Bosnia, Herzegovina)

In Today's Italy   In Today's Romania

The Austro-Hungarian Empire in the Nineteenth Century

Freud lived his whole life within the bounds of Austria-Hungary—mainly in Vienna, one of the two capitals of the empire.

Austria today may seem to some to be primarily a vacation spot, out of the mainstream of European commercial, cultural, and military power. But for hundreds of years, Austria was one of the most influential European nations, straddling the trade routes between eastern and western Europe (especially the Danube River) and between northern Europe and the Mediterranean countries (particularly the mountain passes through the Alps). From the tenth century onward, Austria marked the eastern frontier of the Holy Roman Empire, successor of the old Roman Empire, and it became an important defensive line against invading Slavs and, later, Turks. From the thirteenth century to the twentieth, Austria was ruled by the Hapsburg family, whose political domination in a number of European states gave Austria immense power and territorial claims.

As Holy Roman emperors, the kings of Austria were considered primary defenders of the Catholic faith, even though they occasionally found themselves in conflict with the pope. (Austria today remains about ninety percent Catholic.) Nevertheless, because of Austria's territorial expansion, the royal family ruled over a motley population. Most of its citizens were German speakers, but there were also speakers of Czech, Polish, Flemish, Hungarian, Slovakian, Yiddish, Romanian, Serbo-Croatian, Turkish, and Italian. (Austria controlled large sections of Italy at the time of Freud's birth.) A series of political and military reversals between 1750 and 1860, in which Belgium and parts of Italy were lost to local nationalist revolts, diminished Austria's power. In 1806, Franz II had to abandon his title of Holy Roman emperor and resign himself to being merely "emperor of Austria."

In 1836, twenty years before Freud's birth, the Magyars (Hungarians) rebelled and declared their independence. When the Russian czar intervened on the side of Austria, Emperor Franz Joseph was able to put down the rebellion, but his success was only temporary. Ultimately, the Austrians had to compromise with the Magyars and negotiate a "dual monarchy"—Austria-Hungary. The Austro-Hungarian monarchy adopted the old flag of the Holy

Oh no! Don't take away my **big** crown. I **love** my big crown!

Roman Empire: The double eagle now showed one head looking west toward Austria and the other looking east toward Hungary.

This new "empire" had the appearance of strength but was deeply fractured and, with competing ethnic and linguistic groups demanding self-government, seemed doomed from the start. The Austro-Hungarian military policies, moti-

The Coat of Arms of Austria-Hungary When the Empire Collapsed in 1918

vated by the memories of ancient glories, exacerbated the tense situation. In 1878, Austria-Hungary occupied the Turkish provinces of Bosnia and Herzegovina, and thirty years later annexed them outright. It was, in fact, in Sarajevo, capital of Bosnia, in June 1914, that a Serbian nationalist assassinated the Austrian Archduke Franz Ferdinand, initiating the series of events that would quickly escalate into World War I. The loss of this war by the German and Austro-Hungarian axis in 1918 would prove to be the undoing of the empire, separating its German-speaking population from its Hungarian-speaking citizens and from the polyglot grouping of its Czech and Balkan holdings. In 1936, the chancellor of Germany, Adolf Hitler (an Austrian by birth) sent troops into Austria and annexed it to Germany. The majority of Austrians approved of the new union with Nazi Germany, thereby once again sealing Austria's fate for the immediate future.

It was into the crumbling Austro-Hungarian Empire and doomed Austria that Sigmund Freud was born in 1856. Vienna, the Austrian capital to which Freud was brought by his parents when he was four years old, was in some ways an anachronism by the end of the nineteenth century. Vienna acted as if it were the center of a mighty empire when, in fact, it presided over an awkward, artificial concatenation of peoples held together by a myth of greatness and power. Nevertheless, considering its near-posthumous condition, Vienna was an amazingly culturally endowed city, producing musicians, artists, philosophers, and industrialists who hobnobbed to produce a highly charged creative environment. It also had a large, well-educated Jewish population that supplied many of Vienna's most talented artists, intellectuals, and businesspeople. Vienna became associated with the *fin de siècle* (end of the century) artistic movement with its suggestions of the glorification of decadence. It may well be that there is a connection between this artistic movement and Freud's obsession with sex and death. For one reason or another, it was there, in late-nineteenth-century Vienna, that one of the most amazing theories of human nature was spun out, as we shall soon see.

Biography

Sigmund Freud was born May 6, 1856, in Freiburg, Moravia, at that time part of the Austro-Hungarian Empire, and now called Pribor in Czechoslovakia. He was the first of eight children born to his father's second wife. His father, Jacob Freud, had trouble making ends meet as a small-time Jewish merchant in a provincial town, many of whose inhabitants harbored anti-Jewish sentiments. Seeking a better climate for his business, he moved his family first to Leipzig, Germany, and then to Vienna, while Sigmund was still a small child. Some of Freud's earliest memories were of his father stoically enduring anti-Semitic insults by local bullies in his hometown. In fact, despite his early abandonment of his father's religion, anti-Semitism played a role throughout Freud's life. A liberal government in the Austrian half of the empire had emancipated the Jews in

Sigmund Freud (1856–1939)

the 1880s and granted them citizenship, but the conservatives soon overthrew the liberals; from that point on, anti-Semitism was on the rise, culminating in Hitler's ascent to power.

Even as a student, anti-Semitism determined what fields Freud could choose to study. As a child, he was an avid scholar, reading translations of Shakespeare when he was eight years old and soon studying the classics of the literature of Greece, Rome, France, and Germany in the original languages. But only certain careers were open to Jewish students at Austrian universities, and Freud chose medical research. In his first published paper, he reported his discovery of the location of eel gonads. (People knew that eels had gonads, because there were so many eels around, but nobody knew exactly where those organs were.)

In 1879, Freud became engaged to Martha Bernays, but they could not afford to marry for seven years. He was unable to maintain a household on a researcher's salary, so he turned to the clinical practice of neurology. Impressed by Dr. Joseph Breuer's successes using therapeutic hypnosis as a treatment for "hysteria," he went to Paris to study hypnotic technique with Dr. Jean-Martin Charcot. When Breuer distanced himself from Freud because of what he perceived as Freud's obsession with sexuality as a primary cause of hysteria, Freud took solace in the friendship of the eccentric Wilhelm Fliess and allowed himself to be influenced by some of Fliess's wacky ideas—such as his belief in an important connection between the soft, mucous membranes of the nasal passages and parts of the female reproductive system.

Wilhelm Fliess Smitten

But Freud managed to find his own niche through self-analysis and observation of his patients. In 1899, he published what would prove to be the first work in the new field of "psychoanalysis," *The Interpretation of Dreams* (though Freud insisted on putting the publishing date as 1900 so the book would be the first work of the twentieth century rather than the last of the nineteenth century). After the book's publication, a number of physicians began to gather around Freud, and the weekly meetings at his home at Bergasse 19 became known first as the Vienna Psychoanalytic Society and eventually as the International Psychoanalytic Association. In 1909, Freud was invited to lecture at Clark University in Massachusetts. This would prove to be his only trip to America, a country that did not impress him even though psychoanalysis received a warmer reception there than in Europe in its early days.

Many of Freud's original disciples broke with him as the years went by, establishing their own offshoot schools. Most of the defections were caused by Freud's insistence on putting sexuality at the center of the study of emotional disorders. (For example, Carl Jung, who had traveled to America with Freud, started his own school stressing the positive rather than the negative features of the unconscious mind, and Alfred Adler championed Friedrich Nietzsche's "will to power" over Freud's "id" as the main factor in human moti-

vation. On the other hand, Wilhelm Reich seemed to think Freud had not put enough emphasis on sexuality. For his part, Freud expelled Reich from the International Psychoanalytic Association not for that offense, but for having joined the Austrian Communist party.)

World War I was a shock to Freud, as it was to all European intellectuals. His theories became darker after the war, no doubt partly in response to its horrors and the pessimism it generated in him about Europe in particular and civilization in general. Also, the discovery that his jaw was infected with cancer contributed to his somber mood, as did his observation of the Nazi rise to power in neighboring Germany. In fact, when Hitler annexed Austria in 1936, Freud fled to London to continue his work—and, indeed, to save his life. Unfortunately, several of his relatives died in the Holocaust. Freud himself succumbed to cancer in London on September 23, 1939, after thirty-three surgical operations and seventeen years of chronic pain, which he had born with great patience. He had lived long enough to see his name ensconced in every corner of culture, even if controversially, and to see one of his daughters, Anna, achieve prominence as a great psychoanalyst in her own right.

Freud's Theory

The cornerstones of Freud's psychoanalytic conception of human nature are the ideas of the unconscious mind and of infantile sexuality. The first of these notions (and the most important for our purpose) was not actually invented by Freud. We can find traces of it in Plato, in medieval and Renaissance mysticism, in the poetry of the Romantics, and in the philosophy of Freud's nineteenth-century predecessors Arthur Schopenhauer and Friedrich Nietzsche. But it was Freud who tried to create a science around that idea. Let's inspect that effort.

The Unconscious

The background to Freud's specific version of the unconscious mind is his view that a major portion of human biology is at odds with the goals of civilization. In our biology, unlike the biology of, say, ants and bees, there is nothing corresponding to a social instinct (as we might claim to find in Greek philosophy or in Marx or Darwin). Rather, our main biological motivation is provided by the "pleasure principle"—namely, desire for immediate gratification of basic "instinctual" demands (demands for food, sex, and aggression).

Such an egoistic biological organization may have been sufficient to permit the survival of the species in the ancient past—for example, when our ancestors of a half-million years ago lived in the lush jungles of eastern Africa with few natural enemies, surrounded by edible animals, plants, berries, and roots. But at some point, social skills became necessary for survival, perhaps when the floor of present-day India collapsed, creating the Himalayas, which changed the world's weather patterns,

Our Most Ancient Ancestors

reducing the jungles of north-eastern Africa to semi-arid savannas and leaving the proto-humans alone and defenseless, the "naked ape," as Desmond Morris called us.[1] The development of these social skills required the perversion of our biology. Being organically grounded, the demand for pleasure could not be denied, but pleasure could be modified, substituted for, and postponed. And this, for Freud, is precisely the meaning of civilization—the redefinition and restructuring of pleasure in the name of human cooperation, in the form of love, family connections, friendships, and work relationships (or, in Freudian terms, the creation of the "ego" out of the "id").

The Embarrassment
of the Naked Ape

Before

After

Id–Ego–Superego

Freud's term **id** refers to the combination of those old "instincts" that had to undergo transformation in the name of civilization. ("Instinct" is an unfortunate translation of the German word *Trieb*. If the biological impulses or drives of which Freud speaks were *truly* instincts, they could not be modified by behavior. Yet precisely the point of Freud's theory is to show the effects, both positive and negative, of the molding of our biology by the forces of civilization. The essence of our biological drives has gone unchanged, but their expression has been "perverted." And the point of psychoanalytic therapy is the alleviation, to the extent possible, of those deleterious effects. But we will continue to employ the word "instinct" here because that's the way the idea appears in all the English translations of Freud.) These instincts could not be tamed by rationality alone. Rationality (reason, logic, common sense — associated with what Freud calls the **ego**) is the *product*, not the cause, of the taming of those instincts. To domesticate the instincts, something as irrational as the instincts themselves was needed. It came in the form

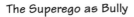

The Superego as Bully

of what Freud calls the **superego**—a tyrannical agency that promotes guilt and uses it in negotiating with the threats of the id.

Despite all the pressure against them, the instincts continue to make their old demands in the form of antisocial wishes, usually sexual and

aggressive wishes, and often directed against members of one's immediate family because they are the people one encounters earliest and most constantly and directly. (In fact, for reasons we will discuss shortly, Freud believes that we are born with a

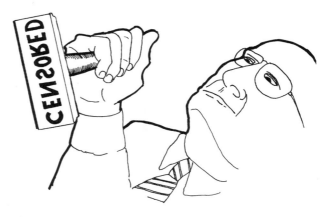

The Ego as Censor

predisposition to be erotically attracted to the parent of the opposite sex and competitive with the parent of the same sex. Freud calls this predisposition the **"Oedipus complex."**) A censoring agent in the ego represses these wishes into the unconscious mind, where they continue to exist and put pressure on the whole organism. Therefore, one kind of mental component in the unconscious is antisocial sexual desire, often incestuous and "œdipal." Another kind is antisocial hostility, and it, too, is often "œdipal."

Censorship and Repression

The function of censorship is to keep the conscious mind clear for everyday activity. If the goals of civilization are to be achieved, consciousness cannot be continuously distracted by antisocial desires or by memories of traumatic events. Anyone who has suffered the loss of a loved one or the end of an important romance knows how the pain caused by these personal tragedies are paralyzing and can prevent one's engagement in everyday life, including even the simplest of tasks. These memories must be **repressed** to the extent possible, especially if the traumatic events they mirror took place in childhood when the personality was still unformed and malleable. In that case, the memories are buried

Screen Memories

deeply in the uncon-
scious and replaced in
consciousness either
by blank spaces or by
"screen memories"—
that is, false memories
that block out painful
memories.

Nevertheless, these
unconscious memories
are still affecting the
individual in terms of
decisions made, things
feared, and people, physical objects, and land-
scapes found attractive
or repellent. Even memo-
ries that are *too* pleasant can be repressed,

according to Freud, for they, too, can be distracting. For example, if one's
most pleasant memory is the total bliss experienced at one's mother's
breast (such feelings of warmth, safety, love, nutritional satisfaction, and
sensuality will never be experienced again), this memory cannot be allowed
to become the retrogressive goal of one's daily actions in the world. If you
are the CEO of a major corporation, and your secretary rushes in to tell

**Saint Teresa of Avila
Contemplates Doing the Dishes**

you of an attempted hostile take-
over of the company, it will do no
good to call your mother (unless,
of course, she is a major stock-
holder or a corporate wizard). For
similar reasons, Freud claims that
the actual experience of sexual
orgasm cannot be fully retained as
a memory. It would be difficult to
repair your car's transmission or
fill out tax forms if *that* were on
your mind all the time. Or, as the
sixteenth-century Spanish mystic
said, After seeing the face of God,
it is difficult to do the dishes.

According to Freud, not only are certain *real* memories repressed into the unconscious, but also certain kinds of *false* memories—what seem to be memories but are, in fact, fantasies. This feature of Freud's theory derives from his belief concerning infantile sexuality, which attacks the cherished Victorian idea of childhood as being innocent of sexual motives. Because we are biologically sexual beings from birth onward, and because there are no socially acceptable outlets for childhood sexuality, sexual fantasies are generated spontaneously in the minds of children and misremembered as real seduction scenes (often "œdipal" in nature involving family members, or involving nurses or teachers). The superego attaches guilt to these fantasies, and they, too, are repressed into the unconscious. (This aspect of Freud's theory has received heavy criticism lately from those who claim that Freud has misread real sexual abuse of children and the role it plays in later emotional problems, and that he led some of his patients to believe that they fantasized, and hence desired, the abuse that they in fact experienced.)

Freud Under Fire

Not only are desires, memories, and fantasies repressed into the unconscious, but so is much of the guilt attached to these mental units by the superego. The conscious mind cannot operate efficiently if it is swamped with feelings of guilt.

Memory Lapses and Guilt

An excellent example of Freud's idea of the repression of guilt can be found in the opening pages of his early book *The Psychopathology of Everyday Life* (1904). This case provides one of the best single instances of Freud's view of how the unconscious mind works in contrast to the conscious mind and how they conflict with each other. Freud tells the following story about an experience he had while traveling south on his annual summer vacation. He is chatting with a fellow traveler in the train coach, and talk turns to Herzegovina and Bosnia, the Muslim region of the Austro-Hungarian Empire. Freud's companion tells of a physician friend who works at a hospital in that zone who is impressed by the fatalism of the Muslims in the face of death. If the doctor must inform one of his patients of a fatal disease, the person typically responds, "Sir [*Mein Herr*], What can I say? I am sure you have done everything you can."

Freud chuckles to himself, remembering (but not sharing) another story by a physician friend of *his* working in the same area. This man agrees that a Bosnian may be fatalistic in the face of death but claims that if you tell the same person that for medical reasons he must abstain from sex, the man cries out, "But Sir, without that, life is not worth living!" Immediately after this slightly improper thought, Freud finds himself abruptly changing the subject to Italian art. He refers to one of his favorite muralists, "The Master of Orvieto," but draws a blank on the artist's name—Signorelli—a name he knows perfectly well. In its place, he thinks of two other Italian artists, Botticelli and Boltraffio, but he immediately recognizes that these names are incorrect.

In the year in which this event took place (c. 1897) probably anybody but Sigmund Freud would have ignored the episode or simply attributed it to a momentary lapse of memory. But not Siggy! He believed that there must be a reason for failing to remember the name of an artist with whose works he was well acquainted, and he traced that reason to the unconscious. His reconstruction of the process leading to the blocking of Signorelli's name is roughly this: The previous year, Freud had been treating a young man in Vienna for a sexual disturbance. When Freud was about to head south on vacation that summer, the patient begged him not to leave, fearing his own suicidal tendencies. Freud assured him that he would survive this brief sojourn, and he left for Italy. When Freud arrived at the city of Trafoi, a telegram awaited him announcing the suicide of the young man. Freud was devastated with guilt, and his vacation was ruined.

The Case of the Missing Italian

Now, in the present occasion, the discussion about the Muslims in Herzegovina and Bosnia (see items 1, 2, and 3 on the chart below) is associated with thoughts of sex and death (item 4), and begins a gravitational pull toward thoughts of guilt (item 5), which the ego's censorship is repressing in order to keep Freud's conscious mind free from tormenting

```
(6) SIGNORELLI   (7) BOTTICELLI   (8) BOLTRAFFIO
(1) HERZEGOVINA   &  (2) BOSNIA        (9) TRAFOI
(3) SIR  [HERR],  I'M SURE...
              (4) SEX & DEATH
        (5) REPRESSED THOUGHTS OF GUILT
```

memories that would spoil his vacation a second year in a row. (We *need* occasional rest, relaxation, and diversion if we are to continue in life.) So the unconscious censorship has broken the deadly gravitational pull toward morbid, painful thoughts by forcing a change of subject. The topic moves suddenly to the happier theme of art. But the superego (whose function is, after all, to tyrannize with guilt) cunningly keeps the conversation targeted on sex and death by having the name of the first artist to be considered—Signorelli—relate metonymically (that is, by the principle of association) with sounds or images already laden with hints of sex and death (because *Signor* [Sir] in Italian means the same as *Herr* in German [item 3]). Thus, for Freud, the word is now connected with suggestions of guilt. The censorship mechanism tries to interrupt this deadly circuit, and Freud "forgets" Signorelli's name (item 6), replacing it with Botticelli's (item 7). But again, the superego triumphs, as the "Bo" in "Botticelli" is related metonymically to the "Bo" of "Bosnia" (and hence indirectly related to sex and death). Once more, Freud misremembers the name of an Italian artist—this time "Boltraffio" (item 8). But the "Bo" in that name is still related metonymically to sex and death by containing the same "Bo" as that of "Bosnia." It is also

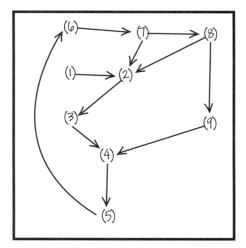

The Deadly Circuit of Guilt

patently related to "Trafoi" (item 9), the city where Freud was overcome with guilt. What we have here is the constant return of repressed guilt and a standoff between two unconscious factions, the superego and the agency of censorship.

We have spent so much time on this complicated example because it is illustrative of Freud's theory of how the mind functions. The conscious mind works commonsensically and ratio-

The Value of Means-to-Ends Analyses

nally in terms of a means-to-ends analysis. (For example, if I want a good grade in my philosophy class, then I should develop good study habits. If I want to learn about the Muslims in Bosnia, then I should read histories of the rise and fall of the Ottoman Empire of the Turks, and the way the Austro-Hungarian Empire tried to profit by its fall.) The logic of the uncon-

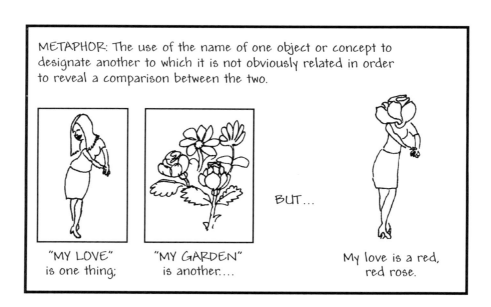

METAPHOR: The use of the name of one object or concept to designate another to which it is not obviously related in order to reveal a comparison between the two.

"MY LOVE" is one thing;   "MY GARDEN" is another....   BUT...   My love is a red, red rose.

demand. In some cultures, certain desires can find no legitimate direct gratification (for example, incestuous, homosexual, polygamous, or cannibalistic desires, and almost all violent desires). These desires can be *displaced* into substitute gratifications, such as professional football in the cases of violence and homosexual desire. Some people can also *sublimate* them into the creation of socially valuable cultural artifacts, such as works of art

or scientific theories. Sublimation is a form of directing the original "gross" desire toward a substitute gratification that produces something "sublime," which is in that sense the opposite of the original desire, but which in effect still contains vestiges of the original impulse. (Think of how much violence and eroticism appear in great art, and how scientific theories are used to control, dominate, or destroy large parts of nature.)

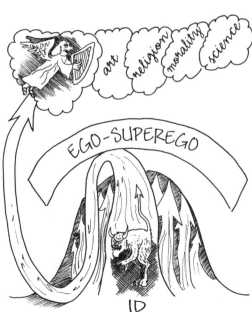

Sublimation

We could also talk about the way repressed wishes manifest themselves in dreams, fantasies, and misdirected behavior (like "Freudian" slips). In some cases, these repressed desires find an outlet in "neurotic" or "psychotic" symptoms. A neurotic symptom is a behavior pattern that interrupts normal life goals in significant ways (like agoraphobia, acrophobia, exhibitionism, or any kind of obsessive behavior). Thus, neurotic symptoms are something one suffers from, but they are also something from which the neurotic derives a certain kind of perverse satisfaction (which is why neuroses are not easy to cure). A psychotic is a mad person. The difference between neurosis and psychosis is only one of degree, as is the difference between neurosis and "normality."

The Psychosexual Stages

Each of us, no matter where we find ourselves on the neurosis-normality scale, brings into adult life our individual past in the form of repressed memories and fantasies that are still acting dynamically on our contemporary conscious life. If we suffered serious traumas (for example, lost a parent to death or were exposed to some terrifying event) during early stages of our lives (what Freud calls the "psychosexual stages"), then we are in a certain sense psychologically trapped in that period—the period in which we knew our last true happiness and the period to which we flee unconsciously under pressure, in moments of panic, or in times of unhappiness.

For instance, suppose you were traumatized in the "oral" stage—that stage during the first eighteen months of life in which pleasure is derived from placing objects in the mouth. Then, in adult life, you would likely exhibit certain behavior patterns related to oral gratification: overeating, drinking, smoking, talking excessively, playing with your lips or teeth, growing a mustache, having mouth twitches, or being obsessive about oral hygiene. Freud calls this syndrome "oral retentiveness." Or,

suppose you were traumatized during the "anal" stage—that period roughly between eighteen and thirty months when (according to Freud) children take pleasure in anal activity and in controlling their bowel movements. Then, in adult life, you would likely be "anally retentive" and exhibit certain symptoms such as suffering from bouts of diarrhea or constipation, using an overabundance of excrementally oriented language, and being obsessed with cleanliness; you would also likely seek a career involving a high degree of mathematical orderliness, such as banking or accounting. (Whole cultures can tend toward anal retentiveness, according to Freud. For example, this trait will be less common in southern cultures—say, Mediterranean societies—than in northern cultures—say, German and Scandinavian—in which, for reasons having to do partly with climate, children are under extreme pressure to become "potty-trained" early.) The philosophically interesting feature of these cases of retentiveness is that they clearly reveal the conflict between nature and culture, our two creators, according to Freud. Nature, for instance, says, "Evacuate your bowels when you feel like it, where you feel like it." Culture says, "Evacuate your bowels NOW, whether you feel like it or not, in this little white hole, . . . OR ELSE!" Culture wins, but at a severe cost in terms of emotional well-being.

The Confrontation between Nature and Culture

Not only does our "ontogenetic" history (that is, the personal history of each of us as individuals) become heavy baggage that we must drag around with us daily, but we lug around "phylogenetic" baggage as well. That is, there is a certain burdensome legacy from the ancient history of the human race that each individual brings into daily life. This feature of Freud's theory of the self is perhaps the most far-fetched part of his doctrine to be presented here so far, but it is certainly an attention-grabber. Besides, it is an idea that Freud refused to give up even though many of his followers were embarrassed by what they took to be its wild implausibility. Therefore, we will take a look at it.

The Luggage with Which No Porter Can Help

The Primordial Patricide and the Racial Memory

We saw that, for Darwin, the transition from nature to culture was a long, slow, incremental process. But for Freud, this development took place overnight. On one fine day, our ancient ancestors were still a part of nature; then, on the next day, they were uprooted from nature forever and, for better or for worse (mostly worse), thrust into culture. The event that propelled them into culture was a murderous act on the part of a group of

Nature   Culture

sons, who, hating their "Primal Father" for his repression of them yet admiring him deeply for his power and sexual domination of all the females under his protection (namely, the sisters, cousins, aunts, and mothers of the brothers), killed and ate him, and had a sexual orgy with what Freud unconvincingly calls "the liberated women."[2]

But the brothers had loved the father they had just killed as much as they had hated him, so in

the aftermath of that event (which Freud calls the "primordial patricide"), guilt set in—the first truly human emotion. According to Freud, this was the ancient origin of the superego. Out of guilt, the sons, who now ruled in place of their dead father, set up the first social laws, the initial one being, "Thou shalt not sleep with thy sister." In this way, they denied themselves the very pleasure for which they had killed their father. In effect, this new "incest taboo" became the primary rule of all future civilizations, and, from a Darwinian point of view, ironically guarantees the triumph of culture over nature.

Ultimately, however, Freud's theory is not Darwinian, for he believes that the repressed memory of the "primordial patricide" and its attendant guilt is passed on genetically from generation to generation, becoming, in effect, a collective unconscious. This **Lamarckian**[3] transmission, then, means that each of us in our unconscious mind knows this truth:[4]

What We All Know

It is this unconscious memory (Freud calls it the "racial memory" because it is a recollection of the origin of the whole human race) that links and explains for Freud a number of cultural and psychological phenomena that otherwise remain disconnected and unexplained. Examples include the nature of primitive religion (the "totem" animal that cannot be killed or eaten, except ritually, when it *must* be killed and eaten, is the symbolic Primal Father), contemporary religion (the Christian religion knows the truth that we, the sons, killed the father, and therefore the Son must die for our guilt; but because the Son *is* the Father, by killing the Son we also kill the Father; we are invited to eat His flesh and drink His blood in a ceremony that unites us all as Christian brothers and sisters), the content of mythology (myths are collective dreams that symbolically express the desire and guilt surrounding the primordial patricide), the content of fairy tales (before Jack can live with his mother happily ever after, he must slay the giant male-figure by chopping down a great phallic column that grows from his mother's garden), and the relation between children and their parents (the racial memory is also meant to explain why we are each born with the Oedipus complex).

All of this indeed constitutes a heavy burden from the ancient past that each of us must carry daily.

But things get worse! As we have just seen, Freud traces the origins of the unconscious first to the infancy of the individual (ontogeny) and then beyond that to the infancy of the human race (phylogeny). But then, in his book written after the ravages of World War I, he traces them back to the beginning of life itself. There, he claims to have discovered in the very first moment of organic existence a death instinct, which he named *Thanatos*, after the Greek god of death. This "god" was as least as powerful as its "equally immortal adversary,"[5] *Eros*, the life instinct, named after the Greek god of love. That is, there is an instinct of self-

The Dance Macabre

destruction built into all biology, and one that eventually triumphs over the life forces. This, if true, is very grave news indeed.

Summary

The picture of the self that emerges here is not a pretty one (which is one reason that Freud is so widely disliked). Freud's "self," whether "normal" or

neurotic, is one that knows very little about itself; it is a self filled with conflict, guilt, and uncertainty. It is also a thoroughly modern self, one that makes old Socrates' exhortation, "Know thyself," both more difficult and more urgent. Kierkegaard's dictum, "Choose thyself," becomes even harder in this model, which smacks heavily of **determinism,** especially in the way in which the individual is trapped in his or her past, both in the ontogenetic past (the history of the individual) and in the phylogenetic past (the history of the human race).

If the psychoanalytic account of human nature is correct, then only a scientific and medical approach to it is proper and efficient (as opposed, for example, to the political approach demanded by Platonism and Marxism, the philosophical approach recommended by the Aristotelian and Cartesian models, the theological approaches offered by the medieval Christian view, the meditative model proposed by the Buddha, or the individualistic approaches required by existentialism). Without such professional intervention, self-knowledge is impossible, or at least, very difficult. (Freud claimed to have psychoanalyzed himself, but he did it as *Doctor Freud*.) This is because the key feature of human psychology is the unconscious. (Freud once suggested that the mind is like an iceberg; the submerged part—ninety percent of it—is the unconscious.) By definition, then, the truth about ourselves cannot be derived directly from looking into our own soul. The conscious mind can only provide hints and clues as to

Freud and the Iceberg Model of the Mind

what is really going on beneath the surface, and these fractured signs must be professionally deciphered. This is extremely difficult in one's own case because there are built-in resistances (defense mechanisms) to discovering that truth.

Where id was, there shall ego be.

Does Freud offer us no possible escape from the clutches of the dark past? He claimed that he was on the side of the ego against the id and the superego, and therefore, optimistically, that he was on the side of reason and culture. The very fact that he developed a therapeutic model shows that he thought it was possible to escape the determinism of the past, or at least to prevent the past from binding us in neurotic ways. Yet, when we turn to his most mature work, we find that the real enemy is not merely the memory of the past, as he had once said. Rather, it is the god of death, Thanatos, who is the source of all violence and destruction, and whose victory is a foregone conclusion. The best advice that Freud can give us in the face of this principle of self-destruction is to fight the good fight for as long as possible; to side with Eros, the god of love, in his eternal struggle with Thanatos; not to "go gentle into that good night," in the words of the Welsh poet Dylan Thomas.

Freud's general theory of psychoanalysis, and with it his picture of human nature, has been the object of blistering criticism from many quarters. Because of its speculative and untestable nature, it cannot meet the criteria that would make it a true science. The therapeutic practice associated with the theory seems no more successful than most of its competitors and is usually much more time-consuming and expensive. Feminists are angered at what seems to be Freud's misogyny and his theory's anti-female bias and insensitivity to women's experiences and needs. Nevertheless, there are important psychoanalytic feminist theorists (who often turn the tables on Freud's misogyny), and, like it or not, Freud's vocabulary is now part of our modern repertoire.

Our age seems to view Freud less as a scientist or even a doctor than as a philosopher with a peculiar but striking reading of the human condition that, despite its excesses and absurdities, resonates in uncanny ways with some experiences we have of this strange world in which we find ourselves. He is like an art critic, suggesting that we view a work of art (the human being) in a special new way. In a sense, he assures us that, if we do, we will see features of it that we had not seen before—features that, once they have been seen, will not be easily forgotten and to which it will be necessary to react.

To my mind, Freud's theory does indeed make us see things differently and is hard to throw off. (I will never read "The Three Billy Goats Gruff" or "Jack and the Beanstalk" the same way as before.) The problem is that it is very difficult to know whether the images that we espy from Freud's perspective are genuine insights, or self-fulfilling prophecies, or illustrations of highly-creative nonsense—or (as I suspect) a combination of all three.

Topics for Consideration

1. In the library, find reproductions of paintings by Egon Schiele and Gustaf Klimpt, two Viennese artists of the *fin de siècle* movement, and comment on them from the perspective of the Viennese situation in general and Freud's theory in particular.

2. In *The Interpretation of Dreams*, Freud claims that dreams are "the royal highway to the unconscious." Based on what you've read here, or on additional reading you have done, explain why you think that Freud believes that the study of dreams will give the psychoanalyst the best access to the unconscious. (If you use external material to answer this question, credit your sources.)

3. According to Freud, the main conflict that we humans experience is that between our natural instincts and the goals of civilization. Explain the sense in which these two systems are in opposition and the way this conflict creates both the unconscious and neuroses, according to psychoanalysis.

4. Describe the nature and function of Freud's three agencies within the human mind—id, ego, and superego—and describe the relationship that exists among them.

5. Based on what you have read here, characterize the "Oedipus complex" and explain what caused it, according to Freud. Then research the Oedipus character in ancient Greek fables, and relate what you learn to Freud's choice of Oedipus's name to designate this complex.

6. Write an essay entitled "The Case of the Missing Italian Painter," showing how Freud's inability to remember Signorelli's name can be attributed to the censorship agency in the ego. (For "extra credit," find a book of reproductions of the murals that Signorelli painted in the cathedral of Orvieto, and discuss the content of these paintings in the light of Freud's analysis of his memory lapse.)

7. Freud's claim that his theories are scientific has been challenged on the grounds that, unlike real scientific theories, his can be neither confirmed nor refuted. By contrasting one of Freud's theories with some scientific theory with which you are familiar, explain this criticism of Freud's theories.

8. Show how the sentence "Ontogeny recapitulates phylogeny" applies to Freud's theory. That is, show how, according to him, the mental infancy of the individual repeats the mental infancy of the human race.

9. Find a short account of World War I in an encyclopedia or a history book. What puzzling features of that war would be explained by Freud's postulation of the "death instinct"?

10. One of the great debates in philosophy has been over the question of freedom versus determinism. Write a paragraph setting forth your understanding of this problem; then show how it arises in Freud's theory.

Suggestions for Further Reading
I. Freud's Main Works[6]
[original publication dates in brackets]

Beyond the Pleasure Principle. Trans. James Strachey. New York: Norton, 1975.

Civilization and Its Discontents. Trans. James Strachey. New York: Norton, 1989 [1930].

The Interpretation of Dreams. In The Basic Writings of Sigmund Freud, ed. and trans. A. A. Brill. New York: Modern Library, 1966 [1899].

Moses and Monotheism. Trans. Katherine Jones. New York: Random House, n.d. [1939].

The Psychopathology of Everyday Life. In *The Basic Writings of Sigmund Freud,* ed. and trans. A. A. Brill. New York: Modern Library, 1966 [1904].

Totem and Taboo. In *The Basic Writings of Sigmund Freud,* ed. and trans. A. A. Brill. New York: Modern Library, 1966 [1913].

II. Secondary Sources on Freud

Crews, Frederick C., ed. *Unauthorized Freud: Doubters Confront a Legend.* New York: Viking/Penguin, 1998.

Gay, Peter. *Freud: A Life for Our Time.* New York: Anchor, 1988.

Gopnik, Adam. "Annals of Psychoanalysis: Man Goes to See a Doctor." *The New Yorker,* Aug. 24 and 31, 1998.

Robinson, Paul. *Freud and His Critics.* Berkeley: University of California Press, 1993.

Wollheim, Richard. *Sigmund Freud.* Cambridge: Cambridge University Press, 1981.

Notes

1. Desmond Morris, *The Naked Ape* (New York: McGraw-Hill, 1967).

2. Sigmund Freud, *Totem and Taboo,* in *The Basic Writings of Sigmund Freud,* ed. and trans. A. A. Brill (New York: Modern Library, 1966), p. 917.

3. Jean-Baptiste Lamarck (1744–1829) was a French naturalist in the generation before Darwin who believed that acquired characteristics could be inherited. Biologists today seem almost universally agreed that Darwin's theory refutes Lamarck's. We see that Freud is indeed consciously a Lamarckian from the following passage, written in the context of a discussion of the racial memory:

   > I must admit that I have argued as if there were no question that there exists an inheritance of memory—traces of what our forefathers experienced, . . . This state of affairs is made more difficult, it is true, by the present attitude of biological science, which rejects the idea of acquired qualities being transmitted to descendants. I admit, in all modesty, that in spite of this I cannot picture biological development proceeding without taking this factor into account.

   Sigmund Freud, *Moses and Monotheism,* trans. Katherine Jones (New York: Random House, n.d.), pp. 127–128.

4. Freud, *Moses and Monotheism,* p. 129.

5. Sigmund Freud, *Civilization and Its Discontents,* trans. James Strachey (New York: Norton, 1989), p. 112.

6. Freud was a prolific writer. His *Collected Works* in English translation take up twenty-four volumes. Here I have listed only the main books upon which this chapter was based, all of which are available in inexpensive editions and accessible to the general reading public.

10

The Atheistic Existential Conception of Human Nature
Sartre

Historical Backdrop

The Treaty of Versailles was signed on October 9, 1919, officially ending "the Great War," which had cost 8.7 *million* lives (France alone lost nearly 1.4 million men) and had changed the political, social, and geographical map of the Western world. The war terminated monarchical rule in Germany, caused the collapse of the Austro-Hungarian Empire, and resulted in the dissolution of czarist Russia, which was replaced by the Communist Soviet Union. The deaths of so many young university-educated British officers severely depleted the British upper classes and invited the working classes to fill the power vacuum. The United States was forced to abandon its policy of international isolationism, and the structure of European colonialism began to disintegrate.

Well, boys. I think among us, we pretty much finished off Europe.

The Treaty of Versailles put the defeated Germany at a distinct political and economic disadvantage, but the Germans ignored the treaty almost from the start, refusing to pay the war indemnities imposed upon them. In 1923, the French occupied Germany's industrialized Ruhr Valley in order to force the Germans to meet their financial obligation, provoking an international crisis. Meanwhile, France itself suffered political destabilization as parties from both the left and the right vied for power. The global financial crisis of 1929 rocked France in 1930 and by 1932 produced general anxiety, which expressed itself in even more extreme political instability. In 1936, the Popular Front under the leadership of the Socialist Leon Blum took over the governmental reins by uniting all the competing leftist factions (Radicals, Socialists, Anarchists, Communists).

In the meantime, Adolf Hitler had been appointed chancellor in Germany after the elections of 1933. France and its old World War I allies failed to prevent Hitler's Germany from annexing Austria and part of the

Czech Republic. Only when Hitler invaded Poland in September of 1939 did France and Britain declare war on Germany. The consequent German invasion of France and its immediate success shocked the French military, whose defense system collapsed. (The Maginot Line, a series of fortifications created to provide a final line of defense, was rapidly breached or circumvented by the German invaders.) Almost at once, the new right-wing puppet government under the leadership of Marshal Phillipe Pétain, the aged hero of the Battle of Verdun in World War I, sued for peace. Pétain's regime, known as the Vichy government, agreed to collaborate with the policies of Nazi Germany—including the arrest and deportation of French Jews, most of whom were put to death in Nazi concentration camps.

During this period, a well-organized and highly disciplined underground resistance movement developed that waged a war of sabotage in France against the German occupying army and the Vichy collaborators. At the same time, General Charles de Gaulle, who had escaped to London, orga-

nized the Free French Forces, which prepared
for the day when they could reenter France
with the invading Allied army of mostly
British, Canadian, and American troops.
This day came on June 6, 1944—
D-Day—when 176,000 Allied soldiers
debarked on the heavily fortified
beaches of Normandy in northern
France. By the end of August, a million Allied troops had occupied a
considerable chunk of French terri-
tory, Paris had been liberated, and
de Gaulle had been installed as pro-
visional president of the Republic.

Field-Marshal Pétain (1856–1951)

Reprisals, both legal and extralegal, were immediately carried out against
the collaborators of the Vichy regime. Marshal Pétain himself was condemned to death, but the former war hero's sentence was commuted to life
imprisonment. He died in disgrace in 1951.

**General Charles de Gaulle
(1890–1970)**

Existentialism was born out of the complicated times in France just before and during
World War II. The political chaos, economic anxiety, and general cultural pessimism of the
prewar years, along with the schizoid conditions in France during the war itself—with
its amalgamation of collaboration and resistance—provided a fertile ground for French
intellectuals to reconsider the human condition in terms of the gloomy worldview of
Søren Kierkegaard (1813–1855) and the
exuberant philosophical anarchism of the
German proto-existentialist Friedrich
Nietzsche (1844–1900). The main spokes-
person in France for these new/old ideas
was Jean-Paul Sartre, who coined the
term "existentialism" in 1943, during the
height of the war.

Biography

Jean-Paul Sartre's mother, Anne-Marie Schweitzer, married Jean-Baptiste
Sartre in 1904. Her new husband, a second lieutenant in the navy, was

Jean-Paul Sartre (1905–1980)

already sick with the tropical fever that would kill him two years later. Jean-Paul was born June 21, 1905, in Paris. After his young father's death, his mother returned to the home of her parents. Her father, Charles Schweitzer, was sixty-two years old and had applied for retirement, but he withdrew his request in order to be able to support his widowed daughter and her son. The domineering old grandfather, a professor of languages, doted on Sartre and became one of the major influences in his life.

When Sartre was seven years old, Dr. Schweitzer sneaked the boy out of the home and, against his mother's wishes, had his curls cut. Aghast when she saw his shorn head, Anne-Marie locked herself in her room, sobbing. Not only had her little boy lost the feminine qualities that she preferred, but with his curls gone, there was no longer any way to avoid noticing that Jean-Paul was an ugly little boy. Besides his homely features, he suffered from a strabismus in his right eye; soon he would lose sight in that eye. Sartre later wrote that he came to realize that he was not the Prince Charming of the fairy tales, but the toad.

However, the attention that a pretty child might get from his looks Jean-Paul got from his writing. Beginning at age ten to the applause of his small family, he produced poems, short stories, and novels, sometimes crossing out parts that were cruel or bizarre so his relatives would not see them. In the meantime, Sartre was only doing so-so in school, an experience that took the wind out of his sails and helped him get over his superiority complex. During World War I, Sartre had his heart broken—not by the loss of a relative on the battlefield, the experience of many of his schoolmates, but by his mother's remarriage. Little Sartre interpreted her act as a betrayal. Now he would have to become his grandmother's darling, because his mother had a new lover.

In 1923, at the age of eighteen, Sartre was drafted into the military, but he was given the routine exemption to finish his studies. He passed his entrance exams and enrolled in the University of Paris's "Ecole Normale" at the Sorbonne, specializing in philosophy with the intention of going into teaching. At first, he did very well in his studies, but when it came time to prepare for his graduation examinations, Sartre allowed himself to be distracted by his writing, university friendships, and love affairs. He flunked a part of his final exam and ended up last in his class. The shock of failure and the wrath of his grandfather convinced him to prepare seriously to retake the exam the next year, 1929. When studying with some other students, he was introduced to another philosophy major, Simone de Beauvoir. So commenced a friendship and

How could you do this to me?

Simone de Beauvoir
(1908–1986)

eventually a love that would last the rest of their lives. However, they elected not to marry, nor even to live together, and they openly had love affairs with others and addressed each other with the word "vous," the formal rather than the informal way of saying "you" in French. They worked on philosophy together and had a deep influence on each other's work. There is still debate today about the depth of Sartre's debt to de Beauvoir for his key ideas. If they were hers—and many of them may well have been—she apparently preferred to let

Sartre have the lime-light. Today their tombs are next to each other in Paris's Montparnasse Cemetery.

Perhaps under de Beauvoir's inspiration, Sartre passed his exams in 1929, achieving first place; de Beauvoir came in second. Sartre's military exemption was immediately terminated, and he spent eighteen months in the service. Upon his discharge, he accepted a teaching job at a "lycée," (a high-powered college preparatory school) at Le Havre on the north coast of France. But Sartre disliked Le Havre and missed Paris. He also missed de Beauvoir, who was teaching at another lycée at Marseilles on the south coast. They would cross France to visit each other or meet at a halfway point to spend a little time together. In 1933, Sartre took a leave and lived in Germany for a term, studying the writings of the influential professor Edmund Husserl, whose philosophy was called "phenomenology." Sartre returned to his teaching job and his writing, incorporating his new phenomenological insights into his own work, along with others he had garnered from the German philosopher Martin Heidegger, a former student of Husserl's. In the next few years, Sartre produced three books—a novel, *Nausea*, and two philosophical essays—all showing the influence of Husserl's and Heidegger's phenomenology. (We'll talk about phenomenology shortly.)

On September 3, 1939, France and Britain declared war on Nazi Germany, and Sartre found himself back in the army. While on duty as a military meteorologist in eastern France, he began reading Kierkegaard and writing the first volume of a massive fictional trilogy, *The Roads to Freedom*. The first German soldier he saw was the one who took him prisoner on June 21, 1940. In the prisoner-of-war camp, he worked on a major philosophical book, to be called *Being and Nothingness* (eventually published in 1943). After nine months of imprisonment, he escaped and sneaked back to Paris,

where he formed a resistance group that engaged in subversive activities against the occupying Germans. He also continued writing—philosophy, plays, and the novel. He called the motivating idea in these works "existentialism" and was surprised by its immediate and enthusiastic public reception. The war ended in 1945, and by the next year, Sartre was known throughout Europe and America. He was flown to many parts of the world to lecture on existentialism and its meaning in the postwar years. The term caught on, and both university students and dropouts everywhere became "Existentialists" overnight, brooding over his ideas in coffeehouses, bars, and dorms into the wee hours.

Yet, ironically, at the very time his ideas had the most influence, Sartre was moving away from his existentialism and toward Marxism. He refused to join the powerful French Communist party, but he visited the former Soviet Union,

How to Be an Existentialist

China, and, later, Cuba. In his speeches, he defended the Soviets against America in the Cold War. His political activities included supporting a Maoist newspaper that had been shut down by the French government, siding with Algerian nationalists in the French war in Algeria, condemning the U.S. role in the war in Vietnam, and supporting the student revolt in Paris in 1968. He so angered the extreme political right that two attempts were made on his life. Nevertheless, he became distraught at the Soviet invasion of Czechoslovakia that same year, and he broke with Fidel Castro in 1971. By 1977, he was forced to admit that he was no longer a Marxist.

The most important work of Sartre's later period is *The Critique of Dialectical Reason*, which was his personal interpretation and defense of Marxism (one attacked by the French Communist party). Its first volume was published in 1960; the second volume appeared only after his death in 1980. He had destroyed his health by too much smoking, drinking, and consumption of drugs, which he took to "wire" himself when he wrote philosophy. Simone de Beauvoir had to be pulled from atop his body by doctors on the night of his death. Though his philosophical star had set by 1980, he still had a huge personal following, and 50,000 people lined the streets of Paris to accompany him on his last journey to the cemetery.

How to Write Existentialist Philosophy

Sartre's Theory

Sartre's existentialism is a combination of certain Kierkegaardian and Nietzschean ideas about freedom and human self-creation presented in terms of the phenomenological method of Edmund Husserl (1859–1938), whose philosophy Sartre had studied in Germany in 1933. In fact, the work of the German philosopher Martin Heidegger (1889–1976) could be similarly described, and some of Sartre's detractors, knowing that Sartre had read Heidegger's *Being and Time* (1929), claim that Sartre's *Being and Nothingness* (1943) is merely an unoriginal reworking of Heidegger's ideas. But Sartre uses Husserl's method in a manner quite distinct from Heidegger's and comes to conclusions substantially different from his. In fact, he draws practical and political implications from his philosophy that are directly contrary to Heidegger's. (Sartre was always dramatically to the left politically, while Heidegger was distinctly a right-winger; Heidegger was at one point a member of the Nazi party and praised Hitler and many Nazi views highly.) In any case, Heidegger refused to call himself an Existentialist. For all these reasons, we will use Sartre as our representative of twentieth-century existentialism and will concentrate only on that period of his work when "existentialist" ideas and "phenomenological" methods dominate his thinking, namely, from about 1938 to 1948.

Phenomenology

Edmund Husserl, like Descartes, wanted to posit consciousness as the starting point of all philosophy. His **phenomenology** is a study of the phenomena (appearances) of consciousness. His method was intended to be a presuppositionless or assumption-free technique of inspecting consciousness, employing no theoretical machinery at all—no "unconscious" (as in Freud), no "false consciousness" (as in Marx), but merely a description of consciousness and its data as they actually exist. It involved a "phenomenological reduction," or an *epochê*, as Husserl sometimes called it. In this act, the philosopher suspends all knowledge, beliefs, and expectations about any particular object of awareness, and replaces the suspended knowledge with a new description of the object in terms only of the characteristics that actually present themselves to consciousness. This method could be applied either to the *objects* of consciousness—for example, to a glass of beer, as Sartre discovered to his delight— or to consciousness itself as that to which the glass of beer presents itself in its multiple aspects.

**Edmund Husserl
(1859–1938)**

In his phenomenological novel *Nausea*, Sartre has his main character, Roquentin, stare deeply into his beer glass while languishing in a seedy bar. He loses himself in this activity, cataloguing each of the qualities presented to consciousness: the long string of bubbles rising from the bottom of the glass, the light shimmering through the golden liquid, the popping of the bubbles of foam, the apparent change in shape of the rim of the glass as he moves his head from side to side, the chill of the glass against his hand, the background noise of the bustling tavern against which all these qualities present themselves to Roquentin's consciousness.

Sartre believes that applying Husserl's method to consciousness itself (in the way that Roquentin applies it to the glass of beer) provides experiential proof of ideas about freedom and the self that were presented by Kierkegaard and Nietzsche in aphoristic and epigrammatic fashion only. He discovers that consciousness does not simply record data passively, nor merely represent external reality in mirrorlike images. Rather, it creates; it generates a bewildering array of possibilities from one moment to the next. (To be aware of an object as a "book" is to see it as a text to be read, or to be used as a paperweight, or as a status symbol to impress a visitor, or as a weapon, or as an object to be ignored.) And he discovers, contrary to Descartes's claims, that the self and consciousness are not identical; rather, consciousness apprehends the self just as it did the book—as an object that is mere possibility. This Husserlian method systematizes what Kierkegaard and Nietzsche had left unsystematic. (Of course, they had done so for a reason, so one can question whether Sartre's systematic phenomenological approach doesn't already falsify "existentialism's" insights.)

Sartre's ideas are presented in two books written before the war— the novel *Nausea*, just mentioned, and *Transcendence of the Ego*, his book on phenomenological psychology—and in his 800-page *Being and Nothingness*, written during the war. The latter is a long, dense, and often difficult book that was so much misunderstood by both friends and foes that, in 1946, Sartre published an essay, *Existentialism is a Humanism*, as a response to his critics. There he tried to popularize and defend his views, which he felt had been twisted by some critics, who presented Sartre as a pessimist and a cynic.

Existentialism Defined

In this essay, Sartre gave his now-famous definition of **existentialism.** An Existentialist is a philosopher who believes that, in the case of human beings, "existence precedes essence." Sartre attributes the opposite view, "essence precedes existence," to the whole Western tradition from the ancient Greeks up to certain maverick thinkers in the nineteenth century, especially Kierkegaard and Nietzsche. An essence is that which a thing is, usually captured in a definition. In Platonic language, it is the "Form" of a thing; in Aristotelian language, it is its "function." It is a thing's "nature." In the Western tradition, then, a thing's "idea," its "Form," its "function," its "meaning," has priority over its existence, and its existence is determined by that essence.

In Platonism the FORM Dominates

If this essence is conceived as a Platonic Form, the essence determines the existence of the individual entity by dictating its necessary conditions. (For any existing thing to be a "triangle," it must be a three-sided closed figure.) If the essence is conceived as a genetic program, it determines the existence of the individual through reproduction. (A mother cat gives birth to a baby cat, which will kill birds, torture mice, tear furniture, and show affection only at mealtime.) If the essence is conceived as an idea in the mind of an inventor, it determines individual existence by instantiating (concretely representing) itself.

Sartre explains this latter conception by asking us to imagine the invention of an artifact like a knife. First comes the idea. (The *essence* is conceived.) Then comes the production. (The thing is brought into *existence* as a representation of its essence.) In the case of the knife, then, essence precedes existence. Sartre claims that, according to the Western tradition, the same picture holds for the human being. God first conceives of human beings in his own mind, and then he creates them. In the cases of both the knife and the human, the value of the product is determined by how well it conforms to the model, its essence. A knife that won't cut is an unsatisfactory knife. A human who will not fulfill his or her function is an unsatisfactory human. But then, says Sartre, along came Nietzsche with

ARTIFACTS
according to all philosophical parties

FIRST THE IDEA
(ESSENCE)

THEN THE INVENTION
(EXISTENCE)

Here, essence precedes existence.

THE HUMAN BEING
according to the Western philosophical tradition

FIRST THE IDEA
(ESSENCE)

THEN THE CREATION
(EXISTENCE)

Here, too, essence precedes existence.

THE HUMAN BEING
according to Existentialism

NO GOD, NO ESSENCE;
JUST EXISTENCE

Existence precedes essence.

his bad news—God is dead! If there is no God to conceive of the human being (or, in a more "naturalistic" vein, if there are no human biological instincts), then there is no human nature to dictate human behavior. The individual human is alone, abandoned, forced to create his or her own nature (essence) through his or her actions. Existence precedes essence. The essence of the human being is to have no essence. The human being is essentially free.

The Relationship between Consciousness and Selfhood

For Sartre, this does not mean that we are born with ready-made selves that happen to have free will. Sartre's point is more radical than this rather conventional picture of freedom. According to Sartre, we are "condemned to be free." This is the one thing about which we have no choice. And with this freedom, we must at every moment create the self that we will be. Here Sartre breaks with his countryman and forebear, René Descartes. Descartes had said, "I think, therefore I am," and he had found in consciousness's depth an absolute self, a pure ego. But Sartre's phenomenological investigation of consciousness does not discover any such thing. Consciousness reveals itself as "an impersonal spontaneity," constantly overflowing its boundaries, "monstrous" in its tireless creation of itself "*ex nihilo*"[1] (out of nothing). You know what Sartre is talking about here. Think of

Need to sleep...leap...beep... Jeep...can't afford new tires... gas...oil...boil...It was hot today...hurray...say...pay... need more money... funny... honey...bees...ants...

those times when you've tried to get a good night's sleep just before an examination or a job interview. You lay your head on the pillow and try to drift off, but useless and shallow thoughts stream through your mind. Finally, you try to stem the flood of ideas by saying sternly, "STOP IT! SHUT UP!" But *to whom* are you addressing this command? Is it your "self," or is it consciousness itself?

Monstrous Freedom

Furthermore, according to Sartre (following Kierkegaard), thoughts present themselves in consciousness as *possibilities*, and because Sartre defines freedom in terms of possibility, freedom is discovered in consciousness. Consciousness is sometimes overwhelmed by the freedom presented to it and, in fact, is terrified by this freedom. Here, we once again have a Kierkegaardian/Sartrean theme that shows how different the existentialist theory of freedom is from most philosophical theories of freedom. Typically, freedom is construed as something that we desire but that has been denied us and for which we must fight. In existentialism, there is no alternative to freedom, and most people spend a great part of their lives looking for ways to escape freedom.

Consider this scenario: You are walking across the Golden Gate Bridge, and at midspan you lean across the guardrail and look straight down into the watery abyss. Suddenly, you push yourself away from the rail. Why? Was it because you feared that someone might push you off the bridge? No. Rather, it was because you feared that you might jump! You were momentarily terrified by your own "vertigo of possibility,"

which demonstrated that you were "monstrously free."[2] There was no one to stop you from jumping but your *self*, and you were not sure that your self was strong enough to do so. At that moment, you experienced what Kierkegaard and Sartre call "anguish" in the face of freedom.

To illustrate his idea, Sartre refers to a case study by the Swiss psychiatrist Jean-Marie Janet of one of his patients. A recently married young woman dreads her husband's departure for work, for she fears that when he leaves she will sit naked in the window like a prostitute and beckon passers-by. We can imagine that this young woman is perhaps beautiful and spoiled, prepared by her parents for the right marriage to the right man from the right family, with the right career and the right connections.

Now, while still young, she has achieved this goal and has little more to look forward to in life (except possibly to have the right number of right-thinking children). She finds that her husband, fatigued after a long day at the office, pays little attention to her upon returning home in the evening. At breakfast, he reads the newspaper without exchanging a word and then rushes off to work. She sits there lonely and depressed, thinking, "I am still young and desirable. I could have

any man I want simply by calling to him from my window." This possibility, once it enters her consciousness, terrifies her, because she fears she may act upon it.

Sartre says that this "neurasthenic" case is only an exaggeration of something that happens to all of us, all of the time. It is anguish in the face of freedom. Normally, we try to marginalize these experiences, telling ourselves that they are insignificant blips of abnormality, but Sartre wants to move them to center stage and to fix our attention upon them. He claims that the experience of anguish is *foundational* to consciousness, deeper than selfhood itself, because anguish is a natural part of consciousness, while selfhood is only a "construct" out of consciousness. In fact, Sartre allows himself to wonder if perhaps the main function of the ego (the self, the "I") is to stabilize experience in such a way as to mask anguish from consciousness. If this suggestion were true, then the self would necessarily be a construction in "bad faith" (Sartre's term for self-deception, for a flight from freedom, from anguish, and from responsibility).

Human beings, then, are always free. No matter the situation in which they find themselves, there are always alternative possibilities. Consider the case of a group of friends on a day hike in the mountains. Their goal is to reach a certain peak and to return to their camp before sunset. They have each packed a lunch that they carry in their backpacks. After several hours of hiking along a narrow trail, they round a corner and are confronted by a huge boulder that has recently fallen and is blocking the path. On one side of the boulder is a deep, uncrossable ravine; on the other, a high, unclimbable cliff. The boulder itself cannot be scaled nor dislodged. Upon seeing it, the first hiker throws his backpack down in disappointment, lies back on a little patch of grass, and says, "Well, that's it. The hike is over. We might as well eat our lunches and go back." According to a Sartrean analysis, this person has chosen the boulder as insurmountable obstacle and chosen himself as defeated. This choice, by the way, probably reflects a pattern in his life. Another member of the hiking party takes out her watercolors and says, "Look at the way that boulder is framed by pine trees on either side of it, and the way the sun glints off it, and the way the snow-covered mountain peak behind it shimmers in the light." This person has chosen the boulder as aesthetic possibility and chosen her-

self as the realizer of that possibility. A third hiker concerns himself with a striation of crystals that runs along the boulder's surface, saying, "Notice that there is no mineral like this in any of the rocks around here. Yet we can see light glittering on the rocks up above. This boulder must have fallen fifty meters from that ledge, and it must have done so in the last twenty-four hours, because there is still green vegetation crushed beneath it." This person has chosen the boulder as scientific sample and chosen himself as scientist. The fourth hiker stares at the boulder defiantly, takes a deep breath, and says, "There must be a way around this thing, and I'm going to find it." This person has chosen the boulder as a challenge and chosen herself as the challenged one. A fifth possibility would be to choose suicidal despair and hurl oneself into the abyss. This alternative is absurd, of course, but the fact that it is always there shows that there are always options. If we have not chosen death (which we may do at any moment), we have chosen its alternative. Therefore, we are free and are responsible for the alternative that we have chosen.

A determinist (that is, someone who denies that freedom exists) may look at the case of our hikers and say that no choices were involved at all. Rather, each was necessarily determined to do what he or she did, perhaps because of habit or conditioning (the view of the behaviorist B. F. Skinner) or perhaps because of the organization of the personality around early childhood experiences (the view of Freud). But for Sartre, the past does not cause the present. At each moment, we rechoose ourselves. It is true that we usually do this by choosing our past and projecting it into our future, but this is often done in "bad faith." Typically, we blame our past for what we are today, and we believe that we could not help what we did. But according to Sartre, we can always choose differently than what we in fact do choose. The defeated hiker *could* choose to interpret the rock as a challenge—but "at what price?" asks Sartre.[3] In other words, for a person who has chosen himself as defeated, discouraged, and cynical, choosing the boulder as a challenge would not be a casual decision. It would be what Sartre calls "a radical conversion." We are all capable of such conversions, but the thought of their possibility terrifies us. We dread the thought that, in the future, we may not be who we are now. Sartre says, "I await myself in the future, where I 'make an appointment with myself on the other side of that hour, of that day, or of that month.' Anguish is the fear of not finding myself at that appointment, of no longer even wishing to be there."[4]

This Is a Job for Superwoman

I Await Myself in the Future

Humans, then, are always free in the sense just outlined, even if we are terrified by that freedom and usually respond to it in "bad faith." Of course, our freedom is not total. We cannot choose to walk through walls (or boulders), nor to be the queen of Sweden. But we are never bereft of choices and must constantly reconstruct our worlds and ourselves through our actions. Freedom is the most important thing about humans. It prevents us from having an "essence" that would both create and constrain our behavior.

Anguish

If we are always free, and if freedom manifests itself as anguish, why are we not in a perpetual state of anxiety? Sartre acknowledges that, in fact, the conscious experience of anguish is rare. He addresses this make-or-break question in the following way: When the alarm goes off in the morning—when I intuit it *as* an alarm—I immediately throw myself into tasks that I perceive as *necessities* about which I have little or no choice. I *must* get up and go to work. But to do that, I must shave, shower, and eat breakfast. At work, I must do this and that. I must talk to Simone and send a letter to Pierre. I

Go ahead. Make my day.

must pay my electricity bill and protest the late charge on my credit card. But if I perform a "phenomenological suspension" of all these "necessary" projects and hold them at a distance, then I realize that nothing forces me to engage in them—"then I discover myself suddenly as the one who gives its meaning to the alarm clock, the one who by a sign forbids himself to walk on a flower bed or on the lawn, . . . the one who makes the values exist in order to determine his action by their demands."[5] All these perceived "necessities" that prove to derive from my own choices are "guardrails against anguish." When I look at them phenomenologically, "all the guardrails against anguish collapse,"[6] disintegrated by the consciousness of my own freedom, and *then* I consciously experience anguish—the anguish of knowing that I am the source of my own values. I cannot dodge this fact; I cannot excuse myself from it. Perhaps the phrase "No excuses!" best summarizes Sartre's existentialism.

It would seem, then, that "good faith"—namely, "authenticity"—would simply be acknowledgment of one's freedom and acceptance of

The Guardrails Against Anguish

responsibility for one's actions. But this picture is too simple. It is complicated by the near impossibility of "good faith" as Sartre construes it. Every *attempt* to be in good faith slips back into bad faith. If we try to be sincere, we are *not* sincere. If we try to be "real," we are a phony. It's like the bumper sticker I once saw:

"BE SPONTANEOUS."

The Other

The possibility of "good faith" is further compromised by the fact that we inhabit a world peopled by other free humans who make demands on our freedom. Sartre is not referring simply to social responsibilities and familial obligations; these are, in fact, part of the system of guardrails against anguish that are our own free constructions. Rather, Sartre is making a phenomenological point: The "other" challenges my freedom every time he looks at me. This is what Sartre calls "the gaze." For example, when you enter a dentist's waiting room and the other patients look up at you, or

when you arrive to class late and the professor briefly glares at you as the other students turn and look at you, you have been objectified by them. You, who as a free being are a subject, have been made into an object—their object. They have robbed you of your space. Your world has suddenly been created out of their space. Perhaps you look down to avoid their gaze and stumble masochistically to the first empty seat. Or perhaps you try to maintain your dignity (after all, you *have* a perfectly good excuse for your tardiness) and maintain your regular gait and demeanor. The trouble is, you can't remember what your normal gait and demeanor are like. Or perhaps you try to turn the tables on your tormentors, and you glare back at them. Or maybe you arrived late intentionally in order to get the attention of others. (There are people who make a profession of such acts.)

L'enfer C'est les Autres

For Sartre, all of these responses to the gaze of the other fail. They are all in bad faith. The existence of other people as proved by their objectification of us in their gaze reveals to us our own contingency and the difficulty of creating a self in good faith. In the words of one of the characters of Sartre's play *No Exit*, "Hell is other people." Unfortunately, Sartre gives us no formula with which to escape the bad faith that seems to be the necessary consequence of not being the only person in the world. Sartre himself sometimes seems discouraged by this impasse, as when he writes, "Man is a useless passion."[7]

Summary

Sartre has produced a paradoxical picture of the human being: a being whose essence is that it has no essence, a being terrified by the very freedom it demands, a being "condemned to freedom," yet whose freedom is compromised by the freedom of other beings like itself. Just as Kierkegaard's hero, "the Knight of Faith," was in "absolute isolation," Sartre's human being (which he calls "being-for-itself") is "abandoned" in the midst of "being-in-itself" (the nonhuman world of inert stuff) and given neither plan nor guidance for the creation of the world that will be his and her responsibility. Furthermore, all such worlds will be equal ("Thus it amounts to the same thing whether one gets drunk alone or is a leader of nations"[8]) and will fail equally.

Equality

No wonder Sartre was accused of pessimism and cynicism by his critics. Yet he denies this charge, for he believes he has revealed us as would-be gods. In traditional Western theologies, it is God who creates the world and who creates the beings that inhabit the world. Moreover, although God is normally characterized by theologians as *causa sui* (a being that is its own cause), according to Sartre, it is we humans who have assumed these functions. God, as he has been conceived in the West, is for Sartre logically impossible, for "he" would have to be both "being-in-itself" (a fullness of being, with no potentiality that he had not already achieved, for in Western theology, God is "immutable"—unchanging and already perfect) and a "being-for-itself" (a free, and therefore unfinished, open-ended being). No being can be both being-in-itself and being-for-itself. Yet, according to Sartre, this is exactly what humans aspire to in every act. We try to create and dominate a world, and we try to occupy it as a "fullness of being," a finished and perfect subject/object. If there is such a thing as "good faith" for Sartre, it is recognizing the contradictory goal of every action, and hence its necessary failure, while at the same time courageously choosing oneself in that unhappy picture. Perhaps the closest that Sartre ever comes to defining "good faith" is in this almost impenetrable assertion:

Jean-Paul Creates Jean-Paul

> A freedom which wills itself freedom is in fact a being-which-is-not-what-it-is and which is-what-it-is-not, and which chooses as the ideal of being, being-what-it-is-not and not-being-what-it-is.[9]

Topics for Consideration

1. Speculate a bit on the connection between Sartre's existentialism and the social, political, and economic conditions in France before and during World War II.

2. Sartre eventually abandoned existentialism for Marxism. Based on your reading of Chapter 8, "The Marxian Conception of Human Nature," what features of Marxism seem to you to be compatible with existentialism? What features seem incompatible?

3. What would you say is the connection between phenomenology and existentialism?

4. Compare and contrast those features of Sartre's theory that make him seem like a pessimist with those that make him seem more positive.

5. Explain in your own words (or with your own diagrams) what Sartre means when he writes, "Existence precedes essence."

6. In what way, according to Sartre, are we terrified by our own freedom?

7. In this chapter, you read about four hikers whose path was blocked by a huge boulder, and you saw how Sartre would use this example to explain "freedom." Based on your reading of Chapter 9, "The Psychoanalytic Conception of Human Nature: Freud," invent a psychoanalytic explanation for each of the four heroes of the story, and contrast them with Sartre's account.

8. Clarify as best you can Sartre's claim that, in choosing the meaning the world has for us, we are choosing ourselves.

9. Why does Sartre believe that "Hell is other people"?

Suggestions for Further Reading

I. Sartre's Main Works

A. Philosophical Works

Anti-Semite and Jew. Trans. George J. Becker. New York: Schocken, 1974.

Being and Nothingness. Trans. Hazel Barnes. New York: Washington Square Press, 1992.

Critique of Dialectical Reason, Vol. 1: *Theory of Practical Ensembles.* Trans. Alan Sheridan Smith. London: Routledge, Chapman & Hall, 1984. (No English translation of Volume 2 is yet available.)

Existentialism and Human Emotions. Trans. Bernard Frechtman and Hazel Barnes. New York: Citadel Press, 1977.

The Transcendence of the Ego. Trans. Robert Kirkpatrick. New York: Farrar, Strauss & Giroux, 1957.

B. Fictional and Dramatic Works

Nausea. Trans. Lloyd Alexander. New York: New Directions, 1964.

No Exit. Trans. Stuart Gilbert. New York: Vintage Books, 1947.

The Roads to Freedom (trilogy)

The Age of Reason. Trans. Eric Sutton. New York: Bantam Books, 1992.

The Reprieve. Trans. Eric Sutton. New York: Bantam Books, 1964.

Troubled Sleep. Trans. Gerard Hopkins. New York: Bantam Books, 1949.

II. Sartre's Philosophy Anthologized

The Philosophy of Jean-Paul Sartre. Ed. Robert Denoon Cumming. New York: Vintage Books, 1972.

III. Secondary Sources on Sartre

Catalano, Joseph S. *A Commentary on Jean-Paul Sartre's "Being and Nothingness."* Chicago: University of Chicago Press, 1980.

Caws, Peter. *Sartre.* Boston: Routledge & Kegan Paul, 1979.

Danto, Arthur C. *Jean-Paul Sartre.* New York: Viking Press. 1975.

de Beauvoir, Simone. *The Ethics of Ambiguity.* Trans. Bernard Frechtman. New York: Philosophical Library, 1948.

Hayman, Ronald. *Sartre: A Biography.* New York: Simon & Schuster, 1987.

Palmer, Donald. *Sartre for Beginners.* New York: Writers & Readers, 1995.

Notes

1. Jean-Paul Sartre, *The Transcendence of the Ego,* trans. Robert Kirkpatrick (New York: Farrar, Strauss & Giroux, 1957), p. 99.

2. Sartre, *Transcendence of the Ego,* p. 100.

3. Jean-Paul Sartre, *Being and Nothingness,* trans. Hazel Barnes (New York: Washington Square Press, 1992), p. 585.

4. Sartre, *Being and Nothingness,* p. 73.

5. Sartre, *Being and Nothingness,* p. 77.

6. Sartre, *Being and Nothingness,* p. 77.

7. Sartre, *Being and Nothingness,* p. 784.

8. Sartre, *Being and Nothingness,* p. 797.

9. Sartre, *Being and Nothingness,* p. 798.

Glossary

(Boldfaced type indicates terms that are cross-referenced within the glossary.)

adaptation The Darwinian process according to which the development of new species (speciation) takes place. Random combinations from the gene pools of individuals and/or genetic mutation produce physical characteristics that may prove to be more suitable for survival and reproduction in a given environment than were those of the individual's ancestors. (See also **natural selection.**)

aesthetics The philosophy of art. The branch of philosophy that investigates questions such as, What makes something a work of art? Are there absolute values in art, or are aesthetic judgments always relative? Can there be rational aesthetic debate, or are aesthetic judgments based only on preference? What is the status of art among other human intellectual and creative endeavors?

altruism Acting to benefit the interests of others at the expense of one's own interest.

Antichrist, the From 1 and 2 John in the New Testament of the Bible, a false Christ or personage appearing in the world in the name of Christ, but, in fact, Christ's opposite.

anti-essentialism The view that in the natural world there are no **essences**—that is, no defining characteristics that naturally determine classification and dictate behavior. Related to **nominalism,** and the opposite of **essentialism.**

a posteriori A belief, **proposition,** or argument whose truth or falsity can be established only through observation. Classical **empiricism** was an attempt to show that all significant knowledge about the world is based on a posteriori truths.

a priori   A belief, **proposition,** or argument whose truth or falsity can be established independently of observation. Definitions, arithmetic, and the principles of logic are usually held to be a priori. Classical **rationalism** was an attempt to show that all significant knowledge about the world is based on a priori truths, which most of the rationalists associated with **innate ideas.**

arianism   A fourth-century heresy named after its leader, Arius, who denied the **doctrine of the Trinity,** holding instead that Christ had his own **essence,** which was divine but which was independent of God's essence.

asceticism   The voluntary practice of austere living, involving self-denial and disdain for sensual gratification.

atheism   The denial of the existence of God or gods.

Bodhisattva   In **Mahayana** Buddhism, a saintly and compassionate person who postpones his or her own permanent passage into **Nirvana** in order to aid other sentient beings in their attempt to achieve escape from suffering and to achieve enlightenment.

Categorical Imperative   The name given by Immanuel Kant to a purported universal law. In one form, "So act that the maxim of your action could be willed as a universal law;" and in another form, "So act as to treat humanity . . . always as an end, and never as merely a means."

causal explanation   A mechanical kind of explanation in which the event or object to be accounted for is rendered intelligible by demonstrating how it is the necessary result of antecedent events. Causal explanations are often represented in terms of natural laws. (Contrast with **teleology.**)

conceptual analysis   The philosophical investigation of concepts to determine their constituent parts, the relationship among the parts, and the relations of the parts to the whole, in such a way that the meaning of the concept is clarified.

cosmological argument   An attempt to establish God's existence by deducing it from observable facts in the world—for example, Thomas Aquinas's claim that from the observation of causal chains in the world, we can deduce the necessity of a "first cause," or God.

determinism   The view that every event occurs necessarily, following inevitably from the events that preceded it. There is no randomness in reality; rather, all is law-governed. Freedom either does not exist (hard determinism) or exists in such a way as to be compatible with necessity (soft determinism).

dialectic   In the philosophies of Hegel and Marx, the mechanism of historical change and progress in which every possible condition exists only in relation to its own opposite. This relationship is one of both antagonism and mutual dependency, but the antagonism (a form of violence—intellectual in Hegel's case and physical in Marx's) eventually undermines the relationship and overthrows it, leading to the next historical stage. (However, sometimes the term *dialectical* is used only to emphasize a relationship of reciprocity between two conditions or processes.)

doctrine of the Trinity   The Christian dogma asserting the union of the three entities—God the Father, Christ the Son, and the Holy Spirit—in one godhead.

dualism   The **ontological** view that reality is composed of two distinct kinds of beings, usually (as in Descartes) minds and bodies.

ego   In psychoanalysis, the name of the rational, mostly conscious, social aspect of the psyche, as contrasted with the **id** and the **superego.**

egoism   Refers to acts motivated by self-interest. (Contrast with **altruism.**)

empirical   An investigation or a **proposition** based on observations and experimentation involving one or more of the five senses. Contrasted with "speculative" and with "mathematical" investigations and propositions, neither of which (for different reasons in each case) admits of empirical confirmation or refutation. (Related to **empiricism.**)

empiricism   The **epistemological** view that true knowledge is derived primarily from sense experience. In the classical versions of this theory, all significant knowledge is **a posteriori,** and **a priori** knowledge is either nonexistent or **tautological.** The existence of **innate ideas** is denied in this school.

entelechy   A term in Aristotelian **metaphysics** designating a supposed force or agency internal to an existing entity, such as a tree or a human being, and related to that entity's **essence.** The entelechy determines the growth and historical development of the entity—directing its potentiality into an actuality. For example, it is the agency that provokes an acorn to become an oak tree and not a goldfish.

epistemology   Theory of knowledge. The branch of philosophy that asks such questions as, What is knowledge? What, if anything, can we know? What is the difference between knowledge and opinion?

essence   The defining characteristic or characteristics of an entity; that which all members of a class have in common by virtue of which they are identified as being members of that class.

essentialism   The view that there are, in the natural world, **essences,** which predetermine classification and behavior of the entities whose essences they are.

ethics   Moral philosophy. The branch of philosophy that asks questions such as, Is there such a thing as the Good? What is "the good life"? Is there such a thing as absolute duty? Are rational moral arguments possible, or are moral judgments based only on preference?

eugenics   The advocacy of controlled breeding to improve the human race.

existentialism   A twentieth-century philosophy associated principally with Jean-Paul Sartre, who coined the term, but also with the work of Karl Jaspers, Simone de Beauvoir, Martin Heidegger, Gabriel Marcel, Albert Camus, and Miguel de Unamuno, among others. Existentialism derived substantially from the nineteenth-century philosophers Søren Kierkegaard and Friedrich Nietzsche. More of a shared attitude than a school of thought, it can nevertheless be roughly defined by saying, with Sartre, that existentialists are those who believe that, in the case of humans, "existence precedes **essence.**" This is the thesis that there is no human nature that precedes our presence in the world. All humans individually create humanity at every moment through their free acts.

false consciousness   A phrase in Marxian philosophy, originating with Friedrich Engels, designating the psychological state of individual members of a society dominated by **ideology** and **false needs.**

false needs   A phrase in Marxian theory naming desires that are artificially provoked in members of a capitalist society in order to enslave them to consumerism. The opposite of "true needs," which are considered to be universal physical, social, and psychological needs based on our true biological nature.

Forms   A term in Platonic philosophy designating those models (archetypes, **essences,** universals) of everything else that exists in the physical or conceptual world, which things are copies of Forms and dependent upon them. Forms are eternal, unchangeable truths that are the ultimate object of all true philosophizing.

Four Noble Truths   The main doctrine of Buddhism concerning (1) suffering, (2) the causes of suffering, (3) the good news that these causes can be overcome, and (4) the **Noble Eightfold Path,** which leads to the liberation from suffering and to enlightenment.

Hinayana   The fundamentalist Buddhists who adhere most faithfully to what are taken to be the original teachings of the Buddha. Hinayana, meaning "small vehicle," was originally a derogatory name coined by the competing **Mahayana** ("large vehicle") Buddhists, because the latter claimed that the fundamentalists carried only one passenger at a time over the troubled surface of existence, while the Mahayana carried many. Eventually a minority form of Buddhism, Hinayana is nevertheless the dominant form in Sri Lanka, Burma, Cambodia, Thailand, and Laos.

Hinduism   The major religion in India today, based on the ancient holy writings of the Vedas, the Upanishads, and the Bhagavad-Gita. A plurality of major and minor deities are worshiped.

id   In psychoanalysis, the name given to the mostly unconscious, antisocial, "animal" self, containing the primitive sexual and aggressive drives, as contrasted with the **ego** and **superego.**

idealism   As used in philosophy, the **ontological** view that, ultimately, reality can be shown to be spiritual or mental, or, at a minimum, that the spiritual or mental features of reality have ontological precedence over the material features of reality.

ideology   A term in Marxian philosophy designating the status of cultural phenomena (such as art, religion, morality, and philosophy) as systems of propaganda supporting a specific socioeconomic system and its beneficiaries.

innate idea   An idea present in the mind at birth, hence **a priori.**

Kantianism   See **Categorical Imperative.**

karma   The doctrine of the religions of India, including Buddhism, according to which actions in one's present life determine the form that one's life will take in its next **reincarnation.**

laity   The members of a religious organization who are not priests, monks, or nuns.

Lamarckism   The evolutionary theory derived from Jean-Baptiste Lamarck according to which the process by which new species are formed (speciation) is explained in terms of biological transmission of acquired characteristics. Changes in the bodies of the parents acquired as a result of habit, use and disuse of limbs, and so on are passed on to their children, who in turn pass them on to their children.

logic   The branch of philosophy that studies the structure of valid inference. A purely formal discipline, logic is interested in the form of argumentation rather than in its content.

Mahayana   The form of Buddhism that eventually came to dominate that religion's more recent history. More elastic than its competitor, **Hinayana** Buddhism, Mahayana universalized the goal of Buddhism to care for all sentient beings. It loosened the strict monastic demands of the Hinayana Buddhists in ways that made Buddhism more open both to monks and to the **laity.**

mandala   In Buddhism, a circular design for the purpose of contemplation, containing geometrical designs and signs symbolizing the different features of reality.

mantra   In Buddhism, a sound bestowed upon a monk by his guru to chant or to use in **meditation.**

materialism   The **ontological** view that all reality can be shown to be material in nature (for example, that "minds" are really brains). Alternatively, materialism refers to obsessive desire to surround oneself with material goods.

meditation   In the Buddhist tradition, a form of spiritual concentration, performed while sitting in a cross-legged position, producing a state of peace issuing into joyfulness (calm meditation), or, in the more advanced form (insight meditation), producing a release or liberation issuing into a state of pure emptiness approaching **Nirvana,** the goal of Buddhism.

metaphysics   The branch of philosophy that attempts to construct a general, speculative worldview—a complete, systematic account of all reality and experience, usually involving an **epistemology,** an **ontology,** an **ethics,** and an **aesthetics.** (The adjective *metaphysical* is often employed to stress the speculative, as opposed to the scientific or commonsensical, features of the theory or **proposition** it describes.)

metonomy   A figure of speech in which an object is named by letting a part of the object stand for the whole (for example, "A thousand sails set out to sea") or by naming another object that is tangential to the object to be named (for example, "Joe likes the bottle too much").

mysticism   The view that a special experience can be achieved that transcends ordinary rational procedures and provides a direct intuition of the presence of God or an extraordinary insight into ultimate truth.

naturalism   As employed in this text, the **ontological** view that all is nature, that there are no supernatural or unnatural phenomena. In **ethics,** naturalism refers to the view that there is no natural hierarchy of value—for example, that humans are no more intrinsically valuable than coyotes.

naturalistic fallacy   Term coined by the British philosopher G. E. Moore for the erroneous belief that a moral conclusion could ever be logically deduced from premises containing no moral terms.

natural selection   The Darwinian process in which the survival and reproductive rates of individuals and species are determined by the harshest features of a given geographical environment, which "selects" those genetic and morphological characteristics that best "fit" the environmental facts. (See also **adaptation.**)

necessary truth   **Propositions** that, within the framework of the conventions of the language in which they are expressed, cannot be false because their negation produces self-contradictions. They usually are thought to comprise definitions, mathematical axioms, and the principles of logic. (See also **tautology.**)

neo-Platonism A version of Platonism revived at the end of the Roman Empire and lasting in various forms throughout the Middle Ages and into the Renaissance. Unlike its Platonic model, neo-Platonism was more **mystically** than mathematically inclined, and it did not despise the images present in the physical world because neo-Platonists believed that these images were cryptic symbols of the spiritual world. Therefore, they also valued art more highly than did Plato.

Nirvana The goal of Buddhism—a liberation from suffering and the achievement of enlightenment in a state of pure emptiness, which is the ultimate reality for the Buddhist.

Noble Eightfold Path The program taught by the Buddha leading to liberation from suffering and to inner peace, involving the perfection of understanding, purpose, speech, action, self-discipline, effort, self-knowledge, and self-transcendence.

nominalism The theory of meaning and language according to which the classes of objects named by abstract nouns and adjectives are determined conventionally or even arbitrarily rather than being classes determined by real **essences** in nature.

normative Pertaining to rules advocating correctness in conduct or expression.

Oedipus complex, the A psycho-biological predisposition that **psychoanalysis** claims to detect in all humans. Children are presumed to be erotically attracted to the parent of the opposite sex and hostile to the parent of the same sex. These feelings become part of the unconscious mind in adult life.

ontological argument An **a priori** attempt to prove God's existence by demonstrating that the very concept of "God" logically entails his **necessary** existence.

ontology Theory of being. This branch of philosophy seeks answers to such questions as, What is real? What is the difference between appearance and reality? What is the relation between minds and bodies? Are numbers and concepts real, or are only physical objects real?

pantheism The view that everything is divine. God's "creation" is, in fact, identical with God. The term derives from the Greek *pan* (all) and *theos* (god).

phenomenology A philosophical school created by Edmund Husserl employing a method of analysis that purports to arrive at the pure data of consciousness and with those data to provide a foundation for **epistemology** and **ontology.** Sometimes the adjective *phenomenological* is used to mean merely "descriptive of subjective experience."

postmodernism   A loosely applied term (1) designating an intellectual posture skeptical of **epistemologies, ontologies,** and institutions (governmental, academic, military, medical, religious) of the modern Western tradition; (2) challenging the basic tenets of liberalism, humanism, individualism, and capitalism; (3) designating a fascination by popular culture and the domination of technology over human endeavors; and (4) dwelling on the contemporary **semiotic** strategies that value signs and images over substance and truth, reproduction over production, and representation over reality.

pragmatism   An American philosophy that claims that the meaning of an idea can be established by determining what practical difference would be produced by believing the idea to be true and that the truth of an idea can be established by determining the idea's ability to "work."

pre-Raphaelites   Mid-nineteenth-century British artistic movement defying current stylistic conventions by returning to the forms and colors of the Italian Renaissance artist Raphael and to the themes of yesteryear. Style, colors, and themes were sensual, sentimental, symbolic, and often mythological or medieval.

pre-Socratic philosophers   Ancient Greek philosophers who lived prior to Socrates. Thales of Miletos (c. 580 B.C.E.) is usually considered the first of these philosophers who tried to discover the ultimate nature of reality from which emerged the four basic elements: earth, water, air, and fire. Some pre-Socratics were monists, believing there exists only one irreducible substance; others were pluralists, holding that there are several such substances. Some believed that motion is real and inertia an illusion; others argued that inertia is real and motion an illusion. One (Pythagoras) believed that only numbers are real.

proposition   As employed in this text, whatever is asserted by a sentence. The sentences "It is raining," "*Es regnet*," and "*Llueve*" all assert the same proposition.

psychoanalysis   The name given by Sigmund Freud to his method of psychotherapy, eventually becoming a theory of the mind, of selfhood, and of culture, in which psychological and social phenomena are traced to their origins in the unconscious mind.

rationalism   The **epistemological** view that true knowledge is derived primarily from the faculty of "Reason." Reason is conceived as the working of the mind on material provided by the mind itself. In most versions, this material takes the form of **innate ideas.** Therefore, for the rationalists, **a priori** knowledge is the most important kind of knowledge. In rationalistic **ontologies,** the mind and the world are seen to be in conformity—the real is the rational and the rational is the real.

reductionism   The attempt to show that all objects and events that operate at one level of analysis can be reduced to simpler objects and events at a more basic level of analysis (e.g., the attempt to demonstrate that all physical objects can be analyzed in terms of molecular structures, or that molecular structures can be analyzed in terms of atomic structures).

reincarnation   In Buddhism, the recombination and rebirth of the elements of the living individual in a new body, either a different human body, or the body of a higher or lower animal, or some divine being.

repression   A term in Freudian theory designating a psychological defense mechanism that prevents certain desires and memories from entering consciousness, and forces them into the unconscious, where they remain active and produce symptoms that manifest themselves in daily behavior.

romanticism   A late eighteenth- and early nineteenth-century European and British artistic movement stressing emotionality, primitivism (the cult of the "Noble Savage"), subjectivity, spontaneity, nature, "natural" religion, individualism, and nationalism.

Saint Vitus's dance   A mysterious affliction that broke out several times in the high Middle Ages. The affliction was similar to epilepsy, but it attacked groups of individuals at the same time and appeared to be contagious, moving from village to village. It was named after the patron saint of epileptics and actors.

salvation history   A medieval Christian conception according to which the whole of history should be understood as a preparation for individual salvation. Salvation history begins with the story of God's creation of the world in the book of Genesis. It emphasizes the Fall of Man due to the first sin and teaches the inheritance of that sin by all descendants of Adam and Eve. Salvation history's centerpiece is the Passion of Christ—the story of his betrayal, trial, abuse, and crucifixion. As part of the process of one's own salvation from eternal damnation, one must understand one's own life in relation to salvation history.

semiology (sometimes called **semiotics**)   The study of the structure of the system of signs and of the signs therein. A "sign" is an arbitrary mark, sound, or image that has become imbued with meaning by virtue of its membership in a system of conventionality. Language is the most obvious case of such a system of signs, but behaviors, rituals, and institutions can also be studied semiologically.

sense data   Data that are received immediately by any one of the senses prior to interpretation by the mind. Sense data include colors, sounds, tastes, odors, tactile sensations, pleasures, and pains. Classical **empiricism** based itself on the supposed **epistemologically** foundational nature of sense data.

social Darwinism   The attempt to apply Darwin's theory of biological evolution to sociology, resulting in the thesis that "superior" individuals and cultures have a natural right to triumph over "inferior" individuals and cultures.

solipsism   The view that the only true knowledge one can possess is knowledge of one's own conscious states. According to solipsism, there is no good reason to believe that anything exists other than oneself.

Sophists   A group of philosophers—or, more accurately, rhetoricians—contemporary with Socrates who traveled ancient Greece teaching argumentative skills as the vehicle to political power. Philosophically, the Sophists defended relativism, skepticism, and subjectivism.

species-being   A term in Marxian philosophy derived from Ludwig Feuerbach designating that supposed feature of human nature according to which humans can understand themselves correctly and solve their problems successfully only by realizing their social, psychological, and biological interdependence with all members of the human species.

superego   In Freudian theory, the component of the psyche that counteracts antisocial desires and impulses of the **id** by attaching conscious and unconscious feelings of guilt to them.

Tantra   A northern Indian form of Buddhism arriving in Tibet in the sixth century C.E. and dominating there. Tantra teaches that enlightenment can be achieved by uniting all opposites and opposes the traditional Buddhist disdain of bodily pleasures and sexuality, asserting that they, too, can be employed to achieve **nirvana.**

tautology   A redundant assertion in which one part of the **proposition** simply repeats another part. Tautologies are **necessary truths,** but they are empty of information about anything other than their own components. For example, definitions are tautological because their predicates are equivalents of the term being defined.

teleology   An explanation in terms of goals, purposes, and intentions (from the Greek *telos*, meaning "goal"). For example, "Aristotle fled Athens because he did not want to be arrested" is a teleological explanation because it describes Aristotle's actions in terms of his intention. (Contrast with **causal explanation.**)

theism   The assertion of the existence of God or of gods.

Tower of Babel According to Genesis 11:4—9, a tower built in the land of Shinar intended to reach Heaven at a time when all humans still spoke the same language. To prevent this arrogant incursion into heaven, God caused the builders to speak many different languages, which rendered the workers incapable of communicating with one another. Therefore, they abandoned their project and scattered over the face of the earth.

utilitarianism The moral and social philosophy of Jeremy Bentham and John Stuart Mill according to which the value of any action or legislation can be derived from the "principle of utility," which advocates "the greatest amount of happiness for the greatest number of people."

villein A tenant farmer during the Middle Ages who was a serf to his lord but a freeman relative to others.

Zen A school of **Mahayana** Buddhism originating in China, where it was called *Cha'n*, the Chinese word for **meditation.** Zen emphasizes the possibility of sudden enlightenment, as opposed to a lengthy, ritualized process. Zen also highly values simplicity, silence, and manual labor.

Index

Charles the Bald, 98

Christ, 71, 107, 109, 111, 114, 115, 116, 119, 166, 169, 192, 295, 296, 297, 303. *See also* Jesus; Christianity

Christianity, 6, 11, 45, 78, 82, 83, 91, 95–121, 153, 156, 163, 166, 192, 214, 215, 228, 264, 266, 297, 303. *See also* Christ; Jesus

Christina of Sweden, 127

Chronos, 13

Church of England, the, 176

Churchill, Winston, 291

Clovis, 99

Cohen, G. A., 238, 239n

Cold War, the, 277

Collins, James, 174

colonialism, 15, 199, 232, 271

Communism, 163, 176, 199, 207, 211, 213, 227, 228, 229, 232–234, 236, 237, 238, 239n, 271, 272, 277, 278

conceptual analysis, 2, 3, 5–6, 296

Constantine, Flavius Valerius Aurelius, 96

Constitution, the American, 19

Conze, Edward, 90, 93, 94n

Copernicus, Nicolas, 124

cosmological argument, the, 106–107, 296

counterreformation, the, 124

courage, 28, 29, 31, 55, 56, 115

creationism, 201

creation science. *See* creationism

Crews, Frederick C., 270

Crick, Francis, 187

Crimean War, the, 176

Critias, 17

Crito, 33, 34, 35

Croxall, T. H., 173, 174n

Crusades, the, 109

Cunning of Reason, the, 215, 216

Custer, George, 19

Cyclops, the, 13

Danto, Arthur, 9, 12n, 93, 294

Darius I of Persia, 14

Dark Ages, the, 97, 98, 100

da Vinci, Leonardo, 123

Darwin, Charles, 6, 7, 46, 47, 48, 64, 89, 175–204, 247, 262, 263, 270n, 295, 300, 303

D-Day, 273

death instinct, the, 265, 269. *See also* Thanatos

de Beauvoir, Simone. *See* Beauvoir, Simone de

Declaration of Independence, the American, 19

deconstruction, 155

de Gaulle, Charles, 272

democracy, 14, 16, 17, 20, 24, 28, 32, 40, 207, 226

Democritus, 3

Denis, Saint, 111, 116

Dennett, Daniel, 186, 197, 198, 199, 200, 201, 202, 203, 204n

deoxyribonucleic acid (DNA), 181–182, 187

Derrida, Jacques, 118

Descartes, Francine, 127

Descartes, René, 6, 11, 123–149, 157, 158, 168, 171, 172, 200, 225, 239n, 266, 279, 280, 283, 297

Descent of Man, The, 188, 189, 196, 203, 204n

Desmond, Adrian, 203

despair, 162

determinism, 4, 9, 143, 170, 265, 267, 269, 287, 296

Dewey, John, 201, 202, 204

Dharma, 77, 79, 83

dialectic, the, 151, 214, 216, 217, 218, 224, 226, 228, 232, 238, 278, 293, 296

Dickens, Charles, 177

dictatorship, 16, 32, 37, 38, 227, 228, 236

Dion of Syracuse, 18

Dionysos, 63

Dionysos the Elder of Syracuse, 17

Dionysos the Younger of Syracuse, 18

Doctrine of the Trinity, the, 97, 296, 297

Donatello (Donato di Niccolo di Betto Bardi), 123

Renaissance, the, 124, 125, 247, 301, 302
repression, 250–252, 253, 256, 259, 260, 302
Republic, The (Plato), 21, 25, 28, 30, 37, 38
responsibility, 285, 289, 290, 291
Ricardo, David, 220, 231
Robespierre, Maximilien de, 205
Robinson, Paul, 270
Rockefeller, John D., 195, 199, 204n
Roland, 109
Romanticism, 176, 234, 247
Roosevelt, Theodore, 196
Rorty, Amélie Oksenberg, 65
Ross, G. R. T., 148, 149n
Ross, W. D., 64
Rubens, Peter Paul, 124
Rubin, Ronald, 148

Saint Vitus's Dance, 120, 303
salvation history, 107–108, 303
Sangha, 83
Sartre, Jean-Baptiste, 273
Sartre, Jean-Paul, 6, 11, 48, 73, 74, 92, 156, 157, 172, 271–294, 298
Satori, 89
Saxons, the, 97, 98
Say, Jean-Baptiste, 231
Schiele, Egon, 268
Schopenhauer, Arthur, 214, 247
Schweitzer, Anne-Marie, 273, 274
Schweitzer, Charles, 274
science, 1, 2, 3, 4, 5, 6, 7, 9, 10, 11, 44, 56, 126, 128, 129, 139, 140, 147, 153, 179, 180, 183, 184, 187, 192, 193, 197, 201, 207, 217, 218, 235, 247, 259, 266, 267, 269, 270n, 286, 300
screen memories, 251
selflessness, 76–78
semiology, 110, 118, 119, 120, 121, 302, 303
semiotics. *See* semiology
sense data, 135, 138, 139, 303
Sermon on the Mount, the, 199
sexism, 53
Shakespeare, William, 48, 124, 244

Shakti, 87
Shelley, Mary, 176
Shiva, 87
Shudras, 68
Signorelli, Luca, 103, 253–255, 269
simile of the line, the, 21–23, 34, 37
Singer, Peter, 213, 238, 238n
Skinner, B. F., 287
slavery, 15, 16, 18, 40, 44, 189, 196, 215, 216, 219, 220, 225, 226, 227
Smith, Adam, 220, 231
Smith, Alan Sheridan, 293
social Darwinism, 193–195, 203, 303
socialism, 213, 272
sociobiology, 198–199, 201, 204
sociology, 193, 200, 237, 303
Socrates, 1, 17, 21, 24–25, 26, 30, 32, 33, 34, 35, 38, 44, 66, 69, 71, 79, 119, 157, 170, 265, 302, 303
solipsism, 137, 303
Solon, 14
sophism, 1, 303
Sophocles, 15
soul, the, 29, 36, 37, 51, 52, 53, 54, 59, 60, 61, 63, 64, 134, 135, 141, 184, 192, 225, 266
species-being, 221, 223, 234, 303
Spencer, Herbert, 193–195, 204n
spirit, 29, 31, 36, 37, 59, 144, 151, 152, 164, 200, 215, 216, 217, 224
Stalin, Joseph, 228, 229, 236
Starkenburg, Heinz, 240n
Stevenson, Robert Louis, 177
Stoker, Bram, 176
Strachey, James, 269, 270n
sublimation, 224, 259
Summa theologica, 106, 122n
superego, the, 6, 249–250, 252, 255, 256, 258, 259, 263, 265, 267, 269, 297, 299, 304
survival of the fittest, 181, 183, 190, 194, 196
Sutton, Eric, 294
Swenson, David, 172, 173
Swenson, Lillian Marvin, 172

Tantra, 86–88, 304
tautology, 3, 6, 297, 301